Perils in the Transvaal and Zululand

by

H.C. Adams

Perils in the Transvaal and Zululand
by H.C. Adams

ISBN: 978-93-59957-35-7

Published by

DOUBLE 9 BOOKS
2/13-B, Ansari Road
Daryaganj, New Delhi – 110002
info@double9books.com
www.double9books.com
Tel. 011-40042856

ABOUT THE AUTHOR

Reverend Henry Cadwallader Adams (1817-1899) changed into a distinguished English cleric, schoolmaster, and renowned author of kid's novels at some point of the nineteenth century. Born on November four, 1817, he got here from a splendid lineage because the grandson of Simon Adams from Ansty Hall in Warwickshire. Adams acquired his schooling at prestigious institutions, together with Westminster School and Winchester College. Subsequently, he continued his educational journey at Balliol College in 1835 and Magdalen College, Oxford in 1836. His academic interests culminated in becoming a fellow of Magdalen in 1843, reflecting his scholarly achievements. Notably, Adams served as a Commoner Tutor at Winchester College, wherein he contributed to the schooling of young minds. His dedication to schooling and spirituality led to his appointment as the chaplain of Bromley College in 1855. Bromley College turned into an almshouse devoted to the aid of widows of priests, wherein Adams persevered his carrier to the community and the church. In addition to his clerical obligations, Adams made a lasting effect on children's literature together with his creative and engaging novels. His existence's work remains a testament to his multifaceted contributions as an educator, cleric, and writer at some point of the Victorian technology. Henry Cadwallader Adams exceeded away on October 17, 1899, leaving behind a legacy of literary and academic accomplishments.

CONTENTS

Chapter One 7

Chapter Two...17

Chapter Three 27

Chapter Four 37

Chapter Five...48

Chapter Six 59

Chapter Seven 69

Chapter Eight...79

Chapter Nine..89

Chapter Ten..99

Chapter Eleven...110

Chapter Twelve...121

Chapter Thirteen...131

Chapter Fourteen..141

Chapter Fifteen 151

Chapter Sixteen...161

Chapter Seventeen...172

Chapter Eighteen...182

Chapter Nineteen 192

Chapter Twenty 203

Chapter Twenty One..213

Chapter Twenty Two..223

Chapter Twenty Three...233

Chapter Twenty Four...244

Chapter One

School was just over. The boys belonging to Arlingford College poured out into the playing fields, the juniors tumbling over one another in haste and confusion, as though the premises were on fire behind them; the seniors strolling leisurely out, or gathering in small groups near the school door, to arrange their plans for the afternoon. Dr Stansfield, the headmaster, still remained, in conversation with Reginald Margetts, a connection of his wife's, a young man of two-and-twenty, who was passing the Oxford long vacation at his house, and had come in with a message from Mrs Stansfield. One of the assistant masters also, George Rivers by name, sat at his desk, looking over some exercises of which he had not completed the revision. He was near about Margetts' age, a well-built young fellow with an intelligent and pleasant face.

"Well, that will do, Redgy," said the Doctor. "You may tell Mrs Stansfield that I do not know, and cannot conjecture who her visitor may have been; but if he is to return in half an hour, I shall be in the library ready to receive him. At present I must have a little talk with George Rivers here, before I leave the school."

"I am going to walk with Rivers presently, sir," said Margetts. "Shall you be long?"

"A quarter of an hour, I daresay. George will join you when we have done. George," he continued, as Margetts left the room, "I have looked over the papers you have sent me. I intended to have had this conversation, even if you had not invited it. It is time that some conclusion was come to. You have not, I fear, received any fresh information?"

"I am sorry to say I have not."

"I am sorry too; but I hardly expected anything else. You are, I think, more than one-and-twenty?"

"Two-and-twenty in a few months, sir."

"Indeed. Well, there ought to be no further delay in the arrangement of your plans for the future. Do you not think so?"

"Yes, sir; and I believe I have made up my mind."

"What have you resolved to do?"

"Before I go into that, Dr Stansfield, I ought to thank you for the great kirdness you have shown me. I should be a pauper, or something like it, but for you."

"We need not speak of that. Go on."

"Well, sir, I feel that I ought not to remain longer in England. I have already trespassed too long on your bounty."

"If that is your reason for leaving England, you had better reconsider it. Whatever might have been the case three years and a half ago, you are not costing me anything now. Your assistant-mastership, small as the salary is, with what you have of your own, is enough to keep you, and you fully earn it. You have, I believe, once or twice expressed a wish to enter holy orders?"

"It has been my wish for some time past, sir."

"Very well. You could not be ordained for more than a year. Before that I think I could arrange with the Bishop for you to be ordained on your mastership here. There is not so much difficulty made about a title as used to be the case."

"You are most kind, sir. I hope you will not think me ungrateful; but I feel it to be my first duty to find my mother and sister, if I can."

"I cannot blame you. But I should like to know what steps you mean to take. I understood you to say you had obtained no further information."

"No; and I do not expect to obtain any information, so long as I am in England. But if I were out in Australia, it might be different."

"What do you propose to do, then?"

"Well, in the first place, to work my passage out to Australia—to Swan River, you know."

"Ay, to Dalby's Plot, to which it was ascertained that your mother went when she landed in Australia. But you doubtless remember that we ascertained, two years and a half ago, that she had left the colony, and had gone—some said to Tasmania, and others to Cape Town; but no one has ever given us a clue, by which we might discover the place to which she had really removed."

"That is so. But if I were on the spot I think I might be able to hunt out information, which no one, who was not as deeply interested as I am, would be able to obtain."

"You may be right in that. Well, suppose you went out, and succeeded in finding Mrs Rivers—what then?"

"Then I should like to buy land—a small farm. A little money goes a long way out there, you know, sir. Then, when I was getting on pretty well, I might be ordained by one of the colonial bishops, and do clerical work combined with farming. It isn't the same kind of thing out there, I am told, that it is in England. There are no large populations—except, of course, in the towns—which take up a man's whole time."

"You are right, I believe. A number of educated and zealous men supporting themselves by their own industry, and yet having the power of ministering to their neighbours, would be a great boon in the colonies. I would willingly lend you all the assistance in my power towards carrying out your scheme; but, as I have already said, I am afraid I see but little hope of learning what has become of your mother and sister."

"I do not see much more; but I think it my duty to make the trial."

"Be it so then. What money have you?"

"Enough to pay my passage to Australia, sir,—that is, as a third-class passenger, if I should prefer that to serving as a sailor on board one of the steamers,—and perhaps 100 pounds over."

"I think you must go as a passenger. It might prejudice your errand, when you get there, if you had been before the mast. We must contrive to get you a letter of introduction to one of the Australian bishops."

"I'll give him one!" exclaimed a voice. "I know two or three of them as well as I know my own brother."

Dr Stansfield started up in great surprise. "What, Rogers!" he exclaimed. "Are you the visitor whom Mrs Stansfield told me to expect? I knew you were coming to England, but not so soon as this."

"To be sure I am. I was told you would be out of school by a quarter past twelve at latest, and now it is half-past, and you are still there!"

"We had forgotten the lapse of time," said the Doctor. "But tell me what has brought you to England so much earlier than was expected."

"The rows with the Boers and the Zulus," said Mr Rogers. "I have come home—partly at the request of many of the leading men in Natal, partly because my own interests were deeply concerned—to try and induce the Government to put matters on some satisfactory footing."

"I had better leave you, sir, had I not?" said George, rising. "You can speak to me further at another time."

Both the gentlemen turned and looked at the speaker, whose presence perhaps they had forgotten.

"Oh yes," said Dr Stansfield; "I will bear what you have told me in mind, and speak to you about it in a day or two."

George bowed, and left the room.

"Who is that lad?" inquired Mr Rogers. "I don't suppose I can have seen him before; but his face seems strangely familiar to me."

"No; you can't have seen him before," rejoined the Doctor, smiling, "unless it was in a dream. He has never been in South Africa, and you, I think, have never left it since he was a child."

"No; I have never left the Transvaal, unless to visit Cape Town, or Zululand, or Natal, for twenty years. I wonder you knew me, Stansfield; but, to be sure, you were expecting me before long. But as regards this lad— has he any relatives in the Transvaal?"

"His mother and sister may be in the Transvaal for all I can tell. They left England some years ago, and the place where they are living is quite unknown."

"What is his name?" asked Mr Rogers.

"Rivers," answered the headmaster,—"George Rivers." Mr Rogers shook his head. "I know no person of that name," he said. "It must be a mere chance resemblance. But I should like to know his history; for some reason or other he interests me."

"Well, I can tell it you now," said the Doctor. "Sophia will not expect us until luncheon-time, and that is not for another half-hour yet. Sit down in that chair, and you shall hear it.

"George's father was a country doctor; he lived in this neighbourhood, and was a very estimable man, and skilful in his profession, but very poor. He married Farmer Wylie's daughter, a well-to-do man, and able to give his daughter Agnes a very comfortable portion, particularly as she was his only child. But he set himself against the marriage, forbade it for several years, and at last only agreed because he saw nothing could change his daughter's mind. But he would give her nothing more than a hundred pounds, to buy her wedding clothes and help furnish the house. A country doctor's practice is not very profitable, and Mr Rivers, though not an extravagant, was not a saving man. They found it hard work to live, still harder when their children began to grow up. George was born to them two years after their marriage, and Thyrza two years after that."

"Thyrza, did you say?" interposed Mr Rogers suddenly.

"Yes, Thyrza," said the Doctor. "It was an unusual name, but I believe it was her father's fancy. Well, Mr and Mrs Rivers got poorer and poorer. He had sent George to the college here. The lad was clever and hard-working, and he obtained a scholarship, which went a long way towards paying his schooling. But Mr Rivers called upon me one day, when George was between sixteen and seventeen, and told me that he could not longer afford to pay even the slight cost of his son's education. He had had an interview with his son, he said, and had told him the truth. I was interested in the lad, and told Mr Rivers that whatever school fees there were would be remitted in the case of his son. The poor man was very grateful; but when he reached home with the good news, he found it had come too late. The boy had disappeared, no one knew whither. It was not for nearly a month afterwards that a letter arrived, saying that he had resolved he would no longer be a charge upon his parents' scanty means. He had therefore gone on board a ship bound for Australia. He meant to work his passage out there before the mast, and when out there hoped to be able to find employment enough to keep himself. As soon as he reached his destination, they should hear from him again. Mrs Rivers brought me this letter, in the hope that I might be able to assist her. She was wrapt up in this boy, and his departure had nearly broken her heart.

"'We could bear anything,' she said to me, 'if he was only with us.'

"I promised that I would write to the owners of the ship in which he had sailed, and make arrangements for his return to England on the earliest opportunity. But a series of misfortunes ensued, which I have often wondered that she survived. First of all, there was a terrible fire, by which Mr Rivers' house was burnt to the ground. No life was lost, but there was heavy loss, and, what was worse, Mrs Rivers was severely burned. One arm was so much injured that it was thought for a long time she would lose the use of it, and the scars on her wrist and thumb will never be erased."

Mr Rogers again started, and was on the point of speaking. But he checked himself, and allowed the Doctor to go on.

"Before she had recovered from her wounds came the news that the *Boomerang*, in which George had sailed, had been wrecked. The crew had taken to the boats, some of which had landed safe on the Australian coast; but others, it was feared, were lost. Mr Rivers could not bear up against this continual current of misfortune. He took to his bed, lingered some weeks, and then died. That his widow did not speedily follow him has, as I have already intimated, always been a matter of wonder to me. I think the necessity of living for the sake of her daughter was the only thing that bore her up. She was left, of course, quite penniless. I had the not very pleasant task of calling upon old Farmer Wylie to inform him of his daughter's destitute condition. The old man had turned more and more against the match, as it became evident that the Riverses were not thriving in the world. Mr Rivers had felt hurt and affronted at the language used by his father-in-law; and for the last few years all intercourse had been broken off. But it was now necessary to apply to him. I rode over accordingly, but found I had gone on a bootless errand. Old Wylie himself was dangerously ill, and died within a few days, never having recovered consciousness. When his will was opened, it was found that his whole property had been bequeathed to the county hospital. There was a small sum which had belonged to his wife, which it was agreed might be made over to his daughter. It was enough to pay her husband's debts, and leave her about a couple of hundred pounds. She resolved with this to emigrate to Australia."

"That was a strange resolution, was it not, under the circumstances?" remarked Mr Rogers.

"I think it was, but she had a reason for it. She fancied that her uncle Christopher, who had gone thither many years before, might still be living there. I believe, too, that the sight of the familiar scenes around her, associated as they were in her mind with her husband and son, were more than she could endure. At all events she went, and arrived safely in the colony. She wrote to apprise me of it, but I never heard from her again. Nor have I ever been able to discover what became of her, except that she left Australia soon afterwards."

"And what of George, then?" asked Mr Rogers, who had become interested in the narrative.

"He returned to England about six months after his mother's departure. The boat in which he had left the *Boomerang* had been driven out of its course, and had at last reached the Island of Timor. Thence George had obtained a passage to Singapore, and thence again home. He came to me in great distress. His father's death and his mother's departure from England had been terrible shocks to him. His first thought, of course, was of immediately joining his mother, wherever she might be. But I pointed out to him that it would be better for him to wait until we could learn more of her movements. All that I had heard at that time was that she had left Australia soon after her arrival there, her uncle, Mr Christopher Wylie, having gone somewhere else, though no one seemed to know where. Probably, however, she would write home again. Meanwhile, inquiry might continue to be made. George, who was now nearly eighteen, had better re-enter the college for a year. A small legacy left him by a relative would enable him to pay for his board, and the school fees we remitted. He agreed to this, and continued in the school for a year and a half, after which I found him some employment as an extra junior master. He has continued his studies, and is now a very tolerable scholar."

"And he has never discovered his mother's present residence?"

"Never. A friend in Swan River, to whom I wrote, made every inquiry, but could only learn what I have already told you, that Mrs Rivers went away soon after her arrival. She had discovered some clue, it was thought, to her uncle's new place of abode. But even that is conjecture."

"And what does the lad propose to do with himself?" asked Mr Rogers. "He will not, I suppose, remain here much longer."

"No. He will go away at midsummer. He wanted to go at once, but I urged his remaining until the end of the half-year. Indeed, there are preparations which must be made before undertaking a long voyage."

"He is going to Australia, then?"

"Yes. He thinks that, although Mr Welstead's inquiries failed to elicit the required information, he himself might be more successful. I don't agree with him; but it would be hard to discourage him."

"And if he finds his mother and sister?"

"Then he would buy a little land with what remains of his cousin's legacy, and settle in the colony with his relatives, combining farming with a clergyman's work."

"A clergyman's work? Has he any fancy for that?"

"Yes, a very decided one. He is one of those who are anxious to do good, but who combine with it an impatience of settled habits of life, and a thirst for novelty and adventure. I do not know how to blame him. He has all the qualities that would fit him for the course on which he desires to enter. He is resolute, intelligent, and ready; capital at all field sports and outdoor exercises; capable of bearing considerable fatigue and hardships without murmuring; and withal extremely affectionate and right-minded. Whatever purpose he might conceive, he would be pretty sure to carry out, and, unless under very exceptional circumstances, successfully."

"Indeed!" said Mr Rogers. "Then he is certainly the man for the colonies. Well, Stansfield, I have not interrupted you, because I wanted particularly to hear the whole of this story; but you will be surprised, I think, to hear that I not only know the place where young Rivers' mother and sister are living, but am myself personally acquainted with them."

"With Mrs Rivers and her daughter!" exclaimed the headmaster in surprise. "I thought you said just now that you knew no one of that name?"

"Nor do I," said Mr Rogers; "but I do know a Mrs Mansen, the wife of a Dutch farmer, who lives at one of my farms, only a short distance from my station. She has a daughter named Thyrza Rivers, whose age corresponds nearly with that of the Thyrza of your story."

"It is an uncommon name," said the headmaster. "Still there might be two persons so called."

"No doubt. But you said the mother had been disfigured in the hand by a severe burn. Mrs Mansen is a handsome woman past forty; but she has just such a scar as you describe on her wrist. But did I understand you to say her Christian name was Agnes?"

"Yes," said Dr Stansfield; "I am pretty sure it is. But anyway it will be in the School Register. Yes," he added, taking a book down; "here it is: 'September 24, 18—. George, son of George and Agnes Rivers, admitted.'"

"Then I think there can be no doubt of the identity," said Mr Rogers. "Mrs Mansen's name is certainly Agnes. She had occasion to sign her name before me, as a magistrate, a twelvemonth ago, and I remember it perfectly. Mrs Mansen, too, had lost, or rather, believed she had lost her only son, at sea. Well, this simplifies matters, I think, considerably. I conclude this young fellow will give up all idea of proceeding to Australia, and betake himself to Mansen's place—'Spielman's Vley,' as it is called—instead?"

"Spielman's Vley," repeated the Doctor. "Is that in Natal or in Zululand?"

"It is in neither. My station—Umvalosa—is just on the very borders of the three countries, Zululand, Natal, and the Transvaal; and Spielman's Vley lies a short distance only to the north-west, in the Transvaal. It is one of the places which my chaplain,—as I call him,—Lambert, continually visits."

"Ay; his visitations are rather different, I expect, from those of our parochial clergy?"

"Very different. There are at least a dozen places round Umvalosa, which, but for him, would be wholly without spiritual care. He visits these in regular order, as well as he can; but some of them only get a service once in two months or so. Unless there is some special reason, such as some one on his deathbed wanting him, he is unable to visit them oftener."

"That must cause a good deal of spiritual deadness," observed Dr Stansfield. "They must soon forget all about his visits."

"Ah, so you in England fancy; but nothing can be further from the fact. If the parson's visits were looked for in England as they are in my neighbourhood, the English Church would be in a very different position.

Our people never forget the day when Mr Lambert is due. They will come a long distance, and in all weathers, to be present at the services. But that is human nature after all. What a man can have for the asking, he cares little about, let it be ever so valuable; what he can only get by taking much trouble and incurring great risk, that he appreciates. But this has nothing to do with young Rivers. I think I ought to see him, and tell him my conjectures—or rather, I think I may say, my decided convictions—as to the identity of his mother with Mrs Mansen."

"Of course," returned the Doctor. "He must judge for himself; but it appears to me to be a clear case."

"Well, but there is something further. If he is convinced that I am right, he will, I conclude, set out shortly—not for Australia, but for South Africa."

"No doubt of that," assented the headmaster.

"In that case I shall make him an offer, which I hope he will accept. I told you it was the political aspect of things that had brought me home a month or two sooner than I had originally intended; but I had other reasons besides. I wanted to get one or two young men, who would take situations as schoolmasters and readers, and who might ultimately be ordained, and serve churches out there, which I believe I can contrive to get built. Now this lad seems to be the very person I am looking after. I could put him into a small farm, which he could cultivate with the help of some natives, and there would be a salary enough to keep him until the farm began to pay. That it would soon do if he was capable and painstaking, as by your account he is."

"He is all that, I can answer for it. If any young fellow is more likely than another to succeed in such a position, it is George Rivers."

"Very good. If he engages with me, I shall undertake to provide his outfit, and pay his passage to Durban and from thence to Umvalosa. But he must make up his mind at once. I must leave this place for London to-morrow."

"You had better see him without loss of time. He was to go out for a short walk with his friend, Reginald Margetts; but he will be back by dinner-time. I think he will probably accept your offer. I should certainly advise him to do so."

Dr Stansfield proved to be right in his anticipations. George was at first inclined to be somewhat sceptical as to the identity of his mother with Mrs Mansen, and also made many inquiries as to the man who, according to Mr Rogers' theory, was her second husband. He was told that Ludwig Mansen was a very worthy man, well educated, and much respected. George would find him a very desirable relative. He was not rich, but in good circumstances. He and Mrs Mansen were generally thought to live very happily together. As regards himself, Mr Rogers knew that his mother had never ceased to deplore his death, which she supposed had certainly occurred, and that his reappearance would be like new life to her. If George had had no other reason for accepting Mr Rogers' offer, this would have been sufficient to induce him to do so; in fact, the desire of meeting her again grew so greatly on him, that it was with difficulty that he could bring himself to consent to the delay of five or six weeks, which Mr Rogers had declared to be necessary for making the required arrangements. His passage was taken in the *Zulu Queen*,—Captain Ranken, commander,—a large vessel carrying a cargo to Durban, and taking a few first-class passengers at a lower rate than was usually charged by the great steam companies.

About a week after Mr Rogers' departure for London, Redgy Margetts came to Rivers with a letter, which he had that morning received from his father.

"All right," he said, "old fellow! The governor has given his consent, like a brick, as he is!"

"Given his consent to what, Redgy?" inquired George with surprise.

"To my sailing with you for Durban in the *Zulu Queen*" answered Margetts. "I hoped from the first that he would; but I said nothing about it till I was sure."

"You go to the Transvaal, Redgy!" exclaimed Rivers. "What should take you there?"

"Oh, I have always intended to go out to one of the colonies. There is nothing for any one to do in England, you know; and it will be very jolly having you for my messmate and fellow-settler."

"It will be very jolly for *me* anyway," said Rivers, shaking him heartily by the hand. "I really think the thing is quite perfect now."

Chapter Two

The *Zulu Queen* had cleared the Channel and the Bay of Biscay, and was somewhere about abreast of Lisbon, when Redgy Margetts came on deck to join his friend Rivers. The latter was a good sailor, and had some considerable experience of the sea. Even the Channel and the Bay, though they had been more than usually rough, had not discomposed him. But the other passengers, of whom there were not more than seven or eight on board, had had a bad time of it. Two Dutch gentlemen, whose names he had discovered to be Vander Heyden and Moritz, had not left their cabin, and Rivers had heard their groans very distinctly through the thin partition of the cabin. Redgy, whose berth was immediately under his own, had been almost as bad, and had only been comforted by George's assurances that when they were well south of Cape Finisterre, his troubles would be at an end.

The prophecy seemed likely now to be fulfilled. The ship had ceased to pitch and roll, and the bright sky and warm sun were delightful after the confined gloom of the cabin. It was a grand sight indeed that met Redgy's eyes as he stepped on deck. There was the vast blue dome above, hardly flecked by a single cloud. There was the illimitable ocean below, the waves dancing gaily in the sunshine, and in the distance the coast of Portugal, lying like a soft cloud, through which some shadowy outlines of the mountains were visible.

"Well, this is jolly enough!" exclaimed Margetts, as he seated himself by his friend's side. "If the voyage is going to be like this, there won't be so much to complain of."

"It *will* be like this, only a little warmer—a good deal warmer—when we get in the tropics," said Rivers. "But otherwise the appearance of things won't be greatly different from this for a good many weeks to come. How are the Dutchmen, Redgy? Have they ceased groaning?"

"I haven't heard them this morning," returned Margetts. "I fancy they are getting up. The lady has been the worst, I believe."

"Lady! I didn't know there was a lady on board. What, is she the big Dutchman's wife?"

"No, sister. I heard the second biggest Dutchman call to the other, and tell him his sister wanted him!"

"Do you know their names, Redgy? I only saw them for a few minutes when they came aboard at Plymouth. I didn't see the lady at all. I suppose she must have gone straight down into her cabin."

"I know nothing but their Christian names," returned Redgy. "The big one is called Henryk, and the other Frank, or, as they pronounced it, Vrank. The lady, I think, is Annchen. That's their way of pronouncing the name."

"Well, I hope they'll make themselves agreeable. As they are to be our companions for four or five weeks at least, it will make a considerable difference to us whether they are pleasant or not."

"I too should like to know something about them," said Margetts. "Here's the skipper. Perhaps he'll be able to tell us something. Good morning, Captain Ranken," he added, as the captain came up.

"Good morning, gentlemen. Good morning, Mr Margetts," said the skipper; "glad to see you've got over it. Mr Rivers here is an old salt, and doesn't mind even the Bay of Biscay."

"We want you to tell us something about our fellow-passengers," said George.

"Fellow-passengers! We've very few—two Englishmen, besides yourselves. One is Mr Whittaker, a clerk in a house at Pieter Maritzburg, the other Mr Walters, who has some Government appointment in the colony. There's a Portuguese too. He's in the wine trade, I fancy, but he goes no farther than Madeira. And there's a Dutch officer and his sister—Mynheer Vander Heyden and his friend Moritz. They all three hail from the Transvaal. I never had so few passengers on board before."

"Well, you know the old proverb," said Margetts: "the fewer the better cheer. We must try to make that good."

"All right, Mr Margetts! Nothing is pleasanter than these voyages, when the passengers are on good terms with one another. I will do my best, I promise you, to make things pleasant. Here they come," he added a moment afterwards, as the head and shoulders of a tall man came up the hatchway. "Come with me, and I will introduce you."

The two Dutchmen looked round them as they mounted the companion ladder, with the air of persons who were familiar with what they saw. They were both somewhat heavily built, but rather fine-looking men. The taller of the two might be eight or nine-and-twenty. His figure showed great muscular strength, and there was an alacrity in his movements which betokened one well accustomed to bodily exertion. His features were rather handsome, though there was an expression to be traced on them which indicated an imperious, and somewhat irascible, temper. His friend Moritz was of a slighter build, but still wiry and strong. His features were not so regular, but he looked more good-natured than his companion. It may be added that their demeanour accorded with these impressions.

"Mynheer Vander Heyden, Mynheer Moritz, let me introduce you to Mr Rivers and Mr Margetts. You will have much in common with them, I fancy, as their destination is only a few hundred miles short of your own."

Vander Heyden bowed distantly. "English settlers, I suppose," he said. "Do you propose to establish yourselves, gentlemen, in Natal, or Zululand?"

"In neither," replied Rivers a little stiffly, for he did not like the tone in which Vander Heyden spoke. "The place to which I am proceeding is in the Transvaal."

"I thought as much," muttered Vander Heyden. Rivers only half caught the words, but there could be no mistake as to Vander Heyden's demeanour. Some unpleasant altercation might have ensued, if Moritz had not stept forward and said pleasantly, "The Transvaal! that is our country, and it is a very fine one to settle in. May I ask what is the name of your station?"

"Dykeman's Hollow," replied Rivers. "It lies, I am told, some twenty miles from the Zulu frontier."

"Yes, at Umvalosa," assented Moritz. "I know where it is, and have often been by it, though I have never visited there. I believe the land is very good in that neighbourhood."

"Is the hunting good there?" asked Redgy; "are there plenty of wild animals about there?"

"More than perhaps you would desire," returned Moritz, smiling. "The lions and the elephants are not often to be seen; they never continue long in any neighbourhood in which Europeans have settled. Still, in the northern parts of the Transvaal you will meet with them—occasionally, at all events. But of the tigers—or rather the leopards, for that is what they really are—and of the hyenas, there are plenty. There is also no lack of snakes—cobras, ondaras, and puff-adders; there is no dearth of any of them."

"I shall enjoy the lion-hunting, at all events," said Redgy.

"I hardly think you will," observed Vander Heyden with something of a sneer. "You will find that a different matter from what you in England are pleased to call sport—hunting a hare or a fox, or shooting at a bird. Hunting in the Transvaal requires both skill and courage."

"No doubt, Mr Vander Heyden," said George shortly; "but there is no reason, I suppose, why an Englishman may not possess both."

"It is possible that he may," returned the Dutchman coldly.

Captain Ranken looked uncomfortable. He foresaw altercations in the distance, if not open quarrels, and these on board ship were especially to be deprecated. He saw that though George apparently was good-tempered, he was not disposed to submit to insolence; and Vander Heyden evidently entertained the strong dislike to the English for which so many of his countrymen were notorious. Nothing, however, had been said as yet which required his interference. He was looking about for some means of diverting the conversation into another channel, when the arrival of a new person on the scene effected his purpose for him. A delicate white hand appeared on the top of the companion, and immediately after a female figure issued forth. The captain stepped forward to offer his hand.

"I am rejoiced, Miss Vander Heyden, to welcome you on deck. This is a charming morning for your first appearance. It is quite warm, though there is a pleasant breeze."

The young lady untied the woollen scarf she had wrapped round her head, and requited the captain's civility by a bow. The latter would have proceeded to present her to the two Englishmen, but her brother stepped stiffly forward, and, offering his arm, led her to a seat near the taffrail Moritz followed, and the captain turned off to give some directions to the mate.

"I don't like that fellow, George," said Margetts. "He seems inclined to be insolent. I'm afraid we shall have a row with him before long."

"I don't know about a row, Redgy," said Rivers; "that is, if you mean an open quarrel. I don't mean to quarrel with him, or with any one else. But he must be more civil, if we are to be on friendly terms. The other seems inclined to be more sociable."

"And his sister too," observed Redgy. "She looks good-natured enough, and only look how handsome she is! Don't you think so, George?"

"She is not bad-looking," assented Rivers; "I shouldn't call her regularly handsome, but she is certainly both pretty and sweet-looking."

"Her society will make the voyage pleasanter," said Redgy.

"I should doubt that," returned George. "If I don't mistake, this Dutchman doesn't mean us to make her acquaintance."

"She may have something to say to that," observed Margetts. "He isn't either her father or her husband, you know."

"No," said Rivers; "he couldn't prevent our knowing her, if she desired it herself. But I shall take my cue from him, and stand aloof if he shows that he wishes it. But here come two more—and Englishmen evidently. I don't think the Portuguese will show on deck to-day, from what the steward told me. I suppose we needn't stand on ceremony here. Mr Whittaker and Mr Walters, I believe," he added, taking off his hat. "My name is Rivers, and my friend's here is Margetts. As we are to be fellow-voyagers for some weeks, we had better make acquaintance."

"My name is Whittaker," said the elder of the two travellers, a pleasant-looking man of about thirty, "and I am happy to be introduced to you, Mr Rivers. This is Mr Walters. He lands at East London, but all the rest of us, I believe, are going on to Durban."

"I believe so," assented Rivers. "Do you reside in Durban, may I ask?"

"No. I am the chief clerk in the Colonial Bank at Pieter Maritzburg. I have been home on business connected with the bank, and am now returning."

"Do you know these Dutchmen?" asked Margetts, looking as he spoke at the group of three who were still seated by the taffrail.

Mr Whittaker looked in the direction indicated.

"Yes," he said, "I do know them; and I am not particularly glad to have them for my fellow-passengers. I have seen them once or twice in Natal, and I met them at the house of one of our correspondents a week or two ago in London."

"What do you know about them?" inquired Redgy. "I know that they have an especial dislike to Englishmen," said Whittaker; "that is, Vander Heyden has; I don't know about the other. If you knew the colony as well as I do, Mr Rivers, you would be aware that there is a great difference observable among the Dutch settlers. Some of them are kind and friendly enough with all white men—"

"All *white* men?" interposed Redgy. "Not with blacks, then?"

"No, Mr Margetts," returned the other gravely. "A man can know very little about the colony not to be aware that every Dutchman regards the natives as being of little more account than dogs or horses—of a good deal less account than many horses."

"So I have heard. But what about their relationship with other whites?"

"As I was saying, some of them will receive kindly and hospitably all Europeans; but others entertain a rooted dislike to all but their own countrymen. Englishmen in particular they regard as their natural enemies. They will not do them the slightest service, or exchange the most ordinary civilities with them. I have known some Boers refuse even a glass of cold water to an Englishman when he was almost perishing with thirst."

"And this Vander Heyden is one of that sort, hey?" asked Margetts. "By the way, did not Captain Ranken say he was an officer?"

"He has been some years in the Dutch service. He left the Transvaal when his father died; but he is now returning to marry, and live on his property with his wife and sister. Some years ago, when visiting a friend at Maritzburg who is a merchant there, there was a quarrel with an English officer, which attracted a good deal of attention, and made Vander Heyden, for the time at all events, very notorious. That was caused by his manner of dealing with the natives."

"What were the particulars?" asked Mr Walters.

"He was on his way to Maritzburg," said Whittaker, "and on the road he met a servant of Captain Tarleton's, who was taking two horses belonging to his master to Rorke's Drift. The spot where they met was at a small spring in the middle of a long dry tract of country. They arrived nearly about the same time; but Tarleton's servant got there first, and was proceeding to water the horses, when Vander Heyden ordered him imperiously to desist, and wait until his party had watered their cattle. He took the captain's servant for a native,—a Kaffir or Zulu; but the man really was a Sikh, and as bold and fierce as Vander Heyden himself. He angrily refused; and, when the Dutchman thrust him violently on one side, he drew his knife, and would have stabbed his assailant, if the others of the party had not seized him. While the altercation was going on, Captain Tarleton himself rode up, and, having heard the particulars from the bystanders, took up the quarrel. The result was a challenge; and there would have been a duel in Maritzburg a day or two afterwards, if the matter had not reached the ears of one of the local magistrates. He sent for the parties, convicted Vander Heyden of an assault, and required him to find securities to keep the peace, or leave the colony. The Dutchman chose the latter course. But the affair, I take it, has not increased his affection for us English."

"Well, he must keep the peace here," remarked the captain, who had again joined them; "and I shall take care that he does. But I agree with Mr Whittaker that he is not very likely to be over cordial with us English. I have already seen some indications of his feelings towards us."

"The other man—Moritz his name is, I think," observed Redgy— "appears to be more amiably disposed."

"The young lady too seems pleasant," said Mr Whittaker; "but I suppose she will be in a great measure under her brother's orders."

"No doubt," said Rivers. "Well, of course, it rests with herself whether we are to be friendly with her or not."

Several days passed on. Madeira was reached; and then the ship's course was set for Saint Helena, where there was to be a delay of at least twenty-four hours. The anticipations expressed as to Vander Heyden's demeanour were fully verified. He stood aloof himself from all the passengers except Moritz and the Portuguese, Martinez; and it was tolerably plain that he only sought his society as a means of keeping the others at a distance. At the meals, which took place in the principal cabin, he seated his sister at the end of the table, on the captain's right. He himself sat next to her, with Moritz immediately opposite, and Martinez next to him. As he never addressed a single word to the Englishmen, and the Portuguese could not speak English, all conversation with Annchen became almost impossible; indeed, as none of them had been introduced to her, they could hardly under such circumstances presume to address her. Indeed, they felt too much offended at the haughty dislike which Vander Heyden made no show of concealing, to have any desire to do so; and the voyage to the Cape might have been accomplished without the interchange of a word between the young lady and her English fellow-passengers, if it had not been for an occurrence which took place when they were some days' voyage south of Madeira, and approaching the equator.

All the party were on deck. Annchen, dressed entirely in white, and wearing a large hat of the same colour,—the crown being thickened as a defence against the sun,—was sitting on a low stool under the shade of the companion. Rivers, Redgy, and Mr Walters were lying on the deck under an awning which they had constructed with the help of an old sail. A sharp wind had been blowing since daybreak, which threatened to rise to a gale at sundown. Presently one of the sailors, carrying a load of potatoes to the coop, came up the hatchway. He had evidently been drinking, and was extremely unsteady on his legs. A gust of wind caught him as he stepped on deck. He reeled, and struck against Vander Heyden, upsetting him, and knocking him against Annchen, who was standing close by. She lost her balance, and the wind, catching her hat, swept it across the deck. It would have been carried into the sea, if it had not been caught in the rigging. Rivers started up, skimmed nimbly up the ropes, recovered the hat, and, descending, presented it to its owner. Annchen coloured, and glanced hurriedly round at her brother, expecting him to acknowledge the civility.

But Vander Heyden was differently employed. He had regained his feet, and was on the point of angrily reproving the sailor for his clumsiness, when he suddenly exclaimed,—

"Ha! you here, you English scoundrel! What has brought you into this ship? How dare you intrude yourself on me?"

"I want to have nothing to do with you," retorted the man sullenly. "I couldn't help the wind blowing, could I? As for my being an English scoundrel, a Dutch coward is worse any day!"

᾽ "Insolent hound!" cried Vander Heyden, striking him a heavy blow as he spoke; "I will teach you to insult a Hollander."

The man reeled and fell on the deck, knocking over another sailor, named Van Ryk, who was passing at the moment. Their dislike of the Boer seemed to be as great as his of them. They leaped up and rushed together on Vander Heyden, and an angry fray would have ensued, if Wyndham, the first mate, had not interfered. He had seen what had occurred, and desired the combatants to desist.

"Mr Vander Heyden," he said, "this cannot be allowed. Bostock has had more than his allowance of grog, and I shall see that he is punished for that; but I am pretty sure he did not mean to annoy you—"

"Whom do you call Bostock?" interrupted the Dutchman,—"that schelm, Cargill? I know him better than you do, I fancy."

"I know him by the name in which he entered this ship," returned the mate. "But it does not matter what his name is. You had no right to strike him, and should beg his pardon."

"Beg his pardon!" exclaimed the other haughtily; "you do not think I shall do that! He has hurt me a good deal. I believe I have sprained my ankle badly. But, anyway, I am not to be subjected to his drunken insolence. If he intrudes himself on me again, he will suffer sharply for it. Help me down below, Frank," he continued; "I must get my shoe off, and bandage my ankle. The surgeon had better come to me."

"Stop, sir," said the mate. "I shall send for the captain, and inform him of what has passed. You will be pleased to wait till he comes on deck."

Captain Ranken accordingly was summoned, and, having heard Wyndham's statement, asked Vander Heyden whether the matter had been correctly reported; but the latter made no reply.

"I must assume, then, that the thing really occurred as reported. I beg to tell you, sir, that I command this ship; and any one who interferes with its discipline is accountable to me. You will beg this man's pardon, as the mate has most properly required, and give your undertaking not to repeat your violence, or I shall confine you to your cabin. Any repetition of your offence will be punished by your being put into irons."

"I shall give no promise," said Vander Heyden angrily. "Frank, help me to my cabin, and send the surgeon to me. I suppose he will not be forbidden to attend me."

"Certainly not, sir," said Captain Ranken; "I did not know that you had been hurt. Perhaps when below you will think better of this, and give the promise I require. I hope you will forgive me, Miss Vander Heyden," he continued, as the Dutchman was helped down the companion. "I am extremely sorry for what has occurred; but it is necessary for the comfort of the whole ship, that I should maintain strict discipline."

Annchen bowed silently, and, taking her hat from George, who was still standing by, holding it in his hand, thanked him very civilly. She then expressed her intention of going down to her brother, to see if she could render him any help.

"I think you had better not," said George. "The surgeon has just gone to him, and will do all that is necessary. Mr Moritz, too, is with him, and there is hardly room for more in the cabin. But I will go down and inquire."

He went below accordingly, and presently returned with the information that the surgeon said there was a severe sprain. But he had bandaged and fomented the ankle, and it would be better for the patient to remain for the present quite quiet. Moritz also returned on deck with the same report, at the same time thanking Rivers with much courtesy for his services. George replied; and a conversation ensued, which altogether dispelled the awkwardness which had hitherto prevailed. Vander Heyden's sprain was found to be worse than it was at first apprehended. It became evident that for a week at least he would be a prisoner in his cabin, thus rendering the captain's sentence altogether needless. His absence from the deck and the daily meals, made an entire alteration in the relation of the passengers to one another. Annchen passed a considerable part of her time in her brother's cabin, but she was still frequently on deck, and when there showed no disposition to repel the civilities of her fellow-passengers, and the whole party soon became extremely friendly with one another.

One evening Captain Ranken announced that they were now within a day's sail of Saint Helena, and that he intended to make up a party, which he hoped all the passengers would join, to visit Longwood and Napoleon's grave.

"I am afraid your brother will still be a prisoner, Miss Annchen," he said. "But that need not deprive us of your and Mr Moritz's company."

Annchen made no reply, unless a slight tinge of colour which overspread her cheek might be regarded as one. She knew that her brother would in all likelihood insist on her remaining in the ship; but that she was very unwilling to do. She was very fond of him, and always sided with him, so far as she was able; but she was not blind to his faults, and knew that in the quarrel which had recently taken place he was almost entirely to blame. She had saved him from the indignity of giving the promise required by Captain Ranken, by assuring the captain privately that her brother would not repeat the offence, though he was too proud to say so; and Captain Ranken, taking into consideration the confinement which Vander Heyden had already undergone, and influenced doubtless, as all men are apt to be, by appeals from bright eyes and arguments from rosy lips, had agreed to make no further mention of the matter. But she was not disposed to submit to her brother's dictation respecting her fellow-passengers, whom she had found extremely agreeable and friendly; against whom, too, there seemed to be no other objection than that they were Englishmen. George Rivers in particular was a very agreeable companion, and she was greatly diverted with the humorous sallies of Redgy Margetts and young Walters, who kept the whole party in a state of continual amusement. Mr Whittaker, again, was an agreeable fellow-passenger, though graver and less communicative than the others. She was more frank and easy with the young men, because it was generally known that there was an engagement between her and Mynheer Moritz, —one of those family compacts, with which both parties seemed to be satisfied, though there was no display of ardent affection on either side. On the whole, the party in the cabin and on the deck was a pleasant one, Moritz appearing to enjoy it as well as herself. But Annchen felt sure that if her brother should be told of the proposed expedition to visit the interior of Saint Helena, he would object to her joining it; and she was not disposed to forego the pleasure she promised herself, to gratify his fancy. She therefore said nothing on the subject until the captain's boat, which was to convey the party on shore, had been made ready. Then she told Captain Ranken that she had resolved to go on the party with the others.

"Delighted to hear it, Miss Vander Heyden?" answered the captain; "and I think I can promise you that you will not regret your determination. I have already sent a message on shore to order a carriage, which will take us to Longwood. Now then for the detested residence, and the empty grave, of the *ci-devant* conqueror of Europe!"

Chapter Three

"Nature must have intended this island for a prison," remarked Miss Vander Heyden, as she looked up at the inaccessible precipices by which Saint Helena is environed. "Nothing but a bird could make its way into the interior, except by the landing-places, and the narrow paths which lead up the mountain-sides from them."

"True," asserted the captain; "and there are only four landing-places which it is possible for a boat to approach, and three of them are more or less dangerous. This one which we are now drawing near to is the only one in the island which deserves the name of a landing-place."

"And it would be difficult for an enemy to assail that," remarked Rivers, as he glanced at the fortified lines, bristling with cannon, which commanded the quay. "It would take a great many ships of the line to silence those batteries. Even then, from the tops of those cliffs, any force that attempted a landing might be destroyed without the possibility of retaliation. Yes, I agree with you, Miss Vander Heyden; Napoleon's heart, if he ever really contemplated an escape from his captivity, must have died within him when he came within sight of these precipices."

"You are right, sir," said Captain Ranken. "That was his real ground of complaint against Saint Helena. He talked of the unhealthiness of the climate, and the badness of his accommodation, and the rudeness of the officials in charge of him. But the true grievance was that escape was impossible."

"Ay," said Mr Moritz; "your countrymen made better jailors than those who had charge of him at Elba. Small blame to you, too. If he had been shut up in any place, which he could have got out of, he would have lived long enough to turn Europe upside down once more."

"Is the climate unhealthy?" inquired Mr Walters.

"Unhealthy! no, not a bit of it," replied the captain. "I resided here once for two years, as one of the Company's agents. I should say it was a particularly healthy country for Europeans. It is both mild and uniform in its temperature, never excessively hot, and never very cold. An English August and an English January would both of them astonish the natives of Saint Helena. The trade wind gives a succession of steady and equable breezes, and tropical storms are almost unknown."

"It is very bare and ungenial in its appearance, any way," remarked Annchen.

"Ah, Miss Annchen, that comes of trusting to first appearances," said Captain Ranken. "You will find it greatly improve on nearer acquaintance. But here we are, and here are our conveyances waiting for us."

They landed accordingly, and, after crossing the drawbridge, passed under the arched gateway, and entered the principal street of the town. This was not very long, not containing more than fifty or sixty houses, but these were mostly of a handsome appearance, resembling English houses for the most part, two storeys in height, and whitewashed. The population seemed to be almost entirely negro; but a bronzed old soldier, who told them that he had in his youth kept guard at Napoleon's grave, offered himself as their guide, and his services were accepted. Under his guidance they began their ascent, which had been constructed with enormous labour along the side of the almost perpendicular precipices, and which tried the nerves of some of the party, who were not accustomed to climbing. For a long way the ascent exhibited nothing but the spectacle of naked and barren rocks, but after the first two miles were passed, the eyes of the travellers were relieved by the sudden sight of wooded heights, diversified by picturesque villas and cultivated gardens. Trees which were quite new to some of the party grew on either side of the pathway. The Indian banyan and bamboo, the mimosa, the aloe, and the prickly pear of Southern Africa, were to be found side by side with Australian gum trees, and the mulberries of Southern Europe. There appeared also to be a variety of tropical fruits; figs, limes, mangoes, guavas, citrons, bananas, and pomegranates grew and throve, apparently, in the gardens which they passed. The temperature altered sensibly as they approached Longwood, which indeed is nearly eighteen hundred feet above the level of the sea.

"This seems a comfortable house enough," remarked Redgy, as they entered the grounds, — "not an imperial palace, to be sure, but that was hardly to be expected."

"He was comfortable enough, I expect," said Captain Ranken, — "as comfortable as he would have been anywhere. Indeed, he wouldn't go into the big house which the English Ministry had built for him. No, it was the being shut up at all that he didn't like."

"You are right, sir," remarked the old sergeant with a smile. "If they had taken the palace of Versailles over for him, he wouldn't have liked it any better."

"Did you ever see him?" inquired Rivers.

"No, sir; I didn't come to the island till just before his death; but my father-in-law, who died a few years ago, was a soldier under Sir Hudson Lowe's command; and he told me that he had often been set as one of the sentries round Longwood, and had seen Buonaparte again and again. It was a troublesome duty keeping guard on him."

"How so?" asked Walters.

"Why, sir, they were obliged — one of them, that is, was obliged — to see Bony with his own eyes once in every twenty-four hours — to make sure of him, you see, sir. There was always a fancy that he was trying to make his escape to America."

"There was some ground for that, if what I have read is true," remarked Rivers.

"Maybe, sir," said Sergeant Thorpe. "Anyhow, Sir Hudson always acted as though he believed it; and he insisted that one of the men should see Bony every day, and make sure he was there; and nothing that he did made Bony so angry. He would take every means of preventing it that he could. He would shut himself up sometimes for a whole day, and allow no one to enter his room but his own servants. They were all in the same mind as himself about it; and even if they hadn't been, they durstn't for the life of them let any one go into the room where he was. Some of our chaps hung about the entrance for an hour or two, or longer than that, before they could get a sight of him. My father-in-law told me that one day, when he had waited for ever so long without being able to see Buonaparte, he hid himself behind one of the curtains in the hall and stayed there till bed-time. About ten o'clock Bony came out on his way to bed. My father-in-law got a clear sight of him, but Bony caught a glimpse of the end of his shoe sticking out from under the curtain. My father-in-law was hauled out, and had to explain what brought him there. A complaint was sent to Sir Hudson — and to the Government, I believe, too — that an attempt had been made to assassinate him! But there were so many stories of the same kind, none of which had any foundation, that very little attention was paid to it."

"No," said Captain Ranken. "The Government would have had little else to do, if they had attended to all his complaints. So this is the house where the great emperor lived, is it?"

"Lived and died, sir," said Sergeant Thorpe. "This is the room where he used to sit and dictate, and this the bedroom where he died. There was a terrible storm on the day of his death, the 4th of May 1821. I can just remember it, having come here when I was a young boy, a few weeks before. The people in the island say there has never been such a storm known before or since. All the trees about the place were torn up, and among them the willow, under which was his favourite seat."

"Were you present at his burial?" inquired Margetts.

"No, sir, I was too young to be taken. I was left at home with my nurse and little sister, but almost every one in the island was there. We will go down and look at it now, if you please. It lies in a small valley. The spot was a favourite resort of his, and there he had asked to be buried."

The party accordingly quitted Longwood, and followed the sergeant down to the spot he indicated. It was a lovely place, but very little attempt had been made further to beautify it. A mound of about three hundred feet in circumference, overgrown with grass, had been surrounded with a simple palisade. About the middle of this there was a tomb constructed of stone enclosed by an iron railing. There was neither inscription nor monument, the coffin having been deposited in a vault beneath, and the roof cemented over.

"I have stood here sentinel many a day, gentlemen," said the sergeant, "when I was a young man. There used to be a many visitors who came to see it—mostly old soldiers who had fought under him."

"Do you remember the removal of the body to France?" inquired Rivers.

"Yes, sir, I saw that myself," replied Thorpe; "it was nearly twenty years after his burial. The son of the king of France, that then was, came to take the body to Europe. It was a grand sight. I was one of the soldiers on duty that day. The earth was dug away until they came to the vault, which had been overlaid with cement, but this was found to be so hard that the workmen's tools broke one after another, and it was a long time before they could make the slightest impression upon it. At last they did make their way through it, and lifted up the large white stone, and exposed the coffin. When the lid was taken off there lay the great emperor, not the least changed, it appeared, by all the twenty years he had lain there. The features were not even shrunk, and there were the orders on his breast, and the cocked hat by his side, scarcely tarnished. After the coffin had been removed they replaced the stones as they were before. A good many people still visit this place, but not nearly so many, of course, as formerly."

The party now took leave of Sergeant Thorpe, and returned to Jamestown.

"Why didn't Whittaker make one of our party?" asked Margetts of Walters, as they rode side by side down the precipitous path.

"I don't quite know," said Walters. "For some reason or other, he is very unwilling to be absent from his cabin for any long time together. I have noticed that almost every hour he goes down to it. I suppose he has something valuable there, which he thinks it necessary to keep an eye upon."

"I don't know but what he's right," remarked Rivers. "One or two of the crew strike me as being by no means the most desirable shipmates. That fellow Bostock, and Van Ryk, the boatswain's mate, and one or two others, if they are honest fellows, don't look it. I spoke to the captain about it a day or two ago, and he agreed with what I said. But he told me that he and Wyndham kept a sharp look-out upon them, and when the ship reached Port Elizabeth, he meant to get rid of them. It is only a few of whom he has any suspicion; the rest are all right."

The next day the voyage was resumed, and after rather more than a week's run, Cape Town was reached. Here there was a delay of several days. Vander Heyden went ashore with his sister to the house of a friend, with whom he resided during the whole of the ship's stay in harbour.

He had been very angry with his friend and sister for joining the English party to Longwood, and would have broken off all acquaintance with Rivers and his friend, if Moritz and Annchen would have allowed it. But though he succeeded so far to prevent anything like close intimacy, he could not prevent civilities from being offered and accepted; and Vander Heyden had seen too much of Captain Ranken, to venture upon any repetition of the conduct which had brought about the collision between them a fortnight before.

During the stay at Cape Town an unfortunate incident occurred, which caused the captain much greater vexation than the misconduct of his Dutch passenger. Nearly a dozen of his best men, who had been allowed by the second mate, in the absence of his superior officers, to go on shore, were reported missing, and all inquiries after them proved vain. Either they had been bribed to serve on board some foreign ship, or to join some party to the interior. Captain Ranken was obliged to supply their place, as well as he could, with some men whom he had picked up at Cape Town, but whose appearance he by no means liked.

"We must keep a sharp look-out upon them, Wyndham," he said on the morning of the day after that on which they had resumed their voyage. "If it wasn't that it would be impossible to navigate the ship without them, there's hardly one of these fellows with whom I would like to sail. I shall send them adrift at Port Elizabeth, along with Bostock and Van Ryk and Sherwin. I expect there will be no lack of good hands there."

"Well, it won't be very long, sir," said Wyndham,—"not above three or four days at the outside, and there are enough of us to put down any disturbance during that time. I'll speak to Mr Rivers and Mr Whittaker, and the others. They'd be very useful if any disturbance occurs."

"I will speak to Mr Whittaker myself," said the captain. "He told me something yesterday, an hour or two after we left the harbour, which if he had mentioned before, I should have taken certain steps, which it would be too late to take now. I gave him my mind on the subject, though there was no great use in doing that."

"What, he has something valuable on board, I suppose?" observed Wyndham; "I have suspected as much for a long time. That was why he would not go ashore at Saint Helena, then?"

"Yes," said the captain; "I think under the circumstances it is quite as well you should know, Wyndham. He has got 5000 pounds in specie, which he is taking out to the bank at Maritzburg. Of course he was bound to tell me—to give it into my custody, in fact—before we sailed. He declares he did not know that. That may be true, though it seems strange he should be ignorant of it. But, any way, it is no use discussing that matter any further."

"No, sir. I suppose you have it in your charge now?"

"Yes, of course. I have put it away in the strong cupboard, and will not deliver it up till we reach Durban."

"And what made Mr Whittaker tell you about it this morning, more than on any other day?" asked Wyndham.

"That is one of the most unpleasant features in the matter," rejoined the captain. "Mr Whittaker has always kept his cabin locked throughout the voyage, and has never been absent from it for any considerable time. Until this morning, he had no suspicion but what everything was perfectly safe. But last night, after the passengers had gone to bed, he fancied he heard a noise in the passage, and caught a glimpse of some one hurrying away. This morning, on going into his cabin, he found Bostock there; and on his inquiring what business the man had in his cabin, Bostock muttered something about having gone in to clean it out. But it is not Bostock's business to clean the cabins. Mr Whittaker was alarmed, and came to me immediately afterwards."

"Indeed, sir! That looks ugly, certainly. You must get rid of Bostock when we get to Port Elizabeth."

"I have already said that I meant to do so. Indeed, I would have dismissed him at Cape Town, if Mr Whittaker had spoken to me in time.

All that we can now do is to keep a bright look-out. Mr Whittaker and I are alternately to keep watch in my cabin, until we drop anchor in Algoa Bay. You had better keep an eye on Bostock; and it would be as well if you asked Mr Rivers to help you in doing so. Mr Rivers is, to my mind, as stout-hearted and cool-headed a fellow as any we have on board."

"I agree with you in that, sir, and will see Mr Rivers at once. But I don't apprehend much mischief from John Bostock. The man seems to me as if he had lost his head."

If Mr Wyndham could have been present at a conversation which had taken place an hour or two before between Bostock, Van Ryk, Andersen, the captain's servant, and a sailor named Sherwin, he would hardly have expressed this opinion. John Bostock, little as Wyndham suspected it, was by birth a gentleman. He was the son of a Lincolnshire squire of ancient family, but very reduced means. His father was the last of a long series of spendthrifts, who had gradually reduced a noble inheritance to a heap of encumbrances. Langley Cargill, or, as he now called himself, John Bostock, was one of his younger sons. He followed in his father's steps, and was soon hopelessly involved in debt. He tried to live by successful betting and gambling, but failed here also, and was reduced to extreme straits, when a boon companion, a man of some influence, obtained for him a commission in a Dutch regiment quartered at the Hague. Here he was safe from creditors, and had an income upon which it would have been possible to live decently, if strict economy had been observed. But to Cargill economy had become impossible. He fell into his old courses, and would probably have soon been expelled from the Dutch service, if his ruin had not been precipitated by an outrage which drew on him the punishment of the law.

In the second year of his residence he was attracted by the grace and beauty of a young girl, who had just made her first appearance in public. Langley contrived to obtain an introduction, which he tried for several months to improve into an acquaintance. The lady's friends, who were aware of his character, interfered to prevent this. Her brother, in particular, a haughty young officer, had forbidden all intercourse; and on the occasion of a public ball, when Cargill was more than usually importunate, had insisted on his leaving the room. Cargill replied by drawing his sword on Vander Heyden. The police interfered, and Cargill was insane enough to resist, wounding several men, and one severely. He would have received a heavy sentence, if he had not contrived to escape from prison, and enlist as a sailor in a ship just leaving the harbour. After several voyages he found himself in London, and in the autumn of 1879 engaged himself, under the name of Bostock, as an A.B. on board the *Zulu Queen*, about to sail for Durban. Here he found Jans Van Ryk, Amos Sherwin, and Eric Andersen, old companions of his coarse debauches. A day or two after leaving harbour, he also recognised Annchen Vander Heyden and her brother, as the reader has heard in the previous chapter. Annchen had no suspicion that she had even seen him before; but her brother's memory was better, though with the scornful hauteur of his character he paid no further heed to Bostock's presence.

It will readily be believed that Bostock was not so indifferent to their former relations. He had devised a scheme by which he was to revenge himself on Vander Heyden, during the ship's stay at Cape Town. He had resolved to follow him on shore, force him to a personal encounter, in which, being himself a first-rate swordsman, he expected to get the better of his antagonist, and, in event of his wounding or killing him, make his escape to the Transvaal, which was at the time full of lawless characters. He had been baffled by Wyndham, who had refused him permission to leave the ship during the stay at Cape Town. Provoked to fury by this failure, he had resolved to enter Vander Heyden's cabin on the night of his return to the *Zulu Queen*, kill him, or be killed; and, if he should prove the survivor, throw himself into the sea and swim ashore. His purpose was a second time defeated—in this instance by Mr Whittaker, who occupied the next cabin to Vander Heyden, and who, as Bostock could see through the glass in his door, was awake and completely dressed. Surprised as well as disconcerted, he looked through the square of glass, and saw Whittaker engaged in counting a number of packages, which he perceived to be rouleaus of gold. The strong iron-bound chest was evidently full of them; in which case, he must have a very large sum of money with him. This discovery turned his thoughts into a different channel. He took an opportunity the next day of visiting Mr Whittaker's cabin, to make some examination of the chest, but was surprised by the sadden entrance of its owner. Mr Whittaker threatened to complain to the captain, and Bostock had no doubt he had carried out his threat. He felt at once that if he was to execute his designs either on Vander Heyden or the chest of specie, it must be done before the ship reached Algoa Bay. He had therefore invited his three mates in evil to a conference in the hold of the vessel. At this he imparted to them the discovery he had made, and the three worthies between them had hatched a plot, which was that very night to be put into execution.

When Wyndham left Captain Ranken, he went immediately to George Rivers' cabin, to whom he imparted the information received from the captain. George at once agreed to do all that lay in his power, and promised to join the first mate on deck, after he had taken a few hours' sleep. Wyndham, on his part, went to take his supper, which was brought him by Amos Sherwin, one of the quartermasters, his own servant, it appeared, being ill.

The night came on suddenly, as is usual in those latitudes, and the moon was obscured by clouds. About ten o'clock the first mate came on deck to take his watch. He complained of feeling drowsy and heavy; but was nevertheless quite able to take his work. A steady hand was placed at the wheel, and everything was quiet on deck. Walters and Margetts, who had not been disposed to turn in, were seated near the taffrail, smoking. Notwithstanding the darkness, the night was pleasant, and it was possible occasionally to discern the coast-line,—which was distant two or three miles,—though very indistinctly. The first mate seated himself near them, leaning his head on his hand. A few minutes afterwards, some one came up with a message to the steersman, and the latter, surrendering the wheel to the newcomer, went below. The night wore on, and after a while the moon, forcing its way through the clouds, lit up the scene. The two young men now noticed that the ship appeared to be a good deal nearer to the coast than it had been all day. Walters called out to the first mate to point out the fact to him. He hailed him once or twice, but received no answer.

"I say," he exclaimed, "Wyndham must be asleep. Oughtn't we to wake him, Redgy?"

"He can hardly be asleep," returned Margetts,—"a smart hand such as he is. But I'll go and speak to him."

He stepped up to Mr Wyndham's side, and, finding he still took no notice, shook him. But the mate did not bestir himself, and the two young men perceived that he was either seriously ill, or intoxicated.

"I say, this is serious," said Redgy; "we had better go down and bring the captain, hadn't we? Look here, if you'll take charge of him, I'll go to the skipper's cabin."

He hurried to the companion accordingly, and on his way encountered George Rivers, who was coming up, according to promise, to join the first mate. He hastily informed him of what was going on up above; and George, a good deal startled, hastened to the place where Wyndham was still sitting, with Walters leaning over him. But, while crossing the deck, he caught sight of an object which filled him with astonishment and alarm. This was the coast-line, which was now clearly visible in the broad moonlight.

"What can you be about?" he shouted to the man at the wheel. "We are more than half a mile nearer shore than we ought to be. If our course is not immediately changed, we shall run upon a reef; and, by Heaven!" he added, a moment afterwards, "there *is* a reef just ahead of us! Starboard hard!—

starboard, I say! Are you drunk, or mad, that you don't see where you are taking us?" he continued, as the man, paying no heed to his warnings, allowed the ship to drive on straight towards the reef.

George rushed up, and endeavoured to wrest the helm from his grasp; but it was too late. The next moment a grinding noise was heard, as the ship's keel grated over a sunk rock. Then came a tremendous crash, which shook her from stem to stern, and the *Zulu Queen* was lodged hard and fast on the reef. George collared the steersman; but he was a powerful man, and shook off his assailant's hold. Pulling his cap farther over his face, he ran down the hatchway, but not before Rivers had recognised Jans Van Ryk, a Dutch sailor, against whom Wyndham had warned him as one of Bostock's intimate companions.

It was no use following the man. Indeed it would have been impossible to do so; for in another minute the hatchway was crowded with men, who rushed up, half-dressed and in deadly terror, to know what had happened.

"Where is Mr Wyndham?" shouted the captain. "How can he have allowed the ship to run on a rock after this fashion, in a light where everything is as clear as noonday?"

"Mr Wyndham is in a kind of fit, sir," said Margetts. "He has been sitting there without moving for the last hour or two. You had better go to him yourself."

The captain stepped across the deck, and took a look at the first mate's face.

"Come here, McCarthy!" he cried to the surgeon. "He has been drugged, hasn't he?"

The surgeon put his hand to Wyndham's pulse, and, bending down, inhaled his breath.

"Yes, sir; he has been drugged with opium. This has been a preconcerted thing!"

Chapter Four

There was an uneasy silence for a minute or two, and then the captain spoke again.

"There cannot be a doubt of it," he said. "My lads," he continued, advancing towards a number of men who were gathered in a confused huddle on the forecastle, "I have a few words to say to you. We have traitors on board. The ship has been run intentionally on the reef. By and by a searching inquiry will have to be made respecting it; meanwhile I shall take the necessary steps for preserving discipline, and I call upon all here to help me in doing so. Let those who are willing to support me come forward and say so."

The men looked doubtfully at one another; and presently the greater part of them slunk off and went below. About a dozen of the best hands remained, and, going up to the captain, declared their resolution of standing by him whatever might happen.

"Thank you, my hearts," said the captain; "that's cheery! There is nearly a dozen of you, I see. There's Radburn, Marks, Coxwell, Daley, Rutley, Wall, Bateman, Hurd, Hooper, and Cookesley. I am obliged to you all, and I hope your example may help to keep the others right. But we must guard against a possible outbreak. The first thing will be to bring out some of the arms and distribute them. I had them all stowed away in my cabin yesterday, half expecting something of this kind. Come with me, Mr Rivers, and we'll hand them up."

This was soon done, and it was found that enough had been brought up to make an ample supply for all the party. Besides the carbines, revolvers, and cutlasses, there were several rifles belonging to the officers and passengers. The captain had two, the surgeon and first mate one each, Vander Heyden and Moritz, George and Margetts, also had one each; and all these gentlemen were well acquainted with the use of their weapons. They were a formidable party. Even supposing that all the crew, excepting those on deck, joined the mutineers,—as the captain evidently feared they would,—they might well hesitate to attack so well-armed and determined a company. At all events, it looked as if such was the case.

"I wonder where Bostock and the others can be," remarked Walters, when half an hour had passed, and everything remained quiet below.

"I have no doubt where they are," said Captain Ranken. "They are ransacking Mr Whittaker's cabin, fancying that what they want is there, though cleverly hidden away. It is fortunate that they made that mistake, as it has allowed us time to make our preparations. Now the next thing is to send a boat to Mossel Bay—which is the nearest place where any ships are likely to be found—and request that something may be sent to fetch the crew and cargo off this reef."

The pinnace—the most suitable boat for the purpose—was accordingly go ready; and by the time this had been done, and the men chosen who were to go in her, the first mate had recovered sufficiently to take charge of her. When he was informed of what had happened, he said he had no doubt that the opium must have been given him in a glass of grog, which he had taken before going on deck. He had poured it out, he said, and mixed it, when he unexpectedly received a message that the captain wanted to speak with him immediately in the cabin. He had hastened thither, but found the door locked. Supposing that the captain had gone on deck, he had hurriedly drunk off the grog, and followed him. The opium must have been put in while he was out of the cabin. He remembered that there had been something strange in the taste; but he was thinking of important matters, and did not notice trifles, he supposed.

"Do you remember who it was that brought you the message?" asked Captain Ranken.

"Not very clearly," replied Mr Wyndham; "but I fancy it was Sherwin."

"Likely enough," remarked the captain. "He and Van Ryk are this man Bostock's bosom friends. Well, all this must be gone into at a later time. What we have to do now is to get away as quick as we can."

"There isn't any hope of getting the ship off the reef, is there?" asked Redgy.

"Not the slightest. She can never swim again. But we must remember that our chief danger is from these mutinous scoundrels. I am convinced this plot has been hatched since we left Cape Town. I understand that all you gentlemen are prepared to stand by me?" he continued, addressing himself more particularly to Vander Heyden and Moritz, who had hitherto said very little.

"I am prepared to take my part," answered Vander Heyden, bowing somewhat haughtily. "If we are attacked, I shall, of course, protect my sister and property. I have no doubt Mynheer Moritz will do the same."

"Certainly," said Moritz in a more friendly tone; "I am prepared to stand by the captain, whatever may happen."

"I thank you," said the captain. "Then we have twenty men on whom we can rely. I am afraid I must reduce the number to sixteen, as I cannot send less than three men with Wyndham in the pinnace; but sixteen will, I hope, be sufficient for our purpose. We must keep an armed watch,—four of us in my cabin, and four on deck,—relieving every four hours. I will take charge of one party; Mr Rolfe, the second mate, had better take the other. Remember the spirit-room must be carefully watched, and any one fired on who tries to force it."

The dawn had broken before the work was half done, and it was morning when the pinnace, with the first mate and his men on board, took its departure. There was a favourable breeze inshore; and to Mossel Bay it was only an hour or two's sail. But it was quite uncertain how long it might be before she could return, or rather how long it might be before another vessel could be sent, large enough to carry off the crew and cargo. There might not be any such vessel in the bay, and Mr Wyndham might have to go overland to Cape Town, before the required assistance could be procured. In this event, of course, there would be a much longer delay—several days, perhaps. If this should prove to be the case, their situation would be far from agreeable. To say nothing of the danger from the mutinous sailors, if a storm should come on, the ship might go to pieces, and their only hope then would be to get on the reef itself, and shelter themselves as well as they could until help came. Vander Heyden suggested that such as chose it might be allowed to get on board the three remaining boats, and make their way to Mossel Bay, from whence they might get across the country to their destination at Natal. But the captain would not agree to this. He pointed out that of the three remaining boats, the launch had been so damaged when the ship ran on the reef, that it could not swim, another—the long-boat—was in such a position that it could not be got at, unless with the consent of the party below, and the remaining one would not hold more than four or five with safety. They were but just enough as it was to resist an attack. If they should be further reduced in numbers, the safety of those who remained behind would be seriously imperilled.

"And what is to become of my sister?" exclaimed Vander Heyden, "if these scoundrels do attack us?"

"We will all die in her defence, will we not, lads?" exclaimed Captain Ranken, looking round him. He was answered by a cheer.

"Nay, do not think of me," said Annchen; "I am not afraid. Any way, I cannot allow the safety of the others to be endangered, in order to preserve me from harm." There was a second cry of approval.

"None of us will allow a hair of your head to be hurt," cried Margetts.

"No," said Rivers, "you may be sure of that. But I would nevertheless suggest that the boat should be launched, and kept in readiness for an emergency. If we should be attacked and overpowered, that might enable some of us at the last moment to escape. In any case, if a skirmish appears imminent, Miss Vander Heyden and her brother might be put on board, and lie off the reef until the result of the encounter is known."

"Why do you propose that, sir?" exclaimed Vander Heyden angrily. "Do you suppose I am a coward, that I should shrink from an encounter with these scoundrels?"

"I implied nothing of the kind, sir," returned Rivers. "I was only carrying out your own suggestion. I suppose Miss Vander Heyden could not be put into the boat with no one to take care of her?"

Vander Heyden would have made an angry answer, but the captain interposed.

"You are quite wrong, Mr Vander Heyden, and, I must add, ungrateful too. Mr Rivers merits our thanks for his suggestion, which I shall at once put in force. We had better launch the boat at once, while the deck is in our possession. As soon as she is in the water, we can put a few provisions in her, and then she can lie off at a little distance. We had better set to work upon that at once."

All hands went to work accordingly with a will, and presently the gig was lowered, and got ready for sailing. Then dinner was served, and the afternoon passed quietly away. Bostock and his companions, if they had intended any violence, appeared to have abandoned the idea. Probably the captain's promptitude had disheartened them, — so it was thought, — and as they knew the pinnace had been sent off to Mossel Bay, they were aware that assistance would probably come from the shore in a few hours' time.

Late in the afternoon the captain, who was very tired, went down to get a few hours' sleep. He was aroused not long afterwards by Rivers.

"Captain," said the latter, "I fear mischief is brewing."

"What makes you suppose that?" said the captain, who had roused himself on the instant.

"There are two things I don't like. In the first place, the men must have got into the spirit-room —"

"Hasn't careful watch been kept upon it?" asked the captain.

"Yes," said George, "most careful watch. No one has approached the door the whole day. They must have broken into the room another way. Any way, there is furious drinking going on on the lower deck. I clambered round on the outside, and could see what was passing. Bostock, Van Ryk, and Sherwin are inciting the men to drink. Half of them, indeed, are drunk already."

"Could you hear what they are saying?" asked the captain.

"Not very distinctly; there was too much shouting and yelling. But I could make out that they were inciting the men to attack us."

"They would hardly do that," answered the captain. "They know that we are armed, and on our guard."

"No doubt, but they are armed too."

"Armed? are you sure? I myself conveyed all the arms in the ship into the cabin, on the night after we left Cape Town."

"In that case, there is either a traitor among the men who have access to your cabin, or they have brought their own arms on board. All the fellows we suspect are provided with cutlasses and revolvers, and I could see more lying about on the tables and benches."

"Was Andersen, my servant, among them?"

"Yes, he was one of the most forward, apparently, of any."

"He is the traitor, then. But that is of little consequence now. Do you think they will make their attack soon?"

"Not for another hour or two, I should say. They may ultimately succeed in getting the men to join them; but they are not ripe for it yet."

"An hour or two may be time enough. Come with me, Rivers; I shall want your help."

The captain went on deck, and, calling three or four of his best hands together, told them what he had learned. By his instructions, they provided eight or ten stout spars, which they carried down below and placed as a barricade, at the distance of about eight or ten feet from the captain's cabin, lashing the ends of the spars, so as to make it impossible for any one to pass. Then the other hatchways were secured, and a man set to guard each. The captain next went down, accompanied by Rivers and Vander Heyden, taking with him the second mate, Rolfe, as well as Marks, Daley, Wall, and Bateman, four of the stoutest and most trustworthy of the sailors. He placed these in positions which would command the barricade, some inside the cabin, some in the passage. The strictest silence was to be observed, and no one was to fire until the word was given. The captain then lighted his dark lantern, obscuring the light until the moment of action should arrive. Annchen had been sent on deck under the charge of Moritz, Vander Heyden having insisted on remaining below. But Whittaker, Margetts, and Walters had constituted themselves her special bodyguard.

When all had taken their places, a long silence ensued. The shouts of the men below were now more plainly heard. It was evident that they were fast becoming drunk, and at any moment the expected attack might be made. Presently the noise below ceased.

"They are getting ready," whispered the captain to George; "we shall have them up in another moment."

His words had hardly been uttered, before they were made good by the sound of feet stealthily ascending the stairs.

"They think to take us unawares," continued the captain. "They don't suspect anything about the barricade."

Presently there was a cry of surprise, followed by a volley of oaths. Then a light was struck, and the mutineers were seen trying to tear down the spars which blocked their passage.

"You had better leave off that, and go below!" shouted Captain Ranken. "We are prepared for you. If you attempt to remove those spars, you will take the consequences."

"Let fly at them," said a voice, which the captain recognised as that of Bostock,—"let fly at them, and particularly at that Dutchman."

Half a dozen pistols were discharged, three of them directly levelled at Vander Heyden, who was standing close to the captain. He had a narrow escape. One of the bullets would have struck him in the heart if Captain Ranken had not at the moment changed his position, and it struck his epaulet. A second grazed his temple, the third was lodged in the partition behind him.

"Your blood be on your own heads!" cried the skipper. "Fire on them!" A general discharge followed, by which it was evident considerable execution was done. Several were seen to fall, and among them Bostock and Van Ryk; but whether these were killed or dangerously wounded did not appear. They were either able, however, to crawl down below, or were carried off by their companions.

"They got that hot and strong, sir," remarked Rolfe; "I don't think they'll try it again."

"It depends a good deal on whether the leaders are killed or severely wounded," returned the captain. "As for Bostock, you hit him fairly, Mr Vander Heyden. The bullet struck him below the hip. But whether it was a slight or a severe wound, I can't say."

"I think it was only a flesh wound," rejoined the Dutchman. "The other fellow—Van Ryk, his name is, I believe—was more seriously hurt, I fancy."

"I hope he is. If those two men should be silenced, we needn't be afraid of the others. Well, we are safe for the night, I think, and we must hope that help will come to-morrow."

The captain's words were so far made good, that the rest of the night passed in quiet. The forenoon of the next day was a time of great anxiety, which no one felt so keenly as the captain. He knew that if Wyndham did not return, it could be only because some accident had happened to his boat, or because he had been unable to obtain any help in Mossel Bay, and had been compelled to go overland to Cape Town. The distance thither from Mossel Bay was more than two hundred miles, and the means of getting there not easy to procure. Even if he could find horses to carry him the whole distance, it would probably take him a day or two to reach the town. Then, no doubt, a vessel would be fitted with as little delay as possible. But probably two or three days more must elapse before it could reach the reef.

Altogether, it was not unlikely that a full week would pass, during which they would have to remain in their present situation, unless, indeed, they could attract the attention of some passing vessel. As the hours went by, the captain grew more and more despondent; and at last it became only too evident that Wyndham's speedy return could not be looked for.

"We are in for this, Rivers," he said, as they stood together on deck, looking anxiously toward shore, half an hour or so before sunset; "unless we are picked up by some ship, we may have to stay a week on this reef, and there is no disguising that, if it should be so, our lives are in the greatest danger."

"Do you apprehend a storm coming on, sir?" asked Rivers.

"I see no signs of that, though in this climate the changes of weather are so rapid that one is never secure for six hours together; but that is not what I am afraid of. These men will get desperate—the ringleaders, that is. They know there is a rope round their necks in consequence of last night's work, and they will get away from the reef at all hazards before Wyndham's return, if by possibility they can."

"I don't see how they can force their way on deck in the face of our fire, any more than they did last night, sir; I don't see how they could remove the barricade either."

"They might contrive to cut the ropes which hold one of the spars," said the captain, — "that is, if they could work in the dark. But I shall take care that the passage is kept lighted all night, so they won't attempt that I think they will try to blow up the hatchways. They have got plenty of powder, and it would not be a difficult thing to do. They would lose some men in forcing their way up; but their numbers so greatly exceed ours, that, once on deck, we should have no chance with them."

"You think all the ship's company will go along with Bostock and Van Ryk, then?"

"I am a good deal afraid of it. I don't think they'd have done this of their own heads. But these two rascals are exceedingly clever, and will, I have no doubt, make out a plausible story. They will persuade the poor fellows that, if they are caught, they will be charged with mutiny for what has been done already. They'll tell them it is their only hope to get off the reef before help comes, and they must cut all our throats to accomplish that."

"And we can't take to the boats, and be gone ourselves?"

"That is what the Dutchman proposed yesterday. But I then pointed out that we cannot get at the long-boat without exposing ourselves to the fire of the mutineers. Nor would they, of course, let us repair the other boat, even if she could be repaired. I only guessed then that they would attack us. It is unfortunately only too certain now. We should simply be playing their game. If they could overpower us, or, in plain English, murder us, they would no doubt go off in the three boats, or make a raft, if the boats would not hold them all. But while we remain here, that would be impossible.

"No," resumed the captain presently; "we must go on as we have begun. It really looks as though the men were unable to devise any plan of attacking us; in which case it is most probable that they will submit, and throw themselves upon my mercy. It is only against a few, you see, that direct mutiny can be proved. Nor have I quite given up the hope that Wyndham may have found a ship at Mossel Bay, though her sailing may have been delayed. Perhaps the men also are reckoning on the possibility of that, and will not commit themselves further, until they feel sure that he will have to go on to Cape Town for help. But all that we can do is to keep a bright look-out, and be ready for action at a moment's notice. I shall go and lie down now for two or three hours, as I feel quite worn out; but I shall trust to you, Rivers, to rouse me if there should be the slightest necessity. You are the only man on board I can thoroughly trust, for, though Rolfe and

McCarthy are good fellows, they are not equal to an emergency. But you know what you are about."

They parted. George took a turn or two up and down the deck, apparently buried in thought. Then he laid aside his cutlass and pistols, put on a sailor's jacket that was lying on the deck, and tied a handkerchief round his head. Having completed these preparations without attracting notice, he disappeared below.

It was about three hours afterwards that the captain was a second time roused from his sleep by a hand laid on his chest. He started up instantly, and was about to speak, when George Rivers, who was his visitor, stopped him.

"Don't wake the others, sir," he said. "If you will come on deck, I have something important to tell you. I wish to say, sir," he continued when they were seated out of the sight and hearing of any of their companions, "that I have been down among the men, and have learned pretty accurately what they mean to do."

"Down among the men—among the mutineers?" exclaimed the captain. "How did you manage that?"

"Well, it was not so very difficult, sir. Several of the men had left their jackets on deck, as well as a handkerchief or two. I put two of these on, pulling the handkerchief well over my forehead, so that by the dim light on the lower deck it was hardly possible that I could be recognised, even if any one noticed me, which was hardly likely. Then I untied one of the ropes, and so got through the barricade. I went to the head of the ladder and listened. There was loud and angry talk going on, and several of the speakers seemed to be more than half drunk. I crept cautiously down, ready to make a bolt up again if any one hailed me, but they were all too busy to notice me. I crept into a corner and lay down, as if asleep, drawing a sailcloth half over me. I lay there for a couple of hours, I should think, and learned all I wanted to know. After that I took advantage of a violent quarrel which broke out among them, to creep up-stairs in the same way as I had crept down, and then secured the spar."

"You have done nobly?" exclaimed the skipper. "And what have you learned?"

"I learned, first of all, that nothing will be attempted to-night, though an attempt will be made to-morrow. In the first place, it appears that Sherwin was one of those killed in the skirmish, though they contrived to carry him off. Van Ryk and Bostock were wounded, though not severely. Bostock was hit in the right leg, and is unable to use it, though the wound is already greatly better. They won't stir unless he leads them, and that he can't do this evening."

"That is fortunate. They are not afraid of Wyndham's return, then?"

"No; they seem to feel sure that he has failed to find a ship in Mossel Bay. Indeed, one of the men said he had gone over to the bay from Cape Town, only a day or two before the *Zulu Queen* sailed, and there was no ship there, and none expected."

"I feared as much," said the captain. "Well, then, what are the men's intentions? Do they all go along with Bostock?"

"I am afraid they do," returned George. "Bostock has persuaded them that there is an enormous sum of money in gold stowed away in the cabin— enough, as he told them, to make them all rich for life. If it hadn't been for the barricade, he said, of which no one had any idea, this would have been in their possession already. But as it is, it is theirs as soon as they choose to seize it. They evidently believe they can get on deck whenever they please—"

"Did you ascertain how?" interrupted the captain eagerly. "Not exactly, sir, but I fancy they mean to blow a hole in the ship's side, and so get down on to the reef, which at low water extends for several feet beyond the ship—"

"Yes, yes," said the captain, "I was afraid so; no doubt they could do that. Go on."

"Well, I expect they will make their way out in that manner, and, although we may be able to kill half a dozen of them before they knock us on the head, they would certainly do so, sooner or later. None of our party are to be spared, except, I am sorry to say, Miss Vander Heyden. Bostock means to carry her off with him."

"The brute!" exclaimed the captain. "He shan't do that, Rivers."

"No, sir. I would blow out her brains with my own hand sooner than allow it?"

"And so, to do him justice, would her brother, or Mr Moritz either— nay, I am persuaded she would do it herself! Well, Rivers, we are in for this, and we must get out of it the best way we can. But I must own I am at my wits' end. Can you suggest anything?"

"It has occurred to me, captain, that we might possibly, if we were hard driven, get on to the other part of the reef yonder, and take provisions with us enough to last two or three days. They couldn't get at us there, I imagine."

The captain looked in the direction to which George pointed. There was another reef, or, more properly, another part of the same reef, divided from that on which the ship was lying by a deep channel some twenty or thirty yards wide. It rose a good deal higher out of the water, and was so plainly visible at all states of the tide that nothing but design, or the most culpable carelessness, could have caused the disaster.

"That is a good thought," he said. "If ever I command a ship again, I must make you my first mate. That reef will be our salvation. We must not lose a moment in getting across, and taking all we want with us. Go and wake all the hands, and bring them on deck at once. If we wait for the moon, the rascals may see us. It is lucky that we have Marks and Cookesley, the ship's carpenters, among our party."

Chapter Five

The sailors who had remained loyal to Captain Ranken obeyed his summons with prompt alacrity. They were reduced to seven, three having gone with the first mate in the pinnace. The captain gave them their orders, which they proceeded to put into execution as rapidly and with as little noise as possible. The boat was brought immediately under the ship's side, and a number of articles put into it, the first being the carpenter's chests, and a load of spars and planks from the workshop. Then the boat returned for boxes and barrels, containing provisions to last for a fortnight, together with all the firearms and cutlasses on deck. Then a quantity of bedding, knives, forks, and crockery, and a large tarpaulin which had been used to form a shelter from the heat for the passengers. A number of empty boxes and barrels were also lowered into the sea, which, as the tide was then running, would be washed up on the further reef. There was a great deal to be done, but the hands were all active and willing; and by the time when the moon rose all the most necessary articles had been ferried over.

As soon as the light permitted, the men, under the direction of the carpenters, began putting up a hut at the spot indicated by the captain. They fortunately found one or two crevices in the rock, in which uprights could be fixed. A long spar was run across from two of these, and the tarpaulin stretched over it. Then four shorter posts were placed at the corners, but at two of these points there were no crevices, and the spars had to be placed in tall barrels filled with stones. The sides were next filled in with planks, with a door and an opening to serve as a window at the end farthest from the wreck. The gig continued her voyages under the conduct of Captain Ranken, George, and the second mate, and almost everything that would be required was brought over. Mr Whittaker's chest had been one of the first things cared for.

By daybreak a very tolerable hut had been constructed; and the captain directed them, as the next job, to put up a barricade extending the whole length of the hut on the side facing the ship. This was formed of barrels and chests containing large stones, of which there was abundance on the reef, the spaces between them being similarly filled. When this had been completed, it was broad day, and it was impossible to expect that the crew, who by this time must have slept off their drunken debauch, could be kept any longer in ignorance of their officers' proceedings. The second mate was sent, therefore, to inform the passengers of the removal to the further reef, and convey them over to it as quickly as possible. They were taken by surprise, but complied readily enough; only Vander Heyden making some complaint that the cabin party had been kept in ignorance of what they ought to have been told.

While they were being ferried across in the boat, the captain and George returned for the last time to the deck.

"We are well out of this, sir," remarked George; "we shall be safe over there."

"Yes, unless they come across to attack us."

"Come across? what, in the long-boat?"

"Yes, in the long-boat. They can't launch it while we have possession of the deck. But as the ship is left to them, there will be nothing to prevent their doing it."

"It would be a desperate thing to attempt, landing on the reef under such a fire as we could open on them."

"No doubt, if they attempted it by day. But in the dark they could get ashore unseen by us, and perhaps make one or two voyages before we found it out. Besides, the long-boat will hold a great number of men. We must not risk it."

"What do you propose then, sir?"

"To destroy the boat," answered the captain. "It is easily enough done, if you will lend a hand. But first, are all the others safely landed on the reef?"

"Yes. The boat, with Mr Rolfe in her, is just coming back for us."

"Very good. Then we will go to work."

He went below and fetched two iron pots, in each of which he placed a heavy charge of powder, rolling a piece of rag round it to prevent its escape. Then, motioning to George to pick up some heavy blocks of wood, he moved noiselessly across the deck, and laid the pots in the bottom of the boat, one at each end, with the blocks to keep them down. Next he laid a train of powder with a slow match, the end of which he ignited.

They now crept down to the boat, and put off. They had almost got across, when a loud explosion, followed almost simultaneously by a second, was heard. Immediately afterwards the men poured up on deck, having evidently contrived some way for themselves of getting up there. Some of them carried carbines, and they might have fired on the captain and his two companions, if these had not hastily drawn up the boat and made for the shelter of the shed.

"Safe now, sir," remarked Rolfe, "unless they swim across to us."

"They'll hardly try that on," rejoined the captain. "They would be an easy mark for our rifles, and they know we have several and can use them. We roust put a man to watch their movements; but I think that is all that will be needed. If breakfast is ready, we may go to it with an appetite."

This had hardly been completed, when Hooper, the man set to watch, came in with the information that a flag of truce had been hoisted on the vessel, and three men, Gott, Shirley, and Sullivan had come down to the edge of the water to parley with the captain.

"Are they unarmed?" asked the second mate.

"Yes, sir," answered Hooper.

"Can you see anything of the other men?" inquired the doctor.

"There are none on the reef, sir, but I thought I saw one or two peeping over the ship's bulwarks."

"I guessed as much," said McCarthy. "You ought to think twice, sir, before you go to meet these men. You would be an easy mark for any one hiding in the forecastle; and they may think that, if they once got you out of the way, they could do anything they pleased."

"That's possible," said Captain Ranken. "But I can't help that. There is a chance of avoiding bloodshed, and it is my duty to go."

"Well, any way, let us take any precautions we can," urged Rolfe. "Five or six of us can take our rifles, and show ourselves over the top of the barricade. They will see that if they have you at their mercy, we have Gott and Shirley and Sullivan at ours."

"You may do that, if you like," said the skipper. "There is never any harm in showing that one is prepared."

The mate's suggestion was acted on. Half a dozen marksmen, including the two Dutchmen, Rivers, Margetts, Whittaker, and the mate, took their guns, climbed on to the top of the barricade, and then stationed themselves behind it, the muzzles of their rifles projecting from between the stones. Then the captain, accompanied by McCarthy, went down to the edge of the reef, and, hailing the three men opposite, asked what they had to say.

"We're very sorry," said Gott, — "sorry as you're displeased, sir. But the most of us don't know what we've done."

"Do you call running the ship on a reef, and then trying to plunder her, and after that attempting to murder us, nothing?"

"It was only one or two as did that; we didn't wreck the ship, or join in the attack as was made on you, sir," said Sullivan.

"I am glad to hear it. What do you want now?"

"We want you and the others to come over here again, and we'll go back to our duty," answered Gott.

"And what about the mutineers?" asked the captain.

"There was but a few of they, and they was mostly killed in the scrimmage."

"Indeed! were Bostock and Van Ryk killed, may I ask?"

There was no answer. The skipper repeated his question, and then Shirley said sullenly, "I don't know as they was."

"Very good. Van Ryk was the man who ran the ship on the reef; Mr Rivers saw him do it. Bostock fired deliberately at Mr Vander Heyden; *I* saw him do it. I don't want to inquire too closely what others may have done, but these two are clearly guilty. If they are put into irons and brought over here, together with all the arms in your possession, we will return to the ship, and when help comes, no proceedings will be taken against anybody, except the two prisoners. These are the only terms I shall offer you. I shall expect to receive an answer in an hour or two."

The men, after exchanging a few words, sullenly withdrew. The captain, and McCarthy, who had been chosen to accompany the skipper, because the men are always unwilling to hurt the doctor, also beat a hasty retreat, and informed their companions what had passed.

"Do you think they will give in, sir?" asked Whittaker.

"No," replied the captain. "I fear Van Ryk and Bostock have too much weight with them. Besides, sailors on these occasions are apt to stick together. If we don't get an answer within the hour, we must look for broken heads."

The hour passed, and then another hour or two. The after noon slipped away, and there was no return of the deputies. The men kept quite out of sight. But the sound of hammering and sawing and the buzz of voices were plainly audible.

"They are up to something, sir," said Rolfe; "making a raft, most likely, by which they hope to reach the shore. They've plenty of materials, and some smart hands among them. Don't you think that is likely, sir?"

"I think it very likely," answered the skipper; "only I am afraid they are more likely to use it to make an attack on us than to reach the shore—or rather, they will attempt the latter, but only when they have carried out the former. They won't go without the money if they can help it. But the first thing for us will be to ascertain what they are really about, and we can do that, though not without some risk. The boat is still lying off at the place where we moored her when we came across for the last time. If we got aboard her we might row out to the other side of the reef, keeping at a safe distance, and then we should find out what they are doing."

"No doubt, sir," rejoined Rolfe; "but would they let us do it? I am pretty sure there are one or two fellows lying under the bulwarks, watching us from the deck. They could pick off any one who tried that."

"I am afraid that is only too likely," said Captain Ranken; "but it is so important to us to know what they are up to, that I think we must attempt it. Who will volunteer for the service?"

He was answered by half a dozen eager voices, declaring each man's readiness to make the adventure.

"Very good, gentlemen; I thank you heartily," said the skipper. "The men I want must be good divers, if possible, but certainly good swimmers. They must also, of course, understand the management of a boat."

"I can't swim, I am sorry to say," cried Walters.

"I can swim, but I am no diver," said Rolfe.

"And I can swim and dive, but I am a poor hand at managing a boat," added Margetts. "But look here, captain, here's your man—George Rivers. He swims like a fish, and dives like a cormorant, and can manage a boat first-rate."

"He will do for one, no doubt," said the captain. "And I think, Mynheer Moritz, you offered, did you not? You, I know, can both swim and dive, and, I believe, understand managing a boat?"

"Yes, sir," returned Moritz, "I believe, without vanity, I can say I do. I shall be pleased to undertake this in company with Mr Rivers."

"Very good," said the skipper. "That is settled, then. Now, gentlemen, this is what you have to do. You must get into the water here, out of the sight of the ship, and swim round, keeping under water as much as possible. Then get under the lee of the boat, and bring her round, sheltering yourselves under the cover of her side. Of course our fears may be groundless. There may be no one lying in wait. But I fancy I have seen heads looking from time to time over the ship's sides, and it is best to take every precaution. Now be off as quick as possible, for the daylight is dying out."

George and Moritz complied. Going to the farther point of the reef, they stripped, and, slipping silently into the water, began swimming round the reef. When they got to the point where their heads would be visible from the ship, they dived, and swam under water, neither of them reappearing until their heads came to the surface close under the bows of the boat.

"Capitally managed!" cried the captain. "If they get her out from shore, all will be safe. I really hope our apprehensions were unfounded."

But at this moment two or three guns were fired from the ship, and several bullets spattered in the water. Moritz, who had incautiously raised his head, had a narrow escape. George seized and dragged him down, himself only just escaping a bullet which whistled over his head. The boat, however, was by this time in motion, and they were enabled to drag it along with them, without again exposing themselves until they were out of shot. Then they climbed in and rowed to the place whence they had started. Here the captain received them with many commendations and thanks; and, while the two adventurers were resuming their clothes, went off in the boat with two of the men to the other side of the wreck, taking care to keep at a safe distance. He returned in half an hour with a very uncomfortable report.

"Have you found out what they are about, sir?" asked Margetts.

"I am sorry to say I have. They mean mischief, and, I fear, will be only too likely to be able to work it. They are putting together a raft, and are getting on fast with it."

"But may not that be only to enable them to make their escape to the shore?" suggested Walters.

"If that had been their intention, they would not have fired on Rivers and Mr Moritz. There is no use in disguising facts. They mean to attack us."

"But how can they contrive, sir?" asked the second mate. "Neither wind nor tide is favourable to them. A raft is a very difficult thing to manage at all times, and they would have to approach this part of the reef under the fire of all our guns."

"You are right, Rolfe," replied the captain; "but unfortunately the raft is not the only work they are engaged on. Somehow it appears that the launch was not so much injured as I had supposed. Two or three smart hands have been employed on it, and it looked as though it had been made all right again. What they mean to do, I expect, is to launch both raft and boat at nightfall, and the one will tow the other till our reef is reached. Then they will land in the dark, and then either take up a position behind our barricade, from which they can fire upon us whenever we go in or out of our hut, or else make an assault upon us as soon as the moon rises, and overpower us by superior numbers. The first would be the surest plan for themselves, but their dread of Wyndham's return may induce them to adopt the other. They outnumber us, remember, at least six to one."

"It is only too likely that you are right," said George; "but what do you advise?"

"I think, in the first place, we must complete the barricade round the hut. At present we are open on two sides to a sudden rush, which would overpower us by force of numbers. Behind, the rise of the rock is so precipitous that they could only climb it with great difficulty, one by one. We must place our best marksmen up there, and the others behind our barricades down below. We must put a man, when the darkness comes on, at the very extremity of the reef, nearest to the wreck. He will be able to distinguish what they are doing sufficiently well to tell us when they are launching their raft. It cannot, I know, be completed for many hours yet. As soon as it does put off, we can burn a blue light,—I took care last night to bring some with me,—and that will enable us to fire on them, while approaching and landing, with effect. We may be fortunate enough to kill their leaders, in which case the others will submit at once."

"If I catch sight of that Cargill," exclaimed Vander Heyden, "he will not trouble us any more! Ha, Vrank?"

"No," responded Moritz; "he doesn't deserve much mercy, and I don't imagine he would show us much."

"None at all, I fear," assented the captain. "But I don't desire his death on that account, but because he is leading these poor misguided fellows into crime and ruin. But no more of him. If we mean to put up our barricades, we must go to work at once."

"All right, captain!" said Rolfe; "we will not delay a minute."

A quantity of barrels and boxes, with which the reef was still strewn, were brought up, and filled with stones, as well as some heaps of wreck-wood, which had been thrown up above high-water mark. In two hours' time a barricade had been erected sufficiently strong to repel any sudden assault. Then attention was turned to the high ground behind the hut. Large stones and pieces of wood were laid along the highest ridge, behind which the riflemen might fire in safety. This party consisted of McCarthy, Rolfe, George Rivers, Margetts, Whittaker, and Walters, together with

Vander Heyden and Moritz. The captain took the command of the party below, which consisted of the seven sailors. Here also Miss Vander Heyden was placed, under the captain's special protection. When the hut was first erected, a space had been partitioned off to serve as Annchen's sleeping-place, and George, during the captain's absence in the boat, had employed his time in doubling this partition, and filling up the space between the boards with stones, so that even if all the other defences were carried, she would still have a last place of shelter.

When the job was done, the whole party sat down to rest and take some refreshment. The evening came on before they had finished their meal, and in a short time it was quite dark.

"If they mean to come," remarked the captain, "it will be pretty soon now. The noise of hammering has ceased for the last half-hour; they must have completed their job; and now it will be seen whether they are going to make for the shore, or attack us."

It was an anxious moment. The whole party sat in front of their barricade, on the stones or logs of which it was composed, listening intently to catch any sound which might determine the momentous question at issue. Presently the silence was broken by Coxwell, the sailor whom the captain had stationed at the farthest point of the reef. He came up with the information that the boat and raft were both afloat, and by the lanterns they had lighted he could see the men getting on board.

"We must all take our places," said the captain. "I will go down to the water's edge and listen. Mr Rivers, be ready to put a match to the blue lights as soon as I call to you."

All obeyed in silence. Annchen took leave of her brother and Moritz, and bade also a general farewell to the others; her eye, as George could not help fancying, lighting with special kindness on him. When they had all taken up their stations, there was a silence of some minutes, and then the voice of the captain was heard,—"Light up! I hear them coming!" Rivers obeyed; and a lurid flame suddenly sprang forth, by the light of which the boat and raft were both distinctly visible, the former with only five or six rowers aboard, the other following in tow, and crowded with armed men.

"The party on the rocks fire on the boat?" shouted Captain Ranken; "those in the shed on the raft!"

He was obeyed on the instant. Eight rifles cracked almost at the same moment from the rocks. The steersman and two of the rowers dropped dead in their places. The other two flung themselves into the bottom of the boat, wounded, but not killed. Several also on board the raft fell into the sea, or into their companions' arms, and a cry for quarter was raised. But the next moment the voice of Bostock sounded loud and clear.

"Step into the water!" he cried. "We are already on the reef; it is not above our knees."

He sprang out himself as he spoke, and began wading ashore, followed, after a moment's pause, by the other men. Several volleys were discharged from the barricade and rocks, not without their effect, though the mark was now more difficult to hit. In a few minutes the mutineers had found refuge, as the captain had anticipated, on the outer side of the barricade, which the besieged, if they may so be called, had run up for their own protection.

The riflemen were now called down from the rocks, and joined their companions in the shed. The fire not having been returned from either the boat or the raft, no injuries had been sustained. But the situation of Captain Ranken and his companions still appeared to be almost hopeless; as the fight would now be carried on on almost equal terms, and the mutineers still outnumbered them in the proportion of four to one. It seemed most likely now that they would try to surround the shed on all four sides, firing through the crevices, which were as available to them as to those within, and so soon pick off all the defenders. But for this light was necessary, and they were therefore waiting for the moon to rise.

While they were still waiting in anxious suspense, a stone with a paper wrapped round it was thrown through the open window. The captain picked it up and read it. It had no name attached to it, but professed to come from the whole of the crew, except those with Captain Ranken. It stated that the hut was completely surrounded, and that the assailants had the lives of all those within at their mercy. But they wished to avoid further bloodshed. If the five thousand pounds which had been removed from Mr Whittaker's cabin should be given up, together with all the arms in the possession of the besieged party, they would go quietly away without hurting any one. But if this was refused, an attack would be made as soon as the moon rose, and no man's life would be spared. It was added, that if no answer was sent before moonrise, that would be regarded as a refusal.

When the captain had finished reading, no one spoke for a while. At last McCarthy broke the silence, —

"Have you any idea, sir, of complying with their demand? You see they do not ask—what we could not have agreed to—the surrender of Miss Vander Heyden."

"No," said Mr Whittaker; "and I do not think my employers would blame you, if you did comply. I daresay we should all agree to bear some portion of the ransom."

Several of the others broke in together, declaring their willingness to pay any portion in their power.

"What do you say, Mr Rivers?" asked the captain, observing that he had not spoken.

"I would pay my share, sir," answered George; "anything that is in my power. But I fear it would be useless. The best hope these men have in escaping the penalty of their mutiny lies in our death. If we were to surrender ourselves to them, as this letter proposes, I think they would murder us in cold blood—all except—"

"You need not mention her name, sir," interposed Vander Heyden. "But you say well. I know the villain who leads these men; he is quite capable of that, or any other atrocity. We had better die sword in hand, like men, than be stabbed like sheep."

"You speak only too truly, sir," said the captain. "Our choice lies between one kind of death or another; and I, for one, choose that of a brave man, who will have no trafficking with villains."

He looked round him, and read approval in every eye. "You are right, sir," said McCarthy briefly, and the others echoed the sentiment.

No one spoke for the next ten minutes. Each was busy with his own thoughts; such as are likely to fill men's minds when on the verge of eternity. The time seemed painfully protracted, and all wished that the trial was over. Suspense was worse than death itself. At last a sudden burst of yellow light streaming through the window warned them that their time had come. The next moment the door was burst in, and a crowd of men, armed with cutlasses and pistols, endeavoured to force an entrance. They were met by a general volley, which killed or wounded nearly all the foremost assailants. But the rush from behind was kept up. Several forced themselves into the hut, and a hand-to-hand struggle ensued. Miss Vander Heyden had been placed behind the screen which Rivers had strengthened for her; and he shouted to her, when the attack began, to throw herself on the ground, as the best chance there was of her escaping injury. The screen caught the eye of Bostock as he entered in the rush, and he and Van Ryk instantly made for it. Vander Heyden threw himself in Bostock's way, and a fierce encounter began between them; while, George in like manner interposing between Van Ryk and the screen, they were soon engaged in deadly combat.

By this time the hut was nearly filled with the mutineers. The captain, with McCarthy on one side of him and Redgy on the other, was desperately defending himself against two or three assailants. The third mate, Whittaker, and Walters, had been all struck down, and several of the men were mortally wounded, when suddenly there came from the sea a strange and unexpected sound—the boom of a cannon!

The strife was instantly suspended. Each man looked in doubt and wonder upon his opponent's face. Then the captain's voice was once more heard,—

"Throw down your arms, you mutinous dogs, and yield yourselves prisoners, or every man among you shall swing at the yard-arm before another hour has passed!"

Chapter Six

About a week had elapsed. George and Redgy were standing on the deck of the Government steamer Wasp, leaning over the bulwarks and contemplating the appearance of the harbour of Port Natal; which lay immediately in front of them, with the town of Durban in the middle distance, and the Natal country in the background. The ship could proceed no farther. The bar across the harbour mouth, on which seething masses of foam were breaking, presented an insuperable obstacle.

"How are we ever to get in, George?" asked Redgy. "I suppose ships *do* get in somehow. Indeed it is plain they do, for there is a lot of them lying off the quays yonder. But how they surmounted that bar, it is beyond me to imagine. I should think even the Yankee captain, who declared he could run his ship anywhere where there had been a heavy dew, would be puzzled here."

"I don't suppose Captain Deedes will take his ship in," answered George. "He has only to deliver and take back despatches to Cape Town, and these can be brought to him out here."

"What, in a boat, I suppose?" suggested Margetts; "and that is the way we shall go in, then? Well, every man knows his own business best; but I should have thought there was a very comfortable chance of any boat being swamped!"

"Wait, and you'll see, Redgy. Captain Deedes told me we should be safe ashore before twelve o'clock."

"Did he tell you anything about what is going on at Mossel Bay?" asked Margetts. "I know he has had letters from thence. I saw them brought aboard half an hour ago."

"Yes, a good deal. I am sorry to say Rolfe is dead; that is the fifth of our party that was killed. Walters and three of the sailors were dead before we sailed, you know."

"I am sorry for Rolfe. How are McCarthy and the captain and Whittaker?"

"They are all doing well. The captain's was only a slight cut across the hand. He was much more hurt by Bostock's and Van Ryk's escape than by that wound."

"I don't wonder. It is certainly a pity that they were not run up to the yard-arm, as half a dozen others may be, who were less guilty than they were. I can't think how they managed to get off."

"Well, I can understand it. Van Ryk and I were having a desperate tussle, and we had been driven close to the door of the shed. When I heard the gun from the *Wasp*, our encounter was broken off, and I thought nothing more of my antagonist for the next ten minutes. As for Bostock, who was, I noticed, a first-rate swordsman, he had disarmed Vander Heyden, and would, I daresay, have run him through, if the cannon hadn't been fired at that moment. I judge both he and Van Ryk, who had their wits well about them, made off as fast as they could to the place where the gig had been left, when Moritz and I landed from her."

"Ay, just at the farthest point behind the ridge, I remember," said Margetts. "She was almost out of sight."

"Exactly. Well, they fell in with Sullivan and one or two other fellows, got aboard, and rowed straight off for land. I daresay they had reached it, before their absence was discovered."

"Very likely. What do you think they will do, then?"

"Most likely land on some solitary spot, scuttle their boat, and make their way into the interior. They have their carbines, and will have no difficulty in providing themselves with food. Perhaps they will make their way to the diamond fields, and there change their names, and make a pot of money; or perhaps they'll take to hunting or farming, and you'll meet them some years hence, driving bullock waggons, or taking flocks of sheep to the market—thriving men and respectable—at least according to their ideas of respectability; or perhaps, once more, they'll come across a band of criminals, who have escaped from prison, and go about robbing and murdering travellers."

"Nothing more likely, I should say. And what will become of the others?"

"Well, as you suggested, half a dozen or so are safe to be hanged—Shirley and Andersen, for example, who were among the leaders, though not the main movers, of the outbreak. As for the others, the captain is mercifully disposed. You see, the whole thing (as has been proved now) was got up by those three villains, Bostock, Van Ryk, and Sherwin, after the ship had left Cape Town. They persuaded the new men—Shirley and Sullivan among them—to enlist. Only three or four in the first instance were told about Whittaker's money. They expected to find that in his cabin, and they would then have launched one of the boats and gone off, leaving us on the reef. When they learned, as they did from Andersen, that it had been locked up in the captain's cabin, they told half a dozen more about the money, and persuaded them to join in the attack on the officers and passengers. Then they induced the rest of the crew to believe that their only hope of escaping hanging lay in silencing the captain and his men, and getting away from the reef. The men have been the victims of several clever scoundrels, and I hope the law won't be put in force too severely against them."

An hour or two afterwards, the bar having become practicable, the steam-tug arrived which was to convey such of the party as desired it to the shore. But the surf dashing over the bar was still so formidable, that it was judged necessary to secure the passengers against damage, after the very curious fashion resorted to on such occasions. They were sent down below, in what would have been total darkness, if it had not been for the glimmering light of a lantern. Then the hatches were covered over, and the passage accomplished, with an amount of shaking and rolling which was considerably worse than a stiff gale at sea. As Redgy afterwards described it, it was like as though they had been a lot of marbles thrown into a bag, and then shaken up. Happily, however, it did not last very long; and they were presently safely landed on the quay, and free to examine the prospect before them. Land is said always to look attractive in the eyes of those who have just accomplished a long sea voyage, but the scene which George and his companions beheld, when they emerged from the cabin of the steam-tug, did not need this consideration to enhance its beauties.

It was indeed a lovely sight which met their eyes. The streets of the town were spacious, and built at right angles to one another,—most of them of a dark stone, which is said to harden by exposure to the air,—but some of them of brick, or wattle covered with plaster; many of them having deep verandahs, with rows of trees in front. Along the quays, which exhibited a busy scene of cargoes in the course of landing or shipping, a mass of vessels bearing the flags of all nations were lying; and on either side of the town rich forests bordered the whole coast. A little inland were seen pastures, and plantations of sugar-cane. The monotonous appearance which this kind of landscape usually presents was varied by high hills, and valleys here and there intervening. The wonderful blue of both sky and sea, which only those who have beheld it can realise to themselves, formed a glorious background to the picture. George and Margetts, accompanied by the other passengers, made their way to a hotel in one corner of the principal street, and partook of a luxurious repast, which to be duly appreciated ought to be eaten by persons who had just landed after many weeks at sea.

This over, they had next to obtain a conveyance to Umvalosa; and for help in providing this they applied to Mynheer Moritz, who had always been friendly, and more especially since the memorable day of the battle on the reef.

"I will help you as well as I can," he said. "I wish I could ask you to join our party, which will pass Umvalosa on our way to Vander Heyden's place, 'Bushman's Drift.' Henryk, his sister, and myself mean to ride, and the luggage will be conveyed in his bullock waggon, which is one of the best in Natal. But it would be no use for me to propose that."

"None at all," assented George drily.

"Well, I don't defend him. He might, and ought to be, more courteous to you. But you mustn't be too hard on him. He has his good qualities. He is brave, and honourable, and high-minded, and capable of very warm and strong affection. He is very fond of his sister, and there is a lady, Lisa Van Courtland, his cousin, to whom he is almost romantically attached, and whom he is soon to marry. As for you, it is not *you* he dislikes, but your country, and that feeling, I am afraid, is not peculiar to him. A great many of our people believe that they have been hardly used by the English. You see, the whole country once belonged to us—was our undisputed possession for more than a century. We had done nothing to forfeit it—so we feel, because we had nothing to do with the quarrels of the governments in Europe; which were the only grounds on which it was taken from us. Then, when we couldn't live under English rule, and left the Cape to settle elsewhere, giving up the homes to which we were so long used, in order that we might live undisturbed, the English followed us to Natal, and we were again obliged to move elsewhere. And now, since this annexation, many of us fear that we shall not be left alone even in the Transvaal, and may be obliged to break up our homes for the third time, to go to some new country; where, even then, we may not be secure from interference. Henryk is one of those who feel this keenly, and he's apt to show his feelings rather too plainly."

"No doubt of that," said George, smiling. "However, I am disposed to make all possible allowance for him under the circumstances you have mentioned; which are, I ought to add, but very imperfectly known to me. I suppose, as is generally the case, there are two versions of the story."

"Probably there are," said Mr Moritz, returning his smile, "and perhaps it is too much to expect that you should credit my version. However, whatever may come of it, I hope you and I will remain friends. I could never forget the service you have rendered me, and, indeed, Annchen also: for she tells me that she believes she is indebted to you for saving her life on the night of the attack."

"I don't know how that may be," said George. "I did my best to protect her, certainly. But as you and her brother were not so close at hand as I was, to defend her, I do not know how I could possibly have done less. I hope we shall be allowed to take leave of her."

"She will wish that too," said Moritz, "but I am afraid her brother will not permit it. She has, indeed, charged me to give you her adieux, together with her regrets that she cannot speak them in person. But now you want my assistance in getting to your destination. Your best course, I think, will be to make the acquaintance of a Natal farmer, named Baylen; who, I have learned, means to set out in a few days for Horner's Kraal, and will therefore pass very near, if he does not stop at, Umvalosa. He is a thriving man, and knows the country well. He is neither wholly English nor Dutch, his father having been an Englishman and his grandfather a Hollander, but his sympathies are mainly English. I will give you a letter to him. I would go with you to his son's house, 'Hakkluyt's Kloof,' where he now is, but time will not allow it, as Vander Heyden sets out in a few hours."

George thanked him, and they cordially shook hands and parted. The two friends then walked out to Hakkluyt's Kloof, and delivered Moritz's letter; which at once secured a hearty welcome from the old man. He was a fine specimen of a colonial farmer, standing more than six feet high, and strongly, if somewhat heavily built. He introduced the young men first to his wife, a still comely matron of fifty, and his daughter Clara, a handsome girl of twenty, then to his sons, Stephen, the eldest, and owner of the Kloof, Walter, Wilhelm, and Ernest. They were all stout and sturdily-built young men, though hardly equalling their father's height or breadth of shoulder. He readily agreed to convey the Englishmen and their baggage to Umvalosa, naming a very reasonable sum as their passage-money. He also invited them to take up their quarters at his farmhouse until the day of his departure came, an offer which the two lads were thankful to accept. George then went out to look at the waggons in which the journey was to be made—each of which, he found, would be drawn by no less than sixteen oxen. They were in construction not unlike an English waggon, only a good deal stronger and more solid. They were arranged not only for the conveyance of goods, but for the accommodation of travellers. At one end there were seats arranged on either side, and from the roof hammocks might be suspended, in which the females of the party might sleep; the men usually making their beds either under the waggons, or at the farther end. Two entire days were consumed in loading them. As George and Redgy were not to go the whole distance, their boxes were put in last, and then one day more was passed in careful examination of the cattle, to make sure they were all in sound condition. On the morning of the fourth day, however, they set out; the party consisting of the farmer, his wife and daughter and his three sons, three native servants, a boy, and the two young Englishmen. The first thing was to harness, or, as it is termed in that country, to inspan the cattle. This is a curious process for a stranger to witness. The oxen, which in a well-trained team are fully as well experienced in the operation as their masters, are driven close up to the wheel of the waggon, with their heads towards it. Then the waggon driver calls each ox by its name, which it knows as well as any English dog knows his, and the animal bends forward to allow the yoke to be put upon its neck. Then they are arranged in a double line—eight couple, one behind the other, a Kaffir lad, called the fore-louper, leading the way. He brandishes in his hand a huge whip of cameleopard's hide, which he delivers with terrific effect on the shoulders or back of the unhappy animals, generally towards the close of the journey, when the team are becoming weary, or, at all events, lazy.

The farmer and one of his sons accompanied the waggon on horseback, while the rest of the party walked by the side, or took a few hours' siesta in the waggons. Farmer Baylen proposed to George to ride the first part of the journey in his and his son's company, and the latter gladly accepted the offer. He was greatly struck with the beauty of the scenery in the neighbourhood of Durban. The journey for the first two days lay over Cowie's Hill, which rises to a considerable height, affording a wide prospect of the sea-coast, with its rich line of woods; while inland, the country for a considerable distance presents a succession of elevated ridges, extending as far as the Umkomanzi river. The road itself was in the highest degree picturesque. It was November, the May of the Southern Hemisphere. Every now and then the waggons would enter upon a thick undergrowth of shrubs, ploughing their way, as it were, through an inland sea; the fragrance and beauty of the shrubs far exceeding anything that an English landscape presents. When a few miles had been accomplished, the oxen were outspanned, and allowed to graze, while the men took their mid-day meal, and afterwards smoked their pipes, under the shelter of some fragrant shrubs. Just as they reached the first halting-place, George discerned in the distance some singular-looking circular erections, which, the farmer informed him, were a native village; and finding that George was anxious to see it, offered to ride up and make an examination of it. The offer was gladly accepted, and after a short canter the kraal was reached. It was situated on one of the slopes above a rapid stream, and was built after the design usual among the Kaffirs. There were two circular enclosures, one inside the other, the whole being protected by a strong palisade. The outer circle is for the Kaffirs themselves, the inner one for the cattle. As these latter constitute the wealth of the villagers, they are careful to secure them against theft or violence, and by this arrangement they could only be seized after all the resistance the men could offer had been overcome. Each hut is circular in shape, and consists of a framework, constructed of long poles, driven into the ground, and bent towards the top, so as to meet at one point in the centre. Similar poles are laid horizontally at intervals one above another, and secured to the uprights by strips of fibre, so that the whole structure resembles a huge circular crate. The portion which forms the roof is covered with grass pegged down and secured to the poles, something after the way in which ricks are thatched in England. The floor usually consists of clay, when it can be found in the neighbourhood, levelled and beaten hard. It is sometimes even polished, by being rubbed over with a flat stone. There is a circular elevation in the centre of the hut similarly formed, which serves as a fireplace, but there is nothing resembling a chimney, the smoke escaping, as used to be the case in the dwellings of the ancient Britons, through the framework above. There is generally a door formed of wattle-work, which can be closed in inclement weather, and sometimes a kind of screen of similar material can be placed to windward of the fire, when the weather is unusually severe. George was struck with the fine proportions and intelligent faces of the men, many of them exhibiting muscular, stalwart frames and expressive features, which a Greek sculptor might not have disdained to copy. The women, though some of them were not ungraceful in figure, were not nearly equal, either in personal beauty or intelligence, to their male companions. Their features were, indeed, altogether too flat to satisfy the European idea of beauty, a fault which was not observable among the men. On George's remarking this disparity of the sexes to the farmer, he answered it was no doubt caused by the severe and incessant labour imposed upon the women, for which nature had not designed them.

"They are required," said he, "to perform the entire manual labour of the kraal—all the digging, planting, and reaping, which in other lands is performed by the men; while the men themselves sit at home, engaged in sewing their karosses, in which they display great dexterity, and by which they realise considerable sums. There is, however, no lack of manhood among them. Their bravery in the chase and in war is not inferior to that of civilised nations."

"If ever they should learn from us how to fight," said old Baylen to George, "and possess themselves of the Gatling gun and Martini rifle, it would be a bad day for the whites. They outnumber us ten to one, and are as fearless and resolute as any European race."

"But if they are converted to Christianity," said George, "they would hardly rise against their benefactors, would they?"

"Ay," said the old farmer, "so many think. But to my mind that is a rotten reed to lean on. The nations of Europe have been Christianised many centuries ago, but that does not prevent their going to war with one another, when they think themselves wronged, or even when they imagine some advantage is to be gained. How mistaken the idea is, was to be seen in Sandilli's war, only a little time ago. Some of the chiefs, and some of their men too, who had been baptised in their infancy, and had lived as Christians all their lives, nevertheless took part with their heathen countrymen in the struggle with the English. Several of the chiefs—Dukwana among others, who had been a very zealous proselyte—hesitated for some time as to what course they should pursue, and did not renounce their Christianity. But they took part with Sandilli, nevertheless; and if they could have succeeded in exterminating the whites, and regaining possession of Southern Africa, would not have hesitated to do so."

"That is a very serious consideration," said George. "You say they are greatly more numerous than the whites, do you not?"

"There is no proportion between the two," said the farmer. "Our European population in Natal—English, Dutch, German, and all others—is considerably under twenty thousand; the Kaffirs number not less than three hundred and fifty thousand; and, what is more serious still, the Zulu kingdom, which immediately adjoins ours, is governed by a native king, the most powerful that has ever reigned in South Africa. His army alone contains four times as many men as our whole white population, and every man among them is a trained warrior, as fearless of wounds and death, as any man in your English regiments."

"How is it they do not attack you?" asked George.

"There are several reasons," answered Baylen. "In the first place, the native races are not at unity among themselves. They hate one another even more bitterly than they hate the white man, and thus the English are enabled to array one tribe against another. The Basutos and the Fingos will help you to put down the Gaikas and the Galekas; and these, when reduced to obedience, would very possibly aid you against the Zulus, if you were indeed going to war with them. That is one reason. Another is, that so far, whenever your English troops have come into collision with the natives, they have always had the better of them, and there is a very general idea that the English cannot be conquered. If any one race should ever succeed in any campaign against your troops, the consequences would be very grave indeed. Indeed, I believe that the general opinion entertained respecting the

Zulu king, and his irresistible military power, has already done enormous mischief; and he will have to be put down before English supremacy in South Africa can be effectually secured. But here we are back again, and it is time to resume our journey."

About nightfall they reached their halting-place, a small village about ten miles distant from Durban, where they obtained a supply of fresh milk and mealies, resuming their journey on the following day.

For several hours they proceeded without any unusual occurrence; but about noon Matamo, as the principal driver was called, came up to Mr Baylen and exchanged a few words with him, pointing in the direction of a small knoll, which lay at a distance of a few hundred yards. The farmer, who had been on the point of dismounting, put his horse in motion, and rode in company with the driver to the spot indicated. He returned in a few minutes, and ordered the cattle to be outspanned and carefully secured inside a small thicket which lay close at hand.

"Have you ever seen one of our South African storms?" he asked of George, when he had finished these preparations.

"No," was the answer. "But surely you cannot apprehend a storm now, Mr Baylen! It is one of the most calm and beautiful days I ever remember to have witnessed."

"Ay, I daresay you think so," returned the farmer. "But nevertheless we are going to have it sharp and strong, as the saying is, and that within a quarter of an hour. The suddenness with which storms come on, and pass away again, is one of the peculiar features of Southern Africa. You had better get inside the waggon, and that without loss of time. The women have been wise enough to take shelter already."

While the farmer was speaking, he had been engaged in carefully securing his horse by a strong rheim, and then, climbing up after Redgy and George into the waggon, drew down and fastened the curtain in front. While this conversation was going on, the air had perceptibly darkened, and there came a rush of cold wind from the north, the precursor apparently of the hurricane. Then the storm broke out with a suddenness and violence which fairly took George's breath away. The wind swept down with such force that, but for the shelter of the trees, neither man nor horse could have stood against it. The air grew so dark that they could hardly discern each other's faces; and the hail, or rather the blocks of ice, poured down from the skies, beating against the covering of the cart with such violence, that George expected every moment to see it driven in. Presently the hail ceased and a deluge of rain followed. The men had been careful to place the waggon on a piece of ground which was slightly raised above the rest. But for this the water would have risen almost to the level of the floor of the waggon; and the ground on both sides of them was soon converted into a small river, which poured along with the fury of a mountain torrent, sweeping away shrubs and small trees, and even large stones, as though they had been so many straws. It was two hours good before the storm was over. Then the clouds dispersed, the sun came out again, and no other trace of the fury of the elements was left, but what was supplied by the uprooted shrubs and the streams of water which continued to pour along with unabated force.

"We shan't be able to proceed any farther to-day," remarked the farmer. "The ground will be too soft to travel upon for ten or twelve hours, even under this hot sun. We must make ourselves as comfortable as we can for the night."

The necessary arrangements were accordingly made. The horses were hobbled, and turned out to graze. A fire was lighted, at which supper was cooked; and after the meal the males of the party sat down to smoke their pipes by it, for the night air after the rain was chilly. Mrs Baylen and Clara retired to rest in their waggon.

"I should like to hear the history of your life in South Africa," said George, as he threw another log on the fire. "I think you said you came into these parts when you were quite a lad, and that, I judge, cannot be less than fifty years ago. You must remember a great many changes, and probably have gone through some strange adventures. If you don't feel disposed for sleep just yet, I wish you would give us the benefit of your experiences. Redgy and I would be greatly interested to hear them."

"Father won't object to that," said Wilhelm with a smile. "Nothing pleases him better than to tell us stories about his young days."

"And they're worth hearing too," added Ernest. "I suppose I've heard most of 'em more than once, but I always like to hear them again. I only wish Clarchen were with us. She enjoys them even more than I do."

Chapter Seven

"Well, Mr Rivers," began Farmer Baylen, "I don't know why I shouldn't gratify your fancy. It is certain that I and mine have been a long time in the colony, and know pretty well all that has happened in it during this century. And what has happened there during this century is pretty nearly all the history it has. Between the time when my mother's ancestors first settled at the Cape, and the time when the English captured it, it can hardly be said to have had any history at all."

"It was a period of a hundred and fifty years, though, wasn't it?" suggested George.

"Yes, but one day was just like another day, and one year like another year, and one generation like another generation all that time. The Dutch occupied the land, and made the natives work for them; and when more land was wanted, they took more land, and enslaved more natives. So they went on, spreading farther into the country, until the English came.

"My father—I believe his name was Andrew Bailey—was a ship's carpenter on board one of the line-of-battle ships in Sir Home Popham's fleet. There was very little resistance offered to the English. It was generally believed that when the European wars came to an end the colony would be restored to Holland, as it had been before. Consequently the Dutch regarded the English as visitors, rather than masters.

"A good many men got their discharge after the fighting was over, and among them my father. He liked the country, and found plenty of employment, and higher wages than he could get at home. He was a skilled workman, particularly clever at house-building. An English settler wanted a house built at Stellenbosch, and my father undertook the job. He lodged, while employed in the work, in the house of a Dutch farmer named Van Schuylen, and there he soon became very intimate. The farmer was a kind and hospitable old man, as the old Hollanders for the most part were."

"Kind to the whites, that is," interpolated Redgy.

"Ay, Mr Margetts, I understand what you mean, and I am afraid there is too much truth in it. There is a prejudice against 'black blood,' which, with all the years that I've lived in this land, I cannot understand. 'Black blood!'

the very words to me seem to be a denial of what the Bible says, that 'God has made of *one* blood all the nations of the earth.' Yes, you are right about Farmer Van Schuylen. He'd make no more of putting a native to do the most unwholesome work, that might kill him outright, than he would of pitching a stone into a pond. And if they were fractious or lazy, he'd stand by and see them flogged with the jamboks—the rhinoceros whips, that is—till their backs were cut to ribbons. But my father was a free man and an Englishman, and Van Schuylen had none but friendly words for him.

"Well, as I've said, my father became intimate with his family, and by and by fell in love with Rose, the only daughter, and she with him. The old man did not object, but Cornelius Van Schuylen, her brother, did not like the match. He was an out-and-out Hollander. He thought the English had no business in the colony. They were interlopers, he said, and jeered at our ways. He and my father had had some high words, I fancy, about the natives, very soon after they came to Stellenbosch. But Rose, though she was very fond of her brother, took my father's part. He was a handsome and well-made man of five-and-twenty, and she would have had him, I believe, even if her father had objected. Fortunately Cornelius lived ten or twelve miles away. I say fortunately, for there certainly would have been a hot quarrel between him and his brother-in-law, if he had had any share in the business. My father became a great favourite with the old man, and in a few years nearly the whole management of the farm was left to his son-in-law, who persisted in showing favour to the blacks. He wouldn't overwork them, and wouldn't allow them to be flogged. What was worse, he allowed them to attend the church services, and to have their children baptised."

"That was no offence, I suppose, sir," said Redgy.

"On the contrary, it was one of the greatest he could commit," said Baylen. "By the Dutch law, all baptised Christians were free. Therefore baptising a native was the same thing as setting him free, and the presence of free blacks in the colony was what they could not endure. There had been differences with the English authorities on this subject; but little had come of them, because the English were only holding the colony for a time. Two or three years after my father's marriage, however, there came the downfall of Napoleon, and a general peace. To the surprise and indignation of the Dutch, the colony was not restored to Holland, but given permanently over to the English."

"Well," said George, "I must say they had some right to complain of that. I heard what Moritz said about it, and I couldn't help agreeing with him."

"I think the English would have acted more wisely if they had retained simply a naval station, with a fort or two to guard it," said the farmer. "Well, when it was seen that the occupation of the English was to be permanent, and that the English discouraged slavery, and allowed the baptism of the natives, there was great discontent, which occasionally broke out into rebellion. Cornelius was among those who were hottest against the English. It was with the greatest difficulty he was kept from joining the rebels. But his father sent for him, and threatened him with his curse if he did, and the Dutch mind what their fathers say, more than any people I know. In 1834, however, when the English Government made a proclamation absolutely forbidding slavery, he could bear it no longer."

"1834," repeated George. "That was the year, was not it, when they put down slavery in the West Indies?"

"Yes, and it lowered the value of the property there as well as here. I don't say the English Government oughtn't to have done it. Slavery is wrong, beginning, middle, and end, in my eyes. But it might have been done gradually, instead of all at once. Any way, the Dutch wouldn't have it, and they resolved to leave the country rather than submit. Great numbers emigrated: some northwards, into what is now the Orange Free State, and the Transvaal, but more into Natal. Cornelius was one of those who removed to Natal, and my father went there too. He didn't want to go, but my mother had been always so attached to Cornelius, that he saw it would break her heart if they were parted. So, like a good husband, he went too."

"Wasn't it rather rash, sir?" suggested George. "Why, to say nothing of the loss of money, Natal must be a good seven hundred miles from Stellenbosch, and it was at that time quite a new country."

"It is more than eight hundred, I believe, for the matter of that, and there were very few whites in it; but the state of things wasn't so bad as you suppose. In the first place, my father took his time in selling his land. As he wasn't a Dutchman, people knew that he wasn't one of those who were mad to go, and would take anything that was offered for it. He got a very good price for it. Then, again, he knew a great deal about Natal. Lieutenant Farewell, who had obtained a large grant of land from King Chaka, came to Stellenbosch, and made large offers to the farmers there. My father closed with him, and got a large farm, and very good land, where my son is now living, for very little money."

"Who was Lieutenant Farewell?" asked Margetts.

"I believe he was an English officer, who had been sent to survey the country, and had a fancy for founding a colony at Natal. He had been murdered by the natives before we went there; but my father had got all his information from him the previous year. Then, again, his move to Natal was well managed. His farm lay on the south side of Stellenbosch, only a short distance from Simon's Bay. A large vessel was lent him by one of his friends, which took him and his family, his waggons, his household furniture, and such of his stock as he wished to take with him, to Natal, at a small cost, and in a few days."

"Your father knew what he was about, Mr Baylen."

"I think he did, sir. I remember well our arrival at Hakkluyt's Kloof. We lived in the waggons till he and his men had run up the house and farm buildings. We soon found we had made a very good bargain."

"That was in King Chaka's time, wasn't it, father?" asked Walter Baylen.

"No, Walter. It was Chaka who granted the land, or rather, leave to settle on the land, to Lieutenant Farewell. But he had been dead a year or two, and his brother Dingaan was king when we arrived there."

"I have heard a good deal about Chaka," observed Margetts, "and I should like to hear more. I suppose you know all about him, Mr Baylen?"

"More than I can tell you to-night, sir," answered the farmer with a smile. "You shall hear all about it another time if you like it. But it's getting late. We must go to sleep now, as we shall be stirring early to-morrow."

At daybreak the journey was resumed. The ground was still soft from the heavy rain in some places, but a few hours' hot sun dried it. The air was fresh and balmy. It was with a sense of exhilaration that George and Redgy mounted their horses, and scented the fresh morning air. Nothing could be more delicious than their journey in the early hours of the day. Aromatic shrubs, graceful sugar bushes, delicate heaths, wild-flowers of every imaginable colour, such as in England would be accounted the rare beauties of the conservatory, grew in profusion on either side of the track they followed. The air was rich with a thousand fragrant scents. In the middle distance, Kaffir hovels or white-gabled farmhouses occasionally presented themselves, each surrounded by orange or palm groves; and the white-peaked mountains, set in their frame of the richest blue, formed a perfect background to the lovely picture.

Notwithstanding the heat, several casualties occurred, in consequence of the recent rains. Sometimes they descended into dongas, where the sun's rays had not penetrated, and there the wheels would sink several inches into the ground, and it needed all the strength of the party to extricate them. Levers had to be applied on both sides, and the unlucky oxen were lashed with rhinoceros whips, until they presented a pitiable spectacle. On one occasion, as they were passing along a gully between two steep rocky banks, they came upon another ox-waggon journeying in the opposite direction. There was not room to pass by two or three feet. At first it seemed as if there was no mode of overcoming the difficulty, except by taking one waggon to pieces. But at this juncture they were met by a man, who came up riding a stout Cape horse, and who seemed to be well known to the farmer and his sons.

"Ah, Hardy," exclaimed Baylen, "you have come just in time to help us! We've neglected to keep a bright look-out, and have got into this mess."

The newcomer dismounted, and, joining the rest of the party, made a careful examination of the banks on both sides of the pathway. Presently Hardy's voice was heard.

"Here you are!" he cried. "Here, Baylen, Matamo, here's a soft place in the bank which we can dig out, and it will be deep enough to hold the waggon. Bring the picks and spades here."

All the party, more than a dozen in number, went to work with a will, and presently a hollow place of three or four feet deep was dug out, into which Baylen's waggon was drawn, just sufficient room being obtained in this manner to allow the other waggon to go by. This *contretemps* caused a delay of several hours, and instead of outspanning on the bank of the Mooi river, as they had intended, they were obliged to stop some miles short of it.

It was not a bad place, though, for a halt. The oxen were outspanned, and turned out to graze on the veldt, care being taken to prevent their straying. The fires were lighted and supper for nine got ready, Hardy having agreed to join the party.

As they sat down, George took a good view of the newcomer. He was a strong, weather-beaten fellow, not much short of fifty, but still in the full vigour of life, with a face expressing sense and resolution. He had a good deal of the soldier in his appearance and demeanour, and George learned from Ernest Baylen that he had served in India, and under Lord Napier and Sir Garnet Wolseley. He had settled in South Africa as a land-surveyor and architect, though he combined some farming with it. He was a friend and frequent visitor of the Baylens, who were evidently pleased at his arrival. As soon as the supper was finished, and the pipes lighted, Margetts asked the farmer to give him the promised account of King Chaka.

"I want to learn all I can about him," he said; "I have heard some strange stories of him."

"I don't know what the stories may have been, Mr Margetts," rejoined Baylen, "but certainly enough might be told about him to startle any one. He was the first person who brought the Zulus into notice. I don't know whose son he was, or who was king before him; nobody does seem to know. But it was about the year 1820 that he first began to attract attention. The Zulus had been an insignificant tribe before that. But soon after the beginning of his reign, he set about forming a large army, which he developed and disciplined in a manner that had been quite unknown to African chiefs before his time. There is a strange story as to what put this fancy into his head. If I don't mistake, Hardy, it was you who told it to me."

"Very likely," said Hardy. "I know what I heard from some French soldiers in India. They had been in Africa, and had known Chaka."

"What was it, Mr Hardy, if I might ask?" inquired Margetts.

"Why, these men told me they had been the servants of some French officers, who, after the close of Napoleon's wars, travelled in South Africa, and became King Chaka's guests. Chaka was fond of inquiring about what had happened in Europe. One of the officers told him a good deal about the Emperor Napoleon—his splendid army, the vast number of men he had collected under his standard, the perfect discipline to which he had reduced them, and their unbounded devotion to his service. By their help, Napoleon had conquered nation after nation, until nearly the whole of Europe had been subjected by him. 'That was something like a king,' Chaka had remarked, and from that day he began forming his famous army."

"Well, I can believe that," observed Baylen, "because his action corresponded very accurately to it. He got together a force of nearly a hundred thousand men, of whom fifteen thousand were always at his immediate command. He subjected his soldiers to severe and continual discipline. He built large barracks, in which they lived quite by themselves, not being allowed to marry until they were elderly men. The least hesitation in obeying his orders was instantly punished by the most cruel of all deaths, impalement. With this army he attacked and conquered his neighbours in all directions, until he became an object of universal terror."

"A black Napoleon, in fact," returned Redgy,—"what he wanted to be."

"He was curiously like him," remarked Baylen, "allowing for the differences of race. I have heard that Napoleon never spared any soldier who showed want of courage in carrying out an order. That was Chaka's policy certainly, though he pursued it after a somewhat different fashion. After one of his campaigns, he would assemble his soldiers, and cause every regiment to pass before him. As it halted in front of his seat, he would call out, 'Bring out the cowards,' and any man who had not been as forward as the others was straightway dragged out and killed. The shrub, under which he usually sat in this manner to review his soldiers, was known as the 'coward's bush.'"

"Didn't he overrun Natal, father?" asked Wilhelm Baylen.

"Yes, and made it a desert for the time. Before his invasion it was densely populated, and in a most thriving condition. But the carnage caused by his troops was so great, that the population was reduced, I believe, to a few hundreds. That was one reason, probably, why he was willing for the English to settle there."

"But he was dead before you arrived in Natal, wasn't he?" asked Ernest.

"Yes. I told you he had been dead some years, and his brother Dingaan was on the throne. Dingaan, who was quite as bloody, and even more treacherous than Chaka, caused him to be assassinated while he was sitting in his kraal, and then was made king in his place. But Dingaan was not his brother's equal in ability or force of character, and he lost a great deal of the power which Chaka had acquired."

"Did you ever come into contact with him, sir?" asked Wilhelm.

"He never sent his soldiers to attack us, but he was continually threatening us with his displeasure, and making demands, which we were obliged to comply with as well as we could. A Zulu Impi would have been no joke to encounter. We must have all fled for our lives, and our houses would have been burnt and our cattle driven off at the least."

"How long did he reign?" asked Redgy.

"About twelve years. In the year 1836 the discontent of the Boers at Cape Town grew so great, that they too moved off to Natal—some five or six thousand of them. That, of course, made a great difference to our position. We could only have mustered a few hundreds to oppose Dingaan, if we had gone to war with him. But now it would be a few thousands."

"And men who knew how to fight the Zulus, too," remarked Walter.

"Yes. Dingaan found that out in 1837, when a war broke out between him and the Boers. Then the Zulus suffered for the first time a disastrous defeat. They rushed upon the Boers with their assegays, but the moment they came within range they were shot down like a flight of birds. They hardly got within hurling distance, and the stout leathern doublets of the Dutch repelled such assegays as did reach them. Not a single man, I believe, was so much as wounded. But it was an unfortunate victory in some ways.

It caused Dingaan, instead of using force, to resort to treachery—treachery which was very nearly being the death of me, though in the end things turned out well."

"Ah, now you are going to tell us the story of how you first got acquainted with mother," said Wilhelm, laughing.

"Well, I daresay it will interest Mr Rivers to hear it," said Baylen. "But, to be sure, it is a shocking history. It happened forty years ago, or one couldn't speak so coolly of it.

"I daresay, Mr Rivers, you have heard of Peter Retieff—any way you have, Hardy—the man, I mean, who founded Maritzburg. I knew him well. He was a brave, honest, kindly man—kindly even to the natives, which is not a common feature in a Dutchman's character. There was a treaty with Dingaan which obliged us to send back to him all the natives, who had fled into Natal from his tyranny. There were great numbers that did this; and all who were so returned were instantly put to death with most barbarous cruelty. Peter Retieff would not consent to carry this out, and paid a visit to Dingaan, to try to get him to cede Natal to the Dutch as an independent kingdom. He knew the danger of such an attempt; but he was a brave man, and trusted to the justice of his cause. He invited several of his neighbours to take part in his mission. Among others, my father and myself agreed to go. I was a lad between seventeen and eighteen at the time.

"We were received with unexpected civility, and my father and myself lodged at the house of Emilius Scheren, a Dutch missionary, whom Dingaan allowed to live at his kraal, but over whom he kept a very jealous watch—regarding him half as a spy on his actions, and half as a hostage for the good behaviour of his countrymen. He was a widower with one little girl, about twelve years old, named Wilhelmine. Mr Scheren told me some terrible stories of Dingaan's cruelty and rapacity. He had himself, he said, long been anxious to escape from the country. But he was most closely watched, and were he to attempt flight, would most certainly be caught and put to death. He would not mind it so much if it were not for his motherless little girl."

"'No one would hurt her surely,' my father said.

"'Dingaan would hurt any one,' Mr Scheren answered. But he was more afraid of his kindness than his cruelty. He feared that Wilhelmine's beauty had attracted Dingaan's notice, and before long he would insist on having her for one of his wives.

"'Why, she cannot be thirteen years old,' my father observed.

"'No, she is little more than twelve. But they marry young in this country, and in another year or so she will be thought old enough.'

"We comforted Mr Scheren as well as we could, promising him Dutch protection, if Retieff succeeded in his design. The next day we had our interview with Dingaan. He was extremely friendly, and complained of nothing but the theft of his cattle. 'If these were restored,' he said, 'he would be willing to leave the Dutch settlers in possession of Natal, provided they did not interfere with him. But if they stole his cattle, and would not restore them, it was impossible for him to regard them as friends.'

"This sounded reasonable enough, and good Peter Retieff was quite taken in by it. He agreed to recover the cattle, and we all went off with him, nearly two hundred in number, and soon succeeded in tracing the oxen, and obliging those who had stolen them to give them up. We returned in a kind of triumphal procession, driving the cattle before us. We were received with the greatest friendliness; all Retieff's demands were conceded, and we were invited to a royal feast, to be given on the following day to the king's Dutch allies."

"I think I have heard what was the issue of that feast," remarked George. "But I had thought that all who attended it." — He paused.

"That all had been murdered, I suppose," supplemented Baylen. "You heard right: all who attended that horrible feast *were* murdered. But I and my father did not go. We were just setting out when Mr Scheren stopped us. He told us that throughout he had suspected treachery was intended. But half an hour ago one of his converts had warned him that all the white men would be shot or stabbed. He had returned in all haste; but it was too late to warn Retieff and his friends, who were already in the royal kraal. All he could do was to save us. To convince us of the truth of his story, he pointed out to us a large force of armed Zulus, creeping stealthily up and surrounding the kraal. There was nothing to be done but to escape. We went into his stable, — where most fortunately we had kept our horses, instead of the place provided by the king for Retieff's train, — saddling and mounting with all possible expedition. We rode off without a moment's pause, but had not cleared the village, when we heard yells and screams which made our blood run cold."

"None of Retieff's party escaped, did they?" asked Hardy.

"Not one, unless you count my father and myself, and we had the narrowest of narrow escapes. We were seen by an Induna, who was late in attending the feast, and he instantly told Dingaan. He at once sent half a dozen of his fleetest men after us. They were on foot, and our horses, though cumbered with two riders, at first left them a long way behind. But the Zulus are wonderfully swift of foot, and their powers of endurance are still more surprising. When we reached the Tugela, they were not a hundred yards behind us. The river was not high, but it was with the greatest difficulty that our jaded horses could cross it. The Zulus came up before we had reached the bank, and hurled their weapons at us. One of the assegays struck Mr Scheren, who was sitting behind my father, and he fell dead into the river. Another grazed my horse's flank, while a third stuck in the saddle, nailing Wilhelmine's gown to it. Fortunately for us, Dingaan's order forbade any Zulu to pass into Natal, for we could have gone no farther, and could have offered no effectual resistance."

Chapter Eight

"What is to be our next halting-place?" asked George of Ernest Baylen, as they rode out in the rear of the party on the following morning, having waited behind to see that none of the articles removed from the waggons on the previous day had been forgotten. "We have a long day's journey before us, I expect."

"We shall stop at Colenso," replied Ernest, "rather a neat little town, and growing fast in size and importance. It stands near the Little Tugela. After that our next halting-places will be Helpmakaar, then Dundee, and lastly Newcastle. We might go farther to-day, but I expect we shall have some trouble in passing the Mooi. It is a good deal swollen by the heavy rain and the overflow of the Tugela. The flood, as yet, has fallen but very little."

He pointed as he spoke to the river, which lay at the distance of a mile or two. George drew his rein for a moment, quite entranced by the varied features of the landscape before him. There was a stretch of green veldt, reaching almost from the point where they had bivouacked to the river's banks, which were densely fringed with mimosas and willow-trees, through which its waters glanced, here and there, bright in the sunshine. To the right and left the ground was broken into declivities, clothed in many places with brushwood, in others presenting picturesque outlines of rock and shrub, while in the far distance towered the range of the Drakenbergs, the grandest mountains of Southern Africa.

"What are those dark objects I see floating about in the water?" inquired George, pointing with his whip to a broad bend in the river, which for some distance in both directions was free from wood on either side.

"Sea-cows! what you call hippopotamuses, I declare!" cried Ernest in some surprise. "They are not often to be seen in the Mooi; but I suppose they have come down from the Tugela. Yes, they are hippopotamuses; I can see them clearly now. If we can spare the time, we may have a hippopotamus hunt; there are few things that are better fun. It requires caution, though, or there may be an ugly accident."

"What, from an attack of the animals?" suggested George. "I should have thought they were too large and unwieldy for there to be any danger from them."

"Ah, but there is. The banks of the river are for the most part covered very thickly with reeds or rushes, among which these creatures are accustomed to lie. When they think that an enemy is at hand, they will rush out suddenly from their covert, and their weight is so great that a blow from them would probably be fatal. Matamo here had a narrow escape from one of them once, which I daresay he will relate to you, if you like to hear it. He speaks very good English, better than you would expect; and there is nothing that he likes better than relating his adventures, which sometimes border on the marvellous. Shall I call him?"

"By all means," said George. "He is there, riding on your father's left hand."

The Bechuana was accordingly summoned, and he at once expressed his readiness to gratify George's curiosity.

"A scrimmage with a sea-cow?" he said. "Oh yes, I remember it. It was when I was a boy. I went out fishing, and I had no gun, only an assegay with me. I caught lots of fish, but by and by I was tired, and went to sleep on the long grass. Presently I was woke up by a great noise close to me, and I saw a big sea-cow coming out of the river with his mouth wide open. I thought perhaps he was going to eat the fish, or perhaps he was going to eat me. I jumped up and ran off, and the sea-cow ran after me. I was in such a fright that I didn't see where I was running to, until I found I had got into a swamp, and was sinking in it. These swamps are sometimes ever so deep, and there is nothing to hold to, to keep you from going down. The more you struggle, the faster you go down. I was already up to my ankles, and should soon have been up to my knees, when I heard the sea-cow flounder in after me. *He* couldn't stop himself either. He was heavier than I was, and went down faster. I caught him by his great big ear and scrambled on to his back. He grunted, but he couldn't help it. Then I stood on his head, gave a great jump, and just reached the bank. He grunted louder than before, and went down into the swamp. Ho, ho, ho!—I dessay he is still going down, and hasn't got to the bottom yet."

"But I suppose," said George, after bestowing due praise on Matamo's story, "there is no real danger if care is taken."

"No, sir, no danger if you take care. There are some fine sea-cows there. Your father sees them too, Mr Ernest."

Mr Baylen now rode up and asked George whether he and his friend would like to take part in a hippopotamus hunt. George expressed his obligations, and presently the necessary preparations were made. All the party dismounted, leaving their horses in charge of the waggon-drivers, and took their rifles, which they carefully loaded. Then they separated into two companies. One of these mounted to the top of a rocky ledge covered with creepers, among which they carefully concealed themselves; while the other, consisting of Ernest, George, and one or two followers, crept stealthily through the long weeds and grass, until they had reached a point beyond that at which the animals were lying. Some of these were basking in the sun, some standing in the water with their heads above it; others were half concealed by the long rushes, which grew thickly on the bank.

"She will be our best mark," whispered Ernest, as he pointed to a huge female, whose carcase was half in, half out, of the river. "It will be very difficult, as she is lying now, to kill her on the spot. But as soon as she feels the shot, she will probably rush away into the reeds or into the water. In either case my father and Matamo, not to speak of the others, will get a good aim at her as she rises up, and will be pretty safe to kill her. Any way, you will get your shot at her, and mind you aim at her ear or her eyes."

George promised acquiescence, and he and Ernest gradually crept nearer, until they were within tolerably easy distance. Then George fired, but apparently did not greatly injure the beast. The whole herd sprang up with loud snortings, and those lying on the edge of the stream plunged into it. The female whom George had wounded rushed away under cover of the rocky ledge, which at that part bordered the stream, encountering, as Ernest had anticipated, the fire of the party stationed above, and the farmer's ball finished the business. The animal fell dead almost immediately at the foot of the rock, and Redgy and the others crowded to the edge to get a sight of the huge carcase. The farmer calmly reloaded, and it was well that he did so; for almost immediately afterwards there came a rushing noise from the bank above, and he caught sight of a huge male hippopotamus rushing down upon them. It was in all likelihood the mate of the female that had just been killed, and he was charging down to avenge its slaughter. With the instinctive readiness which long habit had produced, Baylen raised his rifle and fired. The bullet was happily aimed. It pierced the heart of the monster, and was instantly fatal. The muscular force carried it on for a few yards, and it fell dead only just short of the spot where the party was standing. Another moment or two, and its blind fury would have carried it and them over the edge of the precipice, on to the rocky ledge beneath.

"A near thing that!" exclaimed old Baylen coolly. "Lads, you should be always on the look-out for this kind of thing in hippopotamus-hunting. You are never safe from a charge."

This exciting adventure would naturally have been the topic of a good deal of discussion; but so much of the morning had now passed, that the farmer told them they had no time to bestow on talking. Prime pieces were cut off from both the slain beasts, and put into the cart, Matamo assuring George that they would be regarded by their friends at Colenso as rare delicacies. The whole party then returned to the waggons, and prepared to cross the river; which, in its present swollen condition, it would be no easy matter to accomplish. The quantity of sand brought down by the flood, it should be remarked, presented a more serious difficulty than the depth of the stream, and all the more so because the extremely turbid state of the water made it impossible to see what the depth of the sand was.

The farmer and his sons, aided by Matamo and the other servants, undertook the convoy of the larger waggon first, arguing that if that could be got across without difficulty, the smaller and slighter one in which Mrs Baylen and Clara were located would follow easily enough. Both spans of oxen were fastened to it, one in front of the other; it was hoped that the line of oxen would thus become so long that the foremost ox would reach the opposite bank before the hindmost yoke had entered it. But the river was so greatly swollen that this could not be accomplished. Matamo had to cross, with a long rope tied to the front bullock's horns, and thus guided the team, nearly all of which were swimming, to the bank. Then with great difficulty the oxen struggled up the opposite shore, and the big waggon was safely landed, though its contents had been completely wetted through.

Men and oxen now returned across the river to undertake the transport of the second waggon. But here a terrible misfortune took place. Just as they were approaching the water, the disselboom broke in half, and rendered the waggon quite unmanageable. Until this disaster was remedied, it became impossible for the oxen to draw; and, as they had not the means of mending the breakage on the spot, the waggon must necessarily remain there all night, until the damage could be repaired by workmen from Colenso. Mrs Baylen and her daughter had the option of either remaining on the bank of the river all night, or being conveyed across the river on horseback. They chose the latter; and the two young Englishmen, riding up, volunteered their services. They placed the ladies in their saddles and swam by their sides, drawing their horses after them. After this fashion Mrs Baylen and Clara reached the bank, though almost as completely soaked through as their cavaliers. A consultation was now held. It was proposed to procure a change of clothes for the ladies; but it appeared that all their wardrobe was in a smaller waggon; and even if they could have allowed the young men a second time to encounter the stream on their account, it would have been next to impossible to bring the clothes across in a dry condition. It was presently agreed that the best course would be for the four who had been soaked through to ride straight into Colenso, with Matamo as their guide, and there procure a change of clothes, while the large waggon followed at a slower pace. The riders accordingly set off, and arrived in due time at the Swedish pastor's house.

Mr Bilderjik and his wife, who were old friends of the Baylens, and were in expectation of their arrival, were in readiness to receive them. The ladies and the young men were soon supplied with dry clothes. Carpenters were despatched to the banks of the Mooi to repair the damage done to the waggon, and a message sent up to the hotel in the main street of Colenso to provide beds for Hardy, George, and Redgy, for whom the house of the Swedish pastor could not supply sufficient accommodation.

A few hours afterwards Farmer Baylen arrived with the larger waggon, and he and his sons, as well as Hardy, who was also an old acquaintance, were hospitably welcomed. In an hour or two after their arrival, the whole party sat down to a comfortable repast, at which, as Matamo had before assured George would be the case, the hippopotamus steaks formed the chief delicacy.

There was nevertheless, independently of these, a very appetising meal provided. Sago soup was served up, fish from the Little Tugela river, which ran close to the town; fowls, and pancakes, as well as abundance of ripe fruits,—loquots, oranges, peaches, bananas, and nectarines—all of them from the missionary's garden,—which could only be tasted in their perfection in the climates of which they are the natives.

All the party appeared to be contented with their quarters, except the indefatigable Matamo, who insisted on returning to the Mooi, where he said his presence would be needed to look after the workpeople who had been sent to execute the repairs, and who, as he affirmed, were never to be trusted. As soon as he had finished his dinner, he mounted his horse and rode off.

"You have a valuable servant in that Kaffir," remarked George. "It would not be easy to find his match, even in England."

"Are you speaking of Matamo?" said Mr Baylen. "Yes, he is a good servant—good at farm labour, and better at hunting; but he is not a Kaffir, nor a Hottentot either, but a Bechuana, though a very dark-skinned one. You haven't been long enough in the country to be aware of the difference, but we old residents see it easily enough."

"A Bechuana!" said George. "I think I know where their country is—on the other side of the Transvaal, isn't it, three or four hundred miles away from here? What brought him into these parts?"

"Well, I brought him," was the answer. "I brought him to Natal about five-and-thirty years ago."

"Five-and-thirty years!" remarked Margetts. "He couldn't have been very old then."

"No; he was an infant," said the farmer. "I was a young fellow of four or five-and-twenty myself, and we hadn't been so very long settled in Natal ourselves. My mother, who had been brought up a Presbyterian, though she conformed to her husband's form of belief, had once heard David Livingstone preach, and had been so impressed by him that she had never forgotten it. After my father's death she fell into low spirits, and there was no one near about us who could give her any comfort. Nothing would satisfy her but that Mr Livingstone must come and see her. We tried to pacify her by telling her that Mr Livingstone, who was a great traveller, would some day come our way. You have heard of him, I suppose, gentlemen?"

"All the world has heard of him," remarked Rivers. "I should think there is hardly an Englishman but knows his history."

"I am not surprised to hear it. But he was a young man at the time I speak of, and was but little known. My mother, however, was bent on seeing him. She had heard that he was living at Barolong, and she was sure that he would come to visit her, and she would die if he didn't. At last I saw there was no help for it; I must travel across the country, and find Mr Livingstone out."

"And you went?" inquired George, as he paused.

"Yes, I went; and a terrible journey I had; and after all I couldn't find the gentleman. He had gone up the country, and it was impossible to say, they told me, when he would come back. But that has nothing to do with Matamo; and my story was to be about him. Well, I took a good stout horse, and rode through what is now called the Orange Free State. It was almost wild in those days. Native tribes were living here and there, with whom I sometimes got a lodging; though, to be sure, their kraals were not the pleasantest places in the world, even to me. Once or twice I came across the house of a Dutchman, who had emigrated thither from the Cape."

"I don't expect you got much of a welcome from them," remarked Hardy.

"As an Englishman, I did not expect that I should," said the farmer. "But you see my grandfather, old Fieter Van Schuylen, had been a leading man among the Dutch, and so was my brother-in-law, Cornelius. I had only to mention their names, and they were ready to do anything for me. I got on well enough until I was within a day or two's ride of the village where Mr Livingstone was believed to be living; but there a misfortune befell me. My horse, which had carried me well up to that time,—indeed, was as quiet a beast as ever I remember to have ridden,—suddenly reared and plunged violently, and very nearly threw me. I got off and tried to quiet him; but he continued to struggle, and would not let me remount."

"He had been bitten, I expect," remarked Hardy.

"That is my opinion too; indeed, there was a swelling on his fore-leg, which looked very like the bite of a snake. But I was not sure even of that, and had no remedy at hand, even if I had known how to apply it. I soon saw that, whatever had been the cause of his illness, there was little or no hope of his recovery. His restlessness soon gave way to a kind of dull stupor. He presently lay down, stretched out his limbs, stark and rigid, and was dead in less than two hours from the time when he had been bitten.

"I was quite at a loss what to do. There were no trees near at hand into which I might have climbed and slept in safety. I did not know what wild animals there might be about. Remember this was five-and-thirty years ago, before the settlers had driven the lions and rhinoceroses away. The country consisted of long undulating downs, covered with tall grass, which might shelter any number of poisonous snakes; and a bite from any one of them could hardly help being fatal, seeing how far I was from any place where a remedy could be applied. So I resolved to keep on. The darkness was rapidly gathering, and the moon wouldn't rise, I knew, for several hours. But there was just enough of a glimmer in the sky to enable me to distinguish the track. So I went on, holding my double-barrelled rifle ready cocked."

"Dangerous work," remarked Margetts.

"No doubt; but it was the least danger of the two. Well, I went on, walking slowly and cautiously, and by and by I got clear of the jungle, and came into some high rocky land, in the midst of which there was a Bechuana village. If it had been daylight, I should have gone in at once and claimed their hospitality as an Englishman, whom I knew they would receive kindly. But by that light I was afraid of being mistaken for a Boer, and then my reception would have been very different. It was as likely as not that I should have been speared, before I could explain the mistake they had made. I resolved to find a shelter somewhere for the night, and make my appearance among the Bechuanas in the morning.

"After looking carefully about, I took up my quarters in a cavern in the side of a long ridge of rock which overhung the village. It was December, and the night was warm, so I did not hesitate to lie down as I was on a heap of dead leaves, with which the cave was half filled.

"I was tired out, and soon fell asleep, and, I suppose, must have lain for two or three hours, when I was awakened by the noise of guns firing and men shouting immediately over my head. I started up and looked out. The dawn had just broken, and diffused a light which made it almost as easy to distinguish anything as if it had been broad day. I perceived that the village was surrounded by an armed enemy, and on a high bank on the opposite side of the village I could see a line of men armed with the long gun which the Boers then carried, while at the two ends of the village strong parties—also of Boers, for they had no black allies with them—were stationed. These, too, were armed to the teeth. I knew in a moment what had happened. The Boers had attacked the village by night, and were shooting the men down as they rushed in alarm out of their huts. There was no possibility of resistance or escape. The rocky ridge over my head was too high to have been stormed, even by trained soldiers, and these poor naked half-armed savages could not approach within ten yards of it. The bank opposite was almost as impossible to attack; but I did see two or three of the Bechuana warriors make the attempt. Some spears were flung, but they did no execution. It was simple wholesale murder, and lasted, I should think, fully an hour; by which time every male Bechuana in the village was either dead or mortally wounded. It was the most shocking sight I have ever witnessed."

"Horrible indeed, sir?" exclaimed Redgy. "What provocation do you suppose they had given the Dutchmen?"

"Most likely none at all," was the answer. "The Bechuanas in general are peaceable enough, but the Dutch—the Boers, that is—are bent on having slaves to work for them; and if they can't get them by what they consider fair means, will get them by foul."

"What do they call fair means?" asked Redgy.

"Buying them of their parents," answered Baylen. "They will go to a village and demand the help of a number of women to work in their fields or gardens. These women, who dare not refuse, take their children with them, and then they will try to bargain for these, in order to make slaves of them. But the Bechuanas are a very affectionate people, and can very seldom be induced to sell their children. Therefore, as the Boers would tell you, they are obliged to take them by force."

"You are joking with us, sir, are you not?" said George.

"Indeed I am not. They think that not only is it fair and right that the natives should work without pay for them, but that it is their duty to oblige them so to work."

"On what possible grounds, Mr Baylen?"

"Because they are an inferior race, over whom the Boers have a natural right. This is no pretence. They really think so. The Boers are, after their fashion, a very religious people. They believe Almighty God has given the black races to be their servants, and that they are only carrying out His will when they reduce them to slavery. Some of them even believe that it is their mission to kill all except those who are thus kept in bondage. They liken themselves to the Israelites when they entered the Promised Land, and the natives to the Canaanites, whom they were to exterminate."

"And their quarrel with us really is that we won't allow them to carry out this idea?" asked Margetts.

"At the bottom I am not sure it is not," replied Baylen. "It is certain that they would carry it out, if it were not for the English. Their usual practice is to do what they did on the occasion I have been telling you about. They circulate a rumour that an attack is going to be made upon them by some tribe. The rumour is almost certain to be false, for the Bechuanas are a very peaceable people. But as soon as the report has taken wind, they march out in force, generally taking with them a number of native allies. These surround the village, keeping the men back with their assegays, while the Boers fire in safety over their heads, until all the males have been destroyed. They then carry off the women, children, and cattle."

"Horrible!" exclaimed Redgy. "I shall hate these Boers like poison. Why, they must be the most awful cowards, as well as hypocrites!"

"I don't know about that, Redgy," remarked George. "They don't want to encounter danger, if they can help it, no doubt. But it doesn't follow that they wouldn't fight, if there was the necessity for doing so. They are like Wilkin Flammock in The Betrothed; you remember what he says. He was 'ready to fight for life or property, if it was needed; but a sound skin was better than a slashed one, for all that.' But I thought you told us, sir, that the Boers in your story attacked the Bechuana village without allies."

"So I did," answered the farmer. "But they knew the ground, and were aware that it would be impossible for the Bechuanas to attack them, so that there was no need for the natives to accompany them on that occasion. But to go on with my story. I told you it was a bright morning, and so it continued for nearly an hour. But after that thick clouds came up, and it grew almost dark. The Boers remained in the position they had taken up till the forenoon.

But about half an hour after the firing had ceased, I heard a noise as if some one was moving somewhere near me. I looked out, and could just make out that a Bechuana woman, who had been mortally wounded by a bullet, had crawled to that spot, with an infant of a year old in her arms. I suppose she had some idea of concealing herself in the hollow of the rocks, not knowing that her hurt was to death. I crept down and took the child from her arms. She was just at the last gasp, but I think she gave it over to me willingly, fancying that I should treat it kindly. I took it back with me into the cave, and remained in concealment until the Boers had departed, which they did about the middle of the next day. I was fortunate enough to reach the farm of a friendly Hollander, who sold me another horse, and provisions enough to carry me through the most dangerous parts of the journey. The infant (which I called Matamo, from the name of the Bechuana village which I had seen destroyed) proved strong and healthy and we both reached Hakkluyt's Kloof safe and sound."

"And your mother?" asked Margetts.

"My mother was at first terribly disappointed about Mr Livingstone. But when she heard the tale of the destruction of the Bechuana village, and the rescue of the infant, she was so moved by pity for it, that I think she forgot everything else. She took it under her special charge. Up to the time of her death, three years afterwards, Matamo was her chief care and delight. The boy grew up strong and healthy, and has, as I told you, been an invaluable servant to us."

"And you have well deserved that he should," remarked Mr Bilderjik. "You have had him baptised and educated, and brought up in the Christian faith; you should add that. I would that many masters in South Africa could say the same."

Chapter Nine

A general assent followed Mr Bilderjik's remarks, to which, however, the farmer made no reply. A silence of some minutes ensued, which was broken by George.

"Mr Baylen," he said, "I was much interested in the history you gave us the other day of the colony, and King Chaka and his brother Dingaan. But all that you told us occurred forty years ago. I should like to know something of what has happened since."

"Well, the last thing I told you of, was the murder of Pieter Retieff and his followers," said Mr Baylen, "wasn't it? Well, the natural consequences ensued; there was war for some years between the whites and the blacks. The English settlers invaded Zululand, and carried off a quantity of women, children, and cattle. But they were attacked by ten thousand Zulus, and a hot fight followed. The English shot them down in such numbers, that they formed high banks over which their comrades had to climb. In spite of this, they advanced and overpowered their enemies by mere force of numbers!"

"Ah," interposed Hardy, "and it would be a good job if our English generals remembered that fact. They persist in despising their enemies, and may take a lesson from the Dutchmen, who are too wise to do so. But go on, Baylen; I beg pardon for interrupting."

"The Zulus," resumed the other, "drove the English beyond the Tugela, overran Natal, and for the second time turned it into a desert. The colonists took refuge in an island in the Bay. There they were personally safe, but their houses and goods were utterly destroyed, and their cattle driven off. We had contrived to take away with us everything of value that could be carried off to the island, and no great injury was done to the farmhouse and buildings. But all the cattle, horses, oxen, sheep, and goats were driven away. If we had not recovered them a few months afterwards, I should have had to begin life again."

"How did you manage to recover them, sir?" asked Margetts.

"Through my brother-in-law, Cornelius Schuylen. He had joined the main body of Dutch settlers from the Cape, and was a leading man among them, and a friend of the Dutch General, Praetorius. They found it necessary to go to war with Dingaan, and there was a pitched battle, in which the Dutch were the conquerors. I agree with Mr Rivers, that the Dutch are no cowards; but that they think that a whole skin is better than a slashed one, and they conduct their campaigns accordingly. I was present at the battle myself, having gone up to the Boer camp about my cattle. The natives outnumbered us, ten to one, I should think, and they fought as bravely as men could fight. But we gained a decisive victory, with very little loss."

"How did you manage it, sir?" inquired George. "I have heard that the Dutch have very little discipline in their armies."

"Very little, but their tactics are the thing. When they knew that a battle was imminent, they laagered their waggons together, and stationed their foot-soldiers in and behind them. The mounted men, of which their force principally consisted, waited at some distance until the Zulu assault on the waggons had begun. Then they opened a fire upon them with their rifles, which killed great numbers, and at last obliged them to turn off and attack them. They waited until the Zulus were almost but not quite within what was called assegay distance, and then fired volley after volley into them. When the Zulus advanced nearer, they galloped off to a little distance, and fired as before, repeating the manoeuvre until the blacks were obliged to retire, with immense loss of killed and wounded, while hardly a man on their own side was touched. It wasn't much better with the Zulus on their attack on the laager. They managed to fling a few assegays into, and under, the waggons; but the Boers fired upon them, under almost complete shelter, and shot them down by hundreds. Dingaan was obliged to make peace, and restore the cattle, mine among the rest."

"That must have been near about the end of Dingaan's reign," observed the Swedish clergyman.

"Yes, in less than two years afterwards the Dutch deposed Dingaan, and made his brother Panda king. Dingaan fled to the Amaswazis, and they put him to death. Panda had a long reign of more than thirty years, and during that period there was very little fighting with the European settlers. He was a different kind of character altogether from his two brothers, and loved ease and quiet. But I believe his disposition was almost as cruel as theirs."

"You are right, sir," said Mr Bilderjik. "He was as bloodthirsty as either of them, though he shed the blood of his own people only. He would inflict the most frightful penalties for the smallest offences. If one of his oxen was over-driven or hurt, he would order the cowherd to be impaled. Even for slighter offences than this, if the smallest thing occurred to annoy or cross him, he would sentence the offender to death, and his soldiers were always ready to execute his commands without hesitation. His barbarity drove his subjects away in such numbers, that Natal was almost peopled with them. He was a weak ruler, however, and for the last twenty years of his reign his son Cetewayo, who is now on the throne, was virtually king."

"Cetewayo!" observed George. "Ah, I want to know about him! We hear plenty in England. There is great alarm, is there not, that he will invade this country? I heard them talking of it at Maritzburg."

"There is great alarm, no doubt," said the farmer, "and it is no great wonder, seeing that Natal has twice been invaded and devastated by the Zulus. But I do not myself believe that he will ever cross the Tugela, unless he himself is first attacked, and drives his enemies before him. But I should like to know what you think about him, Hardy. Living so near to him as you once did, your opinion must be valuable."

"Yes, I lived in Zululand for several years after I left the army," said Hardy, "and I saw and heard enough of Cetewayo during that time, to form a decided opinion about him."

"And what was that opinion, Mr Hardy?" inquired George.

"If I remember right, the English agreed to place him on the throne, on condition that the lawless and indiscriminate shedding of human blood should be put a stop to, and that no one should be put to death, until after a trial and sentence. There are those that say that this compact was faithfully kept to."

"And it was," said Hardy, "so long as Cetewayo was insecure of his throne. At first this was the case, and he knew that the best hope of establishing his power lay in the support of the English. For the first few years of his reign, therefore, he did, as a rule, loyally carry out the promises he had given. But those who watched him most closely know that he never intended to be a tributary sovereign to any one. From the first he revived and developed his uncle Chaka's military policy. He reinstated the old regiments, and formed new ones, carefully choosing men to lead them who were qualified to carry out his designs. He rebuilt the military kraals, and obliged his soldiers to live unmarried, as his uncle had done."

"Ay," interposed George, "as Sultan Amurath did, when he instituted the Janissaries."

"I daresay you are right, sir," said Hardy, "though I never heard of him. Well, the only difference Cetewayo made in his dealings with his men was that he armed them with guns. In all other respects it was the reproduction of Chaka's army—the same enormous numbers, the same close and jealous discipline, the same absolute devotion to the king's will, without hesitation or question. If Cetewayo had ever intended to be faithful to his engagements with the English, of what use could this enormous and costly army have been to him? It is ridiculous to say it would be needed to put down the Tongas or the Swazies, or even to resist the aggressions of the Boers. There is but one use to which he could have intended to put it, and that is to drive the white man out of the land."

"Well, there are many, at all events, that think that," observed Mr Baylen. "You think, then, that he is going to declare war."

"I doubt his doing that," said Hardy. "But I think he will provoke the English to attack him—to invade Zululand, in fact."

"Why should he want them to do that?" asked Redgy.

"He will then fight greatly at an advantage," said Hardy. "In fact, he thinks that he sees his way to victory. I don't say I agree with him in that—indeed, I don't. But there is a good deal to be said on his side. Zululand is a difficult country for an army to traverse. He knows every inch of it, and they do not. The climate is often very unhealthy to white men. Disease would probably break out among them, if he could keep them any time there, whereas his own men are thoroughly inured to it. His numbers, again, are vastly in excess of theirs, and if he could attack them when off their guard, he might inflict frightful loss upon them. All these chances are in his favour, and he knows them well."

"In fact, he is trying to pick a quarrel," said Redgy.

"And he may succeed," added Hardy. "Indeed—" He checked himself and went on, "Then as to his natural disposition—you asked me what I thought about that too. I think he is just like his ancestors, quite as merciless and bloodthirsty, and even more crafty. It was said that during the first few years of his reign he *never* put any one to death unless he had really been guilty of some great offence, and that there was always a regular trial and conviction. How much truth there is in that, you may judge from what I am now going to tell you.

"When I first settled in Zululand, there was a Wesleyan missionary living near me, whose name was Garnett. He was a very good man, and the people about there respected him much. He had made several converts, amongst others an Induna named Usumanzi, a man of means and some local importance. Now it is certain that Cetewayo did not like the missionaries—one can very well understand why. The entire submission to his pleasure, right or wrong, which was the first thing he insisted upon, was a thing which no Christian could fall in with. Is it not so, Mr Bilderjik?"

"Of course he could not," assented the clergyman. "A Christian's first law is obedience to God's commandments, not man's. If the two came into collision, the obedience to human authority must give way."

"Exactly so, sir," pursued Hardy. "Well, then, there is no difficulty in understanding Cetewayo's aversion to the missionaries. But at the same time he knew that the missionaries were strongly upheld by the English, and that any persecution of them on religious grounds would be sternly resented. Cetewayo therefore sent a message to Mr Garnett, desiring him to pay a visit to the royal kraal. He wanted, he said, to talk to him about the good things which he taught the people. Mr Garnett was only half deceived. The king really might have been moved by some desire to know the truth. But it was far more likely that he was only pretending such a feeling, in order to get him entirely into his own power. Usumanzi earnestly advised him not to go. He said he knew that the king had been greatly provoked by his conversion, regarding him, as he did, as a valuable servant lost to him. Cetewayo would either banish him from the country, or, what was more likely, accuse him of some imaginary crime, and put him to death for it.

"But Mr Garnett resolved to go. He said there was a hope of doing a great work for his Master, and he was not to be deterred by the danger to himself. I offered to accompany him, as I thought my presence might be some protection. You see, though I was living in Zululand, I was employed by the Natal Government to collect taxes from the native chiefs every year. As an agent of the British Government, I knew Cetewayo would treat me with consideration, and possibly Mr Garnett on my account."

"Well, you were right, I expect," observed Baylen.

"I was to some extent," assented Hardy. "As soon as I made it understood that I was an officer in the employ of the Governor of Natal, there was a difference in the demeanour of the councillors towards me, and Mr Garnett too. A civil reception was given us, and a good hut assigned for our accommodation. Then there followed a long delay, and at last I was told I was to be sent with letters to Sir Henry Bulwer; and the next day I set out, attended by two of Cetewayo's soldiers. I suspected at the time—and subsequent events confirmed my opinion—that the king wanted to get rid of me, because I stood in the way of his carrying out his designs against Mr Garnett. I was no sooner gone than he was informed there was an accusation made against him of practising witchcraft. The king would inquire into the matter himself. This I learned from the Zulu who was sent with me. But what ensued I could never learn with any certainty. Mr Garnett, I believe, underwent a kind of mock trial, being charged with bewitching several persons. He was found guilty, and was sentenced to be banished from the country. Cetewayo had possibly thought that it would be dangerous to put him publicly to death. But it came eventually to the same thing. Mr Garnett set out, in company with two Zulus, who were directed to convey him to Delagoa Bay, whither his wife and children had already been sent. But he never reached his destination. His guides came back with the story that he had been killed by a lion. The general belief was that he had been murdered, and his body left to be devoured by the hyenas.

"But that was not the worst," resumed Hardy after a pause. "There was something like a trial in his instance, and, besides, he might really have been killed by a wild beast, though the circumstances were full of suspicion. The usage of Usumanzi was a much grosser outrage. No charge was made against him, nor did he receive so much as a hint that the king was displeased with him. But the Isamisi, or prophets, whom, to do them justice, both Chaka and Dingaan had discouraged, had gained considerable influence with Cetewayo, and they resented Usumanzi's conversion, and more particularly when they found that he still adhered to his new creed after Mr Garnett's disappearance."

"I wonder he didn't leave the country," remarked Ernest Baylen.

"He was advised to do so," said Hardy, "but he was a brave man, and said he had done no wrong, and that he put his trust in the God he had newly learned. Nothing was heard about him for some time. But one morning, quite early, I was roused by a number of Zulus living in an adjoining kraal, who told me that the king had sent an Impi to eat up Usumanzi. His house had already been surrounded, and himself, and every one belonging to him, even to the infants in arms, assegayed. The cattle were being driven off at that moment. In an hour or two Usumanzi's kraal had been entirely destroyed by fire, and the ashes scattered in all directions. In a short time not a trace was left of his habitation."

"And was no complaint made of such an outrage?" asked Margetts.

"Who was there to make it?" inquired Hardy. "Usumanzi's relatives, if there were any of them left, were too thankful to have escaped notice, and were little likely to do anything that might cause them to share his fate. Perhaps you think that I might have made some representations to the Governor of Natal; but I had already incurred suspicion, and received a hint to keep quiet. The Government were unwilling at that time to come to a rupture with Cetewayo. I knew, too, that I should be required to produce witnesses; and not one of the Zulus, who knew the facts, could have been induced, by love or money, to say a word on the subject. Most probably they would have said, if they had been brought into a court of justice, that Usumanzi's kraal had caught fire accidentally. No. He knew in this instance that he was safe, and you may be assured that, let him profess what he will, there is no possibility of inducing Cetewayo to respect the rights of his own subjects, or those of other nations, except by putting him down by force of arms. And as for that—" He appeared to be about to add something more, but checked himself, and addressed his host. "It must be time for us to go to bed, Mr Bilderjik," he said. "We have a long day's work before us to-morrow, and must start early. I suppose you mean to set off for Helpmakaar the first thing in the morning?"

"Helpmakaar?" repeated the farmer. "No, I shall not set out for that in the morning, if I do it at all to-morrow. You have forgotten that we have left one of our waggons in a damaged condition on the other side of the Mooi."

"To be sure, so I had. How stupid of me! But if we are not going to be fellow-travellers to-morrow, I should like to have a little talk with you, Baylen, before we turn in for the night. Will you walk with me to the hotel in the village; I can say what I want while we are on the way there."

Mr Baylen assented. They said good-night to their host, and stepped out into the porch, and thence passed through the little garden into the wide street of the picturesque little town, with its white houses—each shaded by its green verandah—and its double row of fruit trees already beginning to spread a pleasant shade. At that hour it was quite deserted, and Hardy presently began,—

"I thought it better not to tell you my reason for riding over from Umvalosa to meet you. I did not want to alarm the ladies."

"What has happened?" asked Baylen anxiously.

"No injury has been done to your property or your servants," said Hardy. "But beyond Umvalosa, from a little distance outside the town, as far as Utrecht, or nearly as far, there is nothing but ruin and destruction."

"The storm two days ago, do you mean?" suggested Baylen.

"No; this storm has been of man's making," said Hardy. "Umbelin,— you know him?"

"Every one knows him too well," was the answer. "If he fell into my hands, I should be disposed to make short work with him."

"He wouldn't come off much better in mine," said Hardy, "if I caught him 'redhanded,' as the saying is. He pretends to act independently of Cetewayo; but nobody doubts he is really under his orders. Well, he has made a raid on the district we have been speaking about, with a large force of Zulus. They have burnt to the ground every house in it; driven off the

Perils in the Transvaal and Zululand | 95

whole of the cattle, and murdered every man, woman, and child that came in their way."

"The district between Utrecht and Umvalosa?" said Baylen. "What can have made Umbelini, or rather Cetewayo, choose that? Why, that is the very district which was in dispute, and which the English have awarded to him! That is strange!"

"Well, the English have awarded it to him, no doubt," assented Hardy. "But they didn't give it to him out and out, as he expected perhaps. The rights of the settlers living in it were to be respected. Probably Cetewayo wishes to show his contempt for their decision. At all events, there is no doubt that he is showing studied disregard of Sir Henry Bulwer's demands. There is this business of the violation of the English territory, and the murder of the two women by Sirayo. His answers about that amount really to an insult. It is what I have long supposed, that, although he will not himself attack the English, he wants to provoke them to attack him."

"I suppose it must be so; and the English will be driven to declare war. But about this raid by Umbelini. How far has it spread? Is it likely to spread further? Will it reach Umvalosa?"

"It has not got there yet, and I don't think it will. The place is incapable of resisting an attack; but I think Umbelini has already got as much spoil as he can carry away. Besides, the English forces are advancing to Rorke's Drift, and he will avoid any collision with them."

"If Umvalosa is not attacked, we might rest as usual on our way there. It is one day's journey, you know, from Horner's Kraal."

"Rest? What, at Rogers' station, Dykeman's Hollow?"

"Yes; we always rest there. I know Mr Rogers is away in England. But we should be made welcome all the same."

"Not a doubt of it. But you would find his station deserted. When they heard of Umbelini's approach, his head men packed his waggons with his household goods and valuables, and drove away his cattle."

"And where have his waggons and cattle been driven to?" inquired Mr Baylen. "To my station—to Horner's Kraal?"

"No; Rogers' men thought of going there; but the cattle and the contents of the waggons would be a tempting plunder. Umbelini, who is notorious for his rapacity, might have sent some of his men in pursuit. No; they have gone off to Rorke's Drift, to be under the protection of the British force assembling there. And that is where Mrs Baylen and all your party and waggons must go, if you take my advice—as soon, that is, as you have recovered the one which has been left on the bank of the Mooi."

"The troops assembling at Rorke's Drift! Ah, so you said just now. Then what we heard at Durban must be true; and an ultimatum has been sent to Cetewayo."

"So I am told; and that thirty days have been allowed him in which to send an answer. If he does not do so, Zululand is to be invaded at three different points. One column, under Colonel Pearson, is to cross the Lower Tugela, and move on by Ekowe. A second, under Colonel Evelyn Wood, is to enter by crossing the Blood river, near Kambula. The third, commanded by Lord Chelmsford himself, will set out from Rorke's Drift, and penetrate to the interior by Isandhlwana Hill. If Cetewayo falls back, as they expect, before them, the columns will meet at Ulundi. There he must fight them or surrender. That is what I am told; but of course it is only rumour."

"Well, Cetewayo certainly intends to fight us, and I hope the plan of operations may be successful. But it does not concern me, and I am anxious to be out of it. Can't we go on, resting at any place where we can find shelter,—at Umvalosa or elsewhere,—and get to Horner's Kraal? There we shall be well out of it all."

"I really don't think you can, Baylen. I don't think you'd be troubled by Umbelini and his Zulus. As soon as Wood and his men move to their station on the Blood river, he is sure to take himself off, and will not return while Wood and his troops remain in that neighbourhood. But the country is full of lawless characters of all kinds,—escaped convicts, bush robbers, and adventurers who have lost everything at the diamond fields. There is no legal authority to keep them in control—no sufficient authority, at all events, and they would murder any one for the value of a tobacco pipe. It would not be safe for the ladies of your party, at all events, to attempt the journey, unless with a military escort, until order has been restored."

"And I suppose there is a general flight to Rorke's Drift?"

"There were a great many on their way there yesterday. I passed young Vander Heyden and his sister, accompanied by Frank Moritz, as I rode out."

"Vander Heyden and Moritz! Why, they were in Durban a week or so ago!"

"Yes; but they travelled faster than you. They reached Vander Heyden's house—Bushman's Drift, as it is called—just in time to see it all in a blaze, and the Zulus plundering and killing every one they encountered. Henryk and the others had just time to escape. If they had got there a few hours earlier, they would have been shot or assegayed too."

"And they have gone now to Rorke's Drift?"

"Yes; I exchanged a few words with Moritz. He was hot enough about what he had witnessed. But he was calmness itself to Vander Heyden. *He* did not say a word; but he looked like a man who meant to do something terrible, when the time came. I fancy some one, of whom he was very fond, must have been killed. But I did not like to ask. I gathered, however, that he was not going to Rorke's Drift for protection, but for revenge on those miscreants. Bitterly and notoriously as he dislikes the English, he means to join their army as a mounted volunteer. The Lord have mercy on the Zulus that come in his way, for he will have none. He is an experienced soldier, and will be a valuable recruit."

"Well," said Baylen, "I don't know that I can greatly blame him. I shall not be at all surprised if a great many should be found to follow his example. It is certainly high time that a stop should be put to these atrocities. Well, Hardy, I shall follow your advice. I shall send off the waggon with Mrs Baylen and Clara, with Matamo to take care of them, to-morrow morning, and I shall follow with the other as soon as we have got it out of the Mooi. I suppose the road to Rorke's Drift is open and safe, is it not?"

"Well, for it to be that, Umbelini and his Zulus must have withdrawn. I expect to hear with certainty about that to-morrow morning, and will come down and tell you about it before I start. Mrs Baylen must not set off until the road is safe."

"Many thanks. By-the-bye, I forgot to ask whether you have suffered much loss yourself from this Impi?"

"Not very much, thank you. I had fortunately sold off my stock a short time ago, and I had the money with me. My servants also got notice in time, and made their escape, with most of the articles of any real value. The house has been burnt and wrecked; but I daresay I shall get compensation when the war is over. Meanwhile, I mean to follow Vander Heyden's example, and take service with the mounted volunteers."

Chapter Ten

Baylen returned to the pastor's house too late to impart any of the information he had received to the rest of the family; and, besides, he judged it better that they should all get a sound night's rest, undisturbed by perplexities and alarms. He was up, however, by daybreak, and soon afterwards Hardy arrived with the information that Umbelini and his warriors had all returned to their mountains without having approached Umvalosa. No doubt this was due to the fact that some of Colonel Evelyn Wood's men were on their way to the Blood river. But the condition of the Transvaal, between Umvalosa and Horner's Kraal, was even worse than he had described it. If Mr Baylen could obtain an escort of soldiers for the first ten miles or so, it might be safe for him to go, but not otherwise.

"Very well," said Mr Baylen. "I shan't be able to get that—not for some time, at all events. And I am more likely to get it at Rorke's Drift than anywhere else. So the plan I agreed on with you last night shall hold good. I shall send Matamo to get the waggon ready as soon as possible. When I have seen that off, the boys and I will go down to the Mooi. Mr Rivers, what will you and Mr Margetts like to do? It will be of no use your going to Mr Rogers' station, after what Hardy has told us, and I don't think it will be any better if you went to Spielman's Vley. It is very improbable that you would find the Mansens there."

"True, sir," said George; "so I was thinking myself. But I should learn there what had become of them, and I am most anxious to join my mother as quickly as possible."

"Spielman's Vley?" interposed Hardy. "What, Ludwig Mansen's old station, do you mean, near Landman's Drift, where I live?"

"Yes," answered George. "Mrs Mansen is my mother."

"Really! ah, and Mrs Mansen's daughter is named Rivers, and you are like her. I have been puzzling my head for a long time who of my acquaintances it was whom you were so like. I know Mrs Mansen and her second husband very well. But I thought that her only son had been lost at sea."

"So she believes," said George. "I was wrecked, and nearly all hands were lost."

"She will be very happy when she learns the truth. But it will be no use for you to go to Spielman's Vley to find her. Six months ago, almost immediately after Mr Rogers' departure, there came news that Mrs Mansen's uncle, who lived near Zeerust, had died, and bequeathed all his property to her. It is a valuable and productive farm, I am told, and I fancy Mansen did not like the look of things in these parts, and resolved to move to Zeerust. He sold Spielman's Vley, and moved off as soon as he could to his new place. He has been gone a good many weeks. He has probably before this settled down at Umtongo, as Christopher Wylie's farm was called."

"And where is Zeerust?" asked George, a good deal disturbed at these tidings. "Zeerust! wasn't that the place you were saying something about last night, Mr Baylen?"

"Yes," answered the person addressed. "I believe I mentioned Zeerust, in the story I told you about Matamo. It is a long way there—three or four hundred miles, I should think. And it was, in the days when I was speaking about, a very dangerous journey. But I have no doubt it is much easier now. You mustn't be cast down, my lad," he continued kindly, observing how much George appeared to be distressed. "You are a stout young fellow, with a head on your shoulders, and a brave heart to boot. You will get there, I have no doubt, quite safe. Don't you think so, Hardy?"

"I have no doubt of it," answered the person addressed. "The only thing is that I don't think Mr Rivers can attempt the journey just now."

"Why not?" asked George. "I heard what you said about Mrs and Miss Baylen, and I quite agreed in it, but there will be no ladies in our party, and I can make my hand guard my head. At least, I have never failed to do so yet."

"I don't doubt it, Mr Rivers," said Hardy. "But the danger to you would not be only from ruffians and robbers; there would be risk from wild animals to any one not acquainted with the country. There are not many lions or rhinoceroses or elephants in those parts, no doubt; you seldom or never meet with them about there in these days. But there are plenty of leopards and buffaloes, and, what is more dangerous, deadly serpents— puff-adders, ondaras, cobras, and the like. And you may catch marsh fever any day, if you sleep in the swamp neighbourhood. You would require one skilful guide at least, and it would be better if you had two or three. Now these are not to be had at present. You must wait till this war is over, which we may hope will not be a long one. Then perhaps Mr Baylen here will lend you Matamo and Utango. They would take you across safely enough."

"I think that might be managed," assented Farmer Baylen. "Hardy's advice is good. You will do wisely to wait till this war is ended."

"I have no doubt of his kindness, or of yours either, sir," said George; "but I own that this delay, coming after so many months of expectation, does vex me. How long do you think it will be before the war is over, Mr Hardy?"

"That is hard to say," answered Hardy. "It depends on how our troops are handled, and how quickly they may be able to force on a battle."

"You have no doubt as to what will be the issue of the battle, when it does take place?" suggested Redgy.

"Well, no. Against disciplined English troops, unless there were great incapacity or great cowardice, the blind courage of these Zulus would avail little. But there can hardly be incapacity, for Colonels Wood and Pearson are undoubtedly able officers, and Lord Chelmsford has the name of being a good general—though that has not been so clearly proved. And such a thing as cowardice in English soldiers is unheard of. I am not so sure, however, about the Natal contingent. There is such a terror of Cetewayo among the natives, that, but for the presence and example of English troops, I do not feel certain that they could be got to face the Zulus. However, the chances are that a few weeks will see the Zulu king defeated and put down."

"Well, I don't think I can do better than take your advice," said George. "I suppose Redgy and I had better go with your party to Rorke's Drift, if you will allow us. Perhaps I may be of some use there."

"Perhaps you may indeed," suggested Hardy. "Why, you and Mr Margetts had better join the mounted volunteers, as I mean to do. They would be delighted to have you, and in a few weeks' time—before the fighting begins at all events—you will have had nearly all the drilling that would be required."

"That is not a bad idea," returned George. "I wonder I did not think of it before. What do you say to it, Redgy?"

"Why, that it has been running in my head all the morning," said Margetts. "You see you and I have been taught to ride pretty well. They won't require of you to have a seat like a life-guardsman in Piccadilly, with the tips of your toes in the stirrup, out here. And we know how to shoot too, and are pretty good hands at single-stick, and will soon learn the use of our swords. We should soon be qualified for the rough and ready work out here. I should like to see these Zulu fellows bowled over, I must say."

"Very good! then that's settled," said George. "We'll ride over with the waggon to Rorke's Drift this morning, and offer ourselves as volunteers; and I think we had better go and saddle our horses at once, as I see they are inspanning the oxen already. We have only to take our leave of Mr and Mrs Bilderjik, and thank them for their hospitality."

"You need not take leave of me yet, Mr Rivers," said the Swedish pastor. "I am going, with Mr Baylen's leave, to make one of the party to the Drift, and Mrs Bilderjik will accompany me."

"I hope you don't imagine there is any danger here from the Zulus," remarked Hardy. "As I have told my friend Baylen, the Zulu Impi has been already withdrawn, nor is there the least chance of its return."

"I do not imagine there is," said Mr Bilderjik. "Nor has Umbelini anything to do with my movements. But I think my brother pastor at Rorke's Drift and his wife will have more on their hands for some time to come than they can manage, and that they will be glad of our help. I can be better spared here, where my schoolmaster will do all that is required in ordinary, and I shall ride over occasionally myself. I am going to fetch my horse, and will ride with you. You may be glad of my presence as a guide, and also, it is possible, to answer questions that may be asked. There are a great many suspicious characters about, and the officers in command require explanations before they allow any one to pass."

"I forgot that," said George, "and so, I suppose, did Mr Baylen."

"No, I imagine he reckoned on your riding by the side of the waggons, in which case you would of course have passed as belonging to his party. But you would find it very dull work, keeping by the side of the waggon the whole way."

In another half-hour they had all set out—Baylen and his sons to the Mooi, and Hardy to Umvalosa. The large waggon jolted off with the ladies seated in it. The missionary and the two young Englishmen cantered off in advance, Haxo, the Hottentot groom and stableman, following on a Kaffir pony.

"Have you been long settled in this country, Mr Bilderjik?" asked George, as they drew rein after a sharp ride of half an hour.

"Do you mean in South Africa, or in Natal?"

"I mean in Africa generally. How long is it since you left Europe?"

"A great many years—five-and-thirty or so. It is certainly nearly that time since I landed at Cape Town, and was sent up to Namaqualand."

"Ah, you have been there, among the Hottentots?"

"I was about five years there."

"Were you settled in one place, or did you travel about?"

"My residence was always in the same place, but I and my wife made continual excursions into different parts of the country."

"Did you find the people willing to receive you?"

"That is a question which it is not easy to answer," said the Swedish minister. "They showed no dislike to us; indeed, they were willing enough to listen, but, I fear, to very little purpose. For the first two or three years, I continually fancied that I was making some progress, getting some hold upon them. But I am afraid it was nearly all fancy."

"What stood in your way?"

"In the first place, the profound ignorance of the people, and their low intellectual capacity. They could understand all that was necessary for supplying their wants, averting dangers, relieving pain, and the like. If Christianity consisted in the proper discharge of duties like these, one might have made good Christians of them without any great difficulty. They might have been taught to be diligent, and kind, and truthful, and forgiving—though those last two qualities were not so easy to teach. But when any one tried to impress upon them the notion of an Unseen Power watching over them, to whom they owed obedience, one entered upon an almost impossible task. They couldn't understand that any being could exist whom they could not see, much less that he could have power or authority over them. Where was any evidence of so extraordinary a thing, beyond my bare word? It was useless, again, to tell them that their relatives, who had been taken away from earth, were not dead, but living elsewhere. They had seen them die, they said, and knew that they turned to dust, and there was no more left of them than there was of the wood they had burned for their fire yesterday. They were on the whole a kindly race, and had received such hard usage from the Dutch that they appreciated in proportion the kindness shown to them. But it was impossible to lift their minds—so at least it seemed—from the degradation to which they had sunk."

"Had you not a better chance with the children, sir?" asked Margetts.

"That is every missionary's hope," answered Bilderjik. "Yes, we succeeded in teaching some of the children to read and write, though, to be sure, not very efficiently; and they could take in some very simple teaching on plain subjects, as, for instance, natural history, or geography. I suppose this might have been further developed, until, in process of time, the intellect was fully awakened. But it would be a long and difficult task, extending probably over more than one man's entire life."

"But to have accomplished any part of such a work would be worth the labour of a life," said George.

The missionary looked pleased. "You are right, Mr Rivers," he said. "That is the true way in which to view it. A man's work is often to be estimated—not by what he himself does, but by what he enables others after him to do. 'One soweth and another reapeth,' is truer, I think, of the work of the gospel than of anything else. Have you any idea of giving yourself to it?"

"I have come out to South Africa mainly with that intention," said George. "It has struck me, since we left Colenso, that entering the Volunteers, as I declared my intention of doing, may not be quite consistent with it. What do you think?"

The clergyman smiled. "A minister of the gospel is a man of peace," he said. "But war is sometimes absolutely necessary to the preservation of peace. And that, I am inclined to believe, is the case in the present instance. If you were actually an ordained minister, I think you ought not to take part in any violent proceedings, unless for the purpose of preventing some actual deed of violence. But you are at present a layman, and the cause is one which every right-minded man ought to uphold. Situated as you are, I don't see why you should not enlist. Did I not hear you say that you were going to Umvalosa?"

"Yes, to Dykeman's Hollow—Mr Rogers' place."

"Oh ay, I know him," said Mr Bilderjik. "He is a good and worthy man, and so is his chaplain, Mr Lambert. He often visits me. We agree that there is very little difference between our churches, in respect either of doctrine or discipline—very little even at home, none at all, it may be said, out here. Are you to be one of Mr Rogers' schoolmasters?"

"Yes," said George; "one of his schoolmasters for some time, and afterwards one of his chaplains."

"You will be doing a good work. He has several at Umvalosa, and at Pieter's Kop, and Spielman's Vley, and Landman's Drift, and several other places. Mr Rogers is one of those who make a good use of the means entrusted to them. I wish we had many like him."

"I wish so too," said George. "But we have got away from what we were talking of, the Hottentots. I had heard that they are as a rule untruthful and sensual, but also that they are kind-hearted and affectionate. What is your experience on this point, I should like to know?"

"In all countries, so far as my experience extends," answered Mr Bilderjik, — "in all countries of the world, I believe, parents are affectionate to their children, unless where some strong motive influences them to be otherwise. It is little more, in fact, than a natural instinct that prompts their affection. But where there is this strong motive, the parental instinct is soon disregarded. In countries, for instance, where boys are a source of profit, and girls a burden and a cost, as in China, female child-murder becomes a common practice. In lands, again, where food is with difficulty obtained, and every additional mouth deprives others of their full supply of sustenance, infants are killed without scruple. The Hottentots are no exception to this. This is the case even where the natural affection of parents might have influenced them to make sacrifices for their own children. Where the children of others are concerned, there is the most absolute indifference to suffering. That Hottentot groom of mine, Haxo, is an evidence in his own person of it."

"Your Hottentot groom yonder? What of him?"

"I have had him ever since he was a baby," said the Swede. "This is the way in which I came by him. While we were on our way to the upper part of Namaqualand, and were a mile or two from the Hottentot village where we meant to pass the Sunday, we fell in with a tribe of Hottentots, who were emigrating to a different part of the country. We sat down to rest at the spring at which the Hottentots had been drinking. We soon got very friendly with them, making them presents of a few toys which we had brought with us, to their great delight. They listened very attentively to all I had to say to them, and we parted with them having formed a very favourable impression of them. There was one family in particular that took our fancy. It consisted of a fine handsome man, a rather delicate wife with an infant, not yet weaned, and two lads almost grown up. They went off in the cool of the evening, taking the same path which we meant to take on the Monday. We passed the Sunday as we intended, and the next day set out. After a journey of an hour or two we came upon a woman who lay under the shadow of a rock with an infant in her arms, evidently dying of exhaustion and hunger. We gave her some nourishment, but it was plain that she was too far gone to be restored. She appeared to know us, and with some difficulty we recognised her as the young mother we had so greatly admired. It appeared that after the party had proceeded some distance, it was reported to them that there was a lion in an adjoining donga, which would probably attack them if it was not destroyed. All the men had gone in pursuit of it and killed it. But before this could be done, the woman's husband had been struck by a blow from the lion's paw, and died in a few minutes. There was a debate held as to what was to be done with the family. The two boys were strong and active, and would soon become useful as hunters. It was worth while keeping them, but they could not, or would not, support their mother. No one was willing to take her as a wife, she being notoriously weak and sickly. She tried hard, she told us, to induce one of the women to take her child, and save its life. Her own, she knew, would soon come to an end. But the baby was to all appearance as sickly as herself. After an hour's talk, the whole party went on, leaving her and her infant to die in the wilderness. I should much doubt whether her boys ever gave her another thought."

"Shocking!" said Margetts. "I suppose the poor thing died, did she not?"

"Yes, died in a few hours. We gave her what sustenance we had with us, and did what we could for her. But she was dying when we fell in with her, and I do not suppose that the most skilful physician in Europe could have restored her."

"And you took the baby and brought it up?" suggested George.

"Yes, that was the only thing that gave her any comfort. We promised that we would take charge of it, and see that it was cared for. She died quite contentedly, when she had seen it go to sleep in Mrs Bilderjik's arms, and we buried her in the same grave to which the remains of her husband had been committed on the previous day."

"How has the boy turned out?" asked Margetts.

"Very well," said the Swede. "He makes a good farm servant, and thoroughly understands the management of horses. But he is better at hunting than anything else. He has all the instincts of his race. I frequently send him out with his pony into the wild country, and he is pretty sure to come back before long with a springbok or two, or a hartebeest, or eland; what we don't eat we can dispose of to our neighbours. Mr Baylen spoke in high praise of his Bechuana Matamo. But I think Haxo is pretty nearly his match."

"Any way, he will be so by the time he reaches Matamo's age," said George. "He must be a good deal younger."

"Yes, Haxo is not much more than thirty. By-the-bye, you were speaking of making an expedition to Zeerust, when this miserable war is over. I did not hear clearly what was passing, but I thought I understood that."

"Yes," said George. "They tell me that my mother has removed there; and my first object in life is to find her."

"Ah, I thought so. Well, I daresay I can lend you the services of Haxo. In fact, it would be as much to my advantage as yours that he should accompany you. There is a message I must send to Kolobeng, and I had thought of sending Haxo with it. If he travelled across the Transvaal with your party, it would be an advantage both to him and to you."

"To us certainly," said Rivers. "And I thank you for the offer. But I have not yet done with my inquiries about the natives. You have told me about the Hottentots, but not about the Kaffirs and Zulus; I want to know more about them than any other of the natives. I am in no way surprised that you found it difficult to make any way with the Namaquas and Bosjesmans. They are by all accounts the very lowest types of humanity. But from what I have seen of the Kaffirs, the case must be quite different with them. They strike me as being a highly intelligent race—as intelligent, I should say, as the lower classes in any European country. The same obstacles that stand in the way of the conversion of the Hottentots cannot surely exist in their instance."

"You are right, Mr Rivers," returned Mr Bilderjik. "There are not the same obstacles. But, unfortunately, there are as bad, or, as some would say, worse obstacles. The Hottentots have, strictly speaking, no religious ideas at all. They are simply intelligent animals, and not too intelligent either. But the Kaffir has a religion, though one so wholly false as to render him in a great measure incapable of conceiving the true one. He believes in a God, and even, in a wild, confused way, in a Creator of the universe. But these are in his view only *men*. The dead, according to his ideas, become potent spirits, which must be propitiated, or they will do the living the most terrible injuries. There is no sense of love or of benefits conferred, but only the power of working evil. If the seasons are mild and genial, and the crops productive, that is the ordinary course of nature, and there is no need to be thankful for it. If there comes tempest, or blight, or wasting disease, it is because the spirits are angered at neglect shown, or insult offered them; and sacrifices, often of the most bloody and cruel kind, must be offered, or the vengeance of the angry gods will fall still more heavily on the people. In short, it is a religion of fear and hate, instead of being what it should be, a religion of love."

"Are they not thankful, sir, to any one who will deliver them from such a yoke of bondage?" asked George.

"One would certainly expect that they would be. But the gospel does not make the progress that might be looked for. It is in direct opposition to two of their ruling passions, their thirst for revenge and their sensuality. The preachers of the gospel especially forbid bloodshed and polygamy; and these are the two things their chiefs live for."

"Polygamy! Ay, I was going to ask you about that. I can understand that you would find yourself in a difficulty there. But I do not quite know what your practice is. If a Kaffir chief, who has a number of wives, is converted, would you oblige him to put them all away but one, as a condition on which you will admit him to baptism?"

"It is a point on which Christian ministers are not fully agreed. I see a difficulty myself. A man has solemnly promised to take and keep a woman for his wife, and she has been faithful to him. If he puts her away, she may not only be distressed for the loss of her husband, whom she loves, but may be placed in very painful and degrading circumstances, which she has in no way merited. It seems contrary to the genius of Christianity, which is replete with justice and mercy, that she should so suffer. The Scripture no doubt allows but of one wife, that being God's primary institution of marriage. It cannot, therefore, permit any to *contract* polygamy, but that hardly meets the case. Scripture also commends the man 'who swears unto his neighbour and disappoints him not.' It is a great difficulty."

"How do you yourself meet it, sir?"

"I do not lay down any hard and fast rule. I make a point of talking the matter over with the husband and with the wives, and try to induce them voluntarily to separate, in every case but that of the wife first married. But if I cannot succeed in this, I do not refuse baptism. We must remember that, though polygamy has always been a thing contrary to the divine intention, it was tolerated 'for the hardness of men's hearts,' until the truth in all its fulness was bestowed upon men."

"It is not the first time that the difficulty has occurred," said George. "The French Church, after the conversion of the northern barbarians, was long embarrassed by the same question."

"True; and the custom gradually died out, and was heard of no more, as Christian light grew stronger," said Mr Bilderjik. "We must hope that the same result will follow in Southern Africa. But here I think we are at last. If I do not mistake, that is the Buffalo river that we see glancing in the distance, and those small specks are the houses at Rorke's Drift."

"Yes, that must be the place," said George. "See the baggage-waggons, and the horses and men on either side the ford. But there is nothing even resembling a village, that I can see."

This opinion was confirmed as they drew nearer. There was a stone kraal, and a storehouse near it, and at a distance of a hundred feet or so another building, which, as they afterwards learned, was used as an hospital for thirty sick soldiers. Nearly a quarter of a mile off, in a hollow between two hills, stood the house in which Mr Bilderjik's brother minister resided.

Chapter Eleven

Mr Bilderjik rode up to his brother pastor's abode, by whom he and his young friends were very kindly received, and they were all invited to enter his parlour; where, considerably to George's surprise, he encountered his old companions on board the *Zulu Queen*, the two Vander Heydens, and Mynheer Moritz. Annchen came forward with a smile and a blush to welcome George and Redgy, and Moritz was extremely cordial in his greetings. Vander Heyden also, though somewhat stiffer in his demeanour, saluted them with courtesy, expressing his satisfaction at meeting them again. He explained what, however, the young men had already been informed of, his intention to join as a volunteer the force which was to be sent for the purpose of putting down Cetewayo's lawless rule. "It is not only," he said, "that I have the barbarous murder of a near relative to avenge, but I feel that there will be neither law nor justice in this land until his power is destroyed. I do not know what brings you here, Mr Rivers; but I should be glad to think that our aims and intentions are the same."

"That is so," said George cordially. "I am persuaded that, whatever may have been said of former wars which England may have waged with this country, the one she has now undertaken is the cause of justice and right. I am glad to think we shall be fellow-campaigners in it. I suppose there is no doubt that they will accept our services."

"None indeed," answered Vander Heyden. "You may assure yourself of that. There will be few recruits that they will welcome more readily."

Vander Heyden's words proved true. George and Redgy were admitted wihout any demur, as was also Hardy, who arrived two or three days afterwards. He was a more valuable recruit than any of the party, having served many years in various campaigns under Havelock, Napier, and Wolseley. His advice and help were most serviceable to George and Redgy, and a close intimacy soon sprang up between the three. Their example proved catching. About a fortnight after their arrival at Rorke's Drift, the three young Baylens and Matamo made their appearance, having persuaded their father, after many entreaties, to allow them to enter the same company as their friends, in the Mounted Volunteers. George was surprised to see them, for the Baylens had been gone more than a week. A message had been sent to the President of the Orange Free State, and it was thought necessary, in the disturbed state of the country, that the messenger should have a military escort. As they would pass very near Horner's Kraal, Farmer Baylen had obtained permission to accompany it. But it now appeared that, as soon as they reached home, the young men had made such urgent representations, as to wring from their father a reluctant consent. He had insisted, however, that Matamo should accompany them, upon whom he laid both his commands and entreaties to keep a careful watch on his sons.

The eight friends, for so they soon became, found the time pass pleasantly enough, while the preparations for the campaign were going on. There was the morning drill and parade, the mess-table, at which the six English and the two Dutchmen sat next each other, and there were sword-exercises, and practices with the rifle, which filled up the time, so as to allow of little leisure. In the evening they would commonly adjourn to a neighbouring seat under the trees, where they beguiled the time with narratives of past adventures, and speculations as to the approaching struggle. Hardy was a particularly pleasant companion. His anecdotes of the Indian Mutiny, the Abyssinian and Ashantee expeditions, had a great interest for young soldiers who had never yet encountered the enemy. He told them of the relief of Lucknow, and how he had stood by the terrible Well of Cawnpore; how he had accompanied Sir Garnet Wolseley in his march to Coomassie; and how he had witnessed the final discomfiture of King Theodore. He regarded the Sepoys, he told them, as more dangerous enemies, than either the Abyssinians or the Ashantees. But none of them could, for a moment, compare with the Zulus. It was not merely the brute courage of these last-named savages that rendered them so formidable, for almost all barbarous nations are indifferent to danger. It was their discipline, their devotion to their king's commands, and their contempt for Europeans, that made them so formidable. They could not be cowed or terrified. Nothing but downright hard blows would quell them; and they would endure an amazing amount of hard blows, before they would knock under.

"Were you ever in very great danger during the Ashantee campaign?" asked Redgy, at one of these evening séances.

"Not more than any one must encounter, who goes on a campaign, I believe," answered Hardy. "No; the greatest danger I was ever in, I think, was during the Abyssinian war, and the danger did not come from a man, but an elephant."

"Tell us about it, Hardy," said Walter Baylen. "I did not know King Theodore used elephants in his army."

"No, it was not in battle, it was during the march," was the rejoinder. "Ours was the advanced guard of the army, and we had entered Abyssinia, and were passing through a very wild country, partly covered with long grass, partly with dense forest, when suddenly an enormous elephant rushed out of the bush upon us. He was the biggest elephant I ever saw. I don't think he could have stood less than some inches over eleven feet."

"I thought they were found much larger than that," said Margetts.

"Ah, so people say," said Hardy. "They talk of their being fourteen, fifteen, and sixteen feet high, but that is all fancy. Matamo here, who has shot plenty of them, would tell you so. How high was the largest elephant you ever shot, Matamo?"

"The bull-elephants are mostly nine or ten feet," said the Bechuana. "Some stand eleven feet, but not many. I once saw one eleven and a half feet high, but never bigger."

"Just so," said Hardy. "Well, this chap, I should think, might have been eleven and a half. He was, I fancy, what they call a rogue elephant—an elephant, that is to say, who has been sent to Coventry, for some offence, by his companions. They are always extremely dangerous, and will sometimes attack a man without provocation; which elephants, as an ordinary rule, will not do. He had the most magnificent tusks I ever saw; I suppose our commanding officer, Captain Sparrow, noticed this, and thought they would sell for a lot of money in Magdala. He gave the order for all of us to fire upon him, and kill him. I was aware of the danger, and ventured to step up to him, and ask him to recall his order. I knew how difficult the elephant is to kill, except to experienced hunters. It was before the days of the Martini-Henrys, you will remember. I suppose the captain thought that out of a hundred shots one must be mortal. The men fired before I could get his attention; and, I suppose, considering the size of the mark, every one must have hit him. He staggered under the shock, and his sides streamed with blood, but he did not fall."

"No, Mr Hardy," said Vander Heyden, smiling; "no more than a man would fall if he was pricked with a hundred needles. Well, what next?"

"The next thing was that he recovered his legs," said Hardy, "and glared round at us with an angry eye, as much as to ask, who was to pay for this outrage? I was nearest to him, and I think he had seen me move out to Captain Sparrow, and had an idea that I might have been the author of the attack. Any way, I felt for a minute or two very uncomfortable; but, if he had suspected me, he changed his mind, and made a rush straight at Captain Sparrow. The captain ran for it, and dodged behind his men. It was no good. The elephant soon caught him with his trunk, whirled him into the air as if he had been a shuttlecock, and, when he came down again, trampled upon him again and again, till he had trodden all human likeness out of him. Then he looked round upon the ranks again, as much as to say, 'That's enough for this time, but you'd better not try this again.' After which he turned quietly round and went into the bush. We dug a grave, and scraped together, as well as we could, the bloody and mangled remains. I shall never forget the look the elephant gave me. It was as much as to say, 'If I thought you had anything to do with it, I'd give it to you too.'"

"Ha! that was a narrow escape, Mr Hardy," said Moritz; "but I think my friend Henryk's here was narrower still. I daresay he will tell it you himself."

The others joining in the request, Vander Heyden complied willingly enough.

"It occurred some years ago," he said. "I was staying at the time at Pretoria, with my relative Pieter Uys, and we had gone out for some bok-shooting in the wild country that runs up towards the Limpopo. It was generally believed that the wild beasts had left that neighbourhood; but I imagine that a hunt must have been going on somewhere near the Limpopo, and a number of elephants, some of them wounded, were making their way south. At all events, they broke upon us without our having had any suspicion of their being in our neighbourhood, bursting through the thick mimosas round us, as though they had been so many bulrushes. We were three in party—Frank, myself, and a Hottentot named Kololo. One of the largest of the herd came so suddenly upon us that we had no time to think of escaping. We did the only thing there was to do: we levelled our rifles and fired, hoping to strike him in the heart or brain. Kololo, poor fellow, aimed right enough; but the elephant tossed his head at the moment, and the ball struck his tusk and glanced off. The movement distracted my aim also, and my bullet only inflicted a flesh wound. Frank's rifle, luckily for him, was at the moment empty. The elephant glared at us, then ran up and caught Kololo round the waist with his trunk and flung him up a great distance into the air, so that he fell among the Tambookie grass. Then he charged me, caught me, as he had Kololo, round the waist, and pitched me up as he had him, as easy as a boy shies a stone into the air. Fortunately for me, there was great motjeerie close at hand. I was thrown across one of the great branches, and was jammed into a fork of the tree, so tight that I could not release myself. The elephant stopped below and waited for me to fall, but, seeing that I did not, he rushed after Kololo, who was still lying half stunned in the Tambookie grass, and trampled him, very much as Mr Hardy describes, into powder. Then he came back to the tree where I was still lying insensible, and, seeing that I was out of his reach, twisted his trunk round the bole and tried to tear it up. Then he put his forehead against it and tried to push it down. Big as it was, it cracked under his enormous weight. But by this time Frank had reloaded his rifle, and got a clear sight of him, as he stood pushing at the tree. The ball passed through his heart, and he fell dead instantly. If Frank had taken a bad aim, I shouldn't have been sitting here to tell the story."

"Well, I think your escape was narrower than Hardy's," said Ernest Baylen. "Halloo, Willikind, what now?"

This question was addressed to his brother Wilhelm, who at this moment approached, accompanied by Sergeant Long.

"Your services are required, Mr Vander Heyden," said the latter. "Our colonel wishes to obtain some information from Mr Pieter Uys, who has joined Colonel Wood as a volunteer at Bemta's Kop. The colonel has been told that you are well known to Mr Uys."

"Yes," said Vander Heyden; "he was my guardian, and I have known him all my life."

"So he was informed. He wishes to send a verbal message, and receive a verbal answer, as any writing might, by some accident, fall into the hands of the enemy. Will you and Mr Moritz go to the colonel, who is waiting for you at his quarters?"

The two Dutchmen rose, put on their swords and helmets, and went off in the direction indicated.

"The colonel thinks I ought to take eight or ten with me," continued Sergeant Long, looking round him, "as the roads are said to be beset by a number of lawless fellows, both black and white, who would show no respect for the British flag. Will any of you gentlemen volunteer to accompany me?"

He was answered by a general cry of assent. Pleasant as their camp life was, there was something of monotony in it, and the young men were glad of a little variety. "I will," and "I will," was the cry on every lip.

"A ride to Bemta's Kop will be some fun," remarked Margetts. "Drill and sword-exercise are very well in their way, but there may be too much even of them."

"You will soon see plenty of fun, sir," observed Sergeant Long. "Cetewayo's time will be up in two or three days now, and there is no chance of his knocking under." In another quarter of an hour the party had set out. It consisted of ten persons—there was Sergeant Long, who was in command, the two Dutchmen, George, Margetts, and Hardy, the three young Baylens, and Matamo. The last-named had been very urgent to be allowed to accompany the party, and, as he was a strong, alert, and active fellow, Sergeant Long had made no objection.

The road lay for some distance along the bank of the Buffalo river, and was at first quite open and safe to travel. Knowing that the whole neighbourhood, except within the immediate contiguity of the camp, was full of dangerous characters of all kinds, Sergeant Long had impressed on the party the necessity of keeping a bright look-out Matamo, in particular, whose long training particularly qualified him for such duties, was told to report to the sergeant anything suspicious that might present itself to him. But for some time there was nothing that could occasion uneasiness. There was neither rock nor wood for a long distance on either side of the road, which could possibly afford shelter to an enemy. But after an hour's ride the character of the country began to alter. Ridges of rock appeared rising one above another, until their height became sufficient to shut out the view beyond. Farther on, these ridges began to be clothed with thorns and shrubs of various kinds, presenting places from which it would be easy to fire unobserved on any one passing by. The farther the road ran, the more dangerous did it appear; and at last, when they were approaching Bemta's Kop, Sergeant Long drew rein, and called up Matamo.

"I don't like this," he said. "Do you know this road? Have you often travelled by it?"

"I know the road pretty well," answered Matamo. "But if the Zulus or the white robbers hide in the bank, it will not be possible to see them till they fire."

"Just so. Are there many bad places before we reach Bemta's Kop?"

"Plenty of bad places—as bad or worse than these. But I chance to know a way round. It is a mile or two longer, but we shall be safe from the robbers there."

"We should lose time by taking that, but I really think it would be safer. What do you say, Mr Hardy?" he continued, drawing him aside. "I don't like the look of the road; and if it is true that there are large gangs of ruffians of all kinds about, it is not safe to proceed farther in a route like this."

"I am quite of your mind, sergeant," said Hardy; "I know Matamo is entirely to be trusted."

"Very good; so be it. Show us the way, Matamo, and we will follow."

The Bechuana complied. Turning back about fifty yards, he urged his horse between two almost perpendicular masses of rock, and then made his way among the boles of the trees for perhaps a quarter of a mile. Then he turned sharp to the right, and followed a similar course, appearing to know his way, as if by instinct, among the yellow woods and oomahaamas, of which the wood chiefly consisted. A bare, open country followed, along which they rode for a long distance without seeing so much as an animal or a bird the entire way. Presently Matamo again turned sharply to the right, and after a short ride through some thickets of scrub, the summit of Bemta's Kop, and soon afterwards Colonel Evelyn Wood's encampment, came in sight.

On arriving there, Sergeant Long presented himself at the quarters of the commanding officer and stated his errand. Mr Uys, it appeared, was in the camp, and Vander Heyden and Moritz were immediately conducted to him. The others were invited to sit down to refreshments offered them. It was seen at once that they were not common soldiers, and the officers entered into friendly conversation with them.

"You are fortunate in having got along that road in safety," observed Captain Forester to George. "It is not everybody who does. Only two days ago some waggons bringing in supplies were attacked by a lot of these fellows in open day, and several of our men were wounded. They got the worst of it, however, and perhaps that has induced them to sheer off. I believe one or two of them were killed—certainly hurt."

"Well, we were not in charge of any valuables," remarked George. "There was nothing to be got from us but our guns, and perhaps our horses."

"Just so; unless they thought you were carrying despatches. Cetewayo would pay them well for any information that might be brought him."

"Well, I suppose no white men would carry any information against their own countrymen to him," remarked Margetts.

"Oh, wouldn't they!" exclaimed Captain Forester. "You have much too good an opinion of our countrymen, Mr Margetts. I am afraid they would not only give information, but supply them with Martini-Henrys and Colt's revolvers, and Gatling guns too, if they could get hold of them, always provided they could make fifty per cent, by the bargain. However," continued the captain, "if they had meant to stop you at all, they would have done so on your way here. Most probably the losses they sustained the other day have given them such a lesson that they won't meddle with our men again."

In another hour the two Dutchmen returned, having had a satisfactory interview with Mr Uys, and received the reply which was to be carried to Rorke's Drift. A consultation was then held, and it was agreed that they had better set out immediately, as it would be possible, by sharp riding, to reach the camp before dusk. It was thought better to follow the same road on their way back, as that by which they had come, it being plain that it was a route known to very few, if to any but Matamo himself. They set out accordingly, and arrived without adventure at the point in the road whence Matamo had turned off. Considering now that all danger was over, they set off at a round trot by the way which ran along the river-side; when suddenly, as they were passing a mass of rock, the top and sides of which were hidden by foliage, a puff of white smoke issued from a bush, and a bullet was fired which would have struck Vander Heyden in the chest, if it had not happened that Walter Baylen's horse plunged forward at the moment, so that the ball intended for the Dutchman entered Walter's shoulder. Hardy instantly fired his revolver at the spot whence the smoke had issued; and all the party, putting spurs to their horses, galloped through the first opening that presented itself into the broken ground which lay on the other side of the rock. Half a dozen rough-looking fellows, alarmed by their approach, were just springing on their horses, and making off in all directions, as they came up. One of the party, who had been wounded, doubtless, by Hardy's shot, was leaning against a tree unable to move. By the sergeant's direction, Hardy and Matamo alighted from their horses, and proceeded to secure him, at the same time tying up a wound in the thigh which he had received. The two Baylens and Margetts lifted Walter from his horse, and proceeded to examine his hurt. The sergeant and Moritz went off in pursuit of one knot of fugitives; George and Vander Heyden after another. The latter were not above two hundred yards ahead, and there was a long stretch of down country without shrub or stone to break the prospect. As their horses were evidently better than those of the robbers, they expected to overtake them. After a gallop of half an hour, they had approached within fire, and George, discharging his pistol, wounded one of the horses in the leg. Perceiving that he could go no farther, the man sprang from his saddle, and confronted his antagonist. An expression of surprise broke from George, as he recognised the leader of the mutineers on board the *Zulu Queen*, John Bostock. Vander Heyden also appeared surprised, though he made no remark.

"You here?" exclaimed Rivers. "I did not expect it, but I am glad you will not escape the punishment you so richly deserve. I suppose you will surrender yourself our prisoner, or we shall fire upon you at once."

"You are two to one, Mr Rivers," said Bostock, "and you are both armed. But I call upon Mr Vander Heyden here, if he is not a coward, to meet me in fair fight. He knows that I am entitled to it. My birth is as good as his own, I have served in the same army as himself, and I have twice challenged him. He is fond of saying that the English would be no match for the Dutch, if it wasn't for the advantages that their position in the colony gives them. Does he dare meet an Englishman now, without advantage on either side? Mr Rivers, here, may stand by, and see that there is fair play."

"Mr Vander Heyden, surely you will not think of allowing this," said George, as he saw the Dutchman alight from his horse, and proceed to secure him to a solitary thorn which grew on the down. "Let him say what he likes, he cannot be entitled to a meeting at your hands."

"It may be he is not, Mr Rivers," said Vander Heyden. "He is no doubt by birth a gentleman, and has held a commission in our army. I agree with you that he has so lowered and degraded himself, that he cannot claim his privilege, either as an officer or a gentleman. But let that be as it may, no soldier, and, above all, no Hollander, can refuse to meet him face to face. You must act for both parties, Mr Rivers, and see that everything is fair. No Englishman shall ever say I refused his challenge."

"If you insist upon it, I suppose I must," said George, who, though greatly vexed and disgusted, knew enough of Vander Heyden to be assured he would not give way on the point. "If this duel is to take place, it had better be immediately. What weapons do you propose?"

"What he pleases," replied Vander Heyden shortly.

"Pardon me, Mr Vander Heyden," said George, "but if I am to have the management of this affair, I cannot allow that. You are the challenged, and, by a rule everywhere acknowledged, have the choice of weapons. I choose pistols for you, and twelve paces is the distance at which you are to fire. I presume no objection is raised to either point." He looked at Bostock, who, though somewhat disappointed, as George fancied, at the proposed arrangement, answered sullenly, "Choose what weapons you like."

"Very well," said Rivers. "Then here is my revolver and Mr Vander Heyden's; they are by the same maker, and as nearly equal as two pistols can be. Take your choice of them, and stand, if you please, on that spot. Now, Mr Vander Heyden, in what manner will you fire—alternately or at the same moment?"

"Alternately; that is the usual practice here," said Vander Heyden. "We can toss for who is to have the first fire."

A florin was accordingly flung up, and it was found the right of shooting first fell to Vander Heyden.

The signal was given, he fired, and his bullet tore a button from Bostock's breast. The Englishman then discharged his revolver, and the bullet struck Vander Heyden's helmet, through which it cut a furrow, without wounding him, though he reeled under the blow.

"I presume that is enough," said George. "He cannot claim more at your hands."

"Does he demand more?" asked Vander Heyden.

"I do," said Bostock. "I claim a second shot."

"Let him have it," said the Dutchman.

"If you must, you must," exclaimed Rivers. "But take notice that I will allow no more. If you persist after this, I shall ride off the ground."

Vander Heyden bowed stiffly, and, raising his revolver, delivered his second shot. It evidently struck his antagonist, who raised, and then dropped his arm, as if in pain. Hastening up, George discovered that he had been hit in the right wrist. The wound did not appear to be a dangerous one, but it was obviously impossible for Bostock to hold a pistol.

"I cannot have my revenge to-day," he exclaimed sullenly, when the bleeding had been stopped, and the wound bound up. "But the day will come when I shall return your fire."

"When you please, sir," answered the Dutchman haughtily. "After an affair of this kind, you must be allowed to go free. If we meet again, it will be different. I shall not feel obliged to answer your challenge a second time."

They parted, Bostock leading away his wounded horse, and the other two, remounting, rode back to their companions.

"Mr Rivers," said the Dutchman when they had ridden, a short distance, "I thank you for your friendly offices. Will you add to them by being entirely silent about this adventure?"

"Certainly," returned George; "it would not be desirable on many accounts to speak of it." No more was said until they rejoined their companions, who were somewhat impatiently awaiting their return.

"Did you kill either of those fellows?" asked the sergeant. "I fancied I heard several shots fired."

"No, they got off," said George vaguely. "I hope Walter is not much hurt."

"Only a flesh wound, George," said Walter Baylen. "The worst of it is that I am afraid it will prevent me from joining the other fellows when they march. They tell me I shan't be able to stir for three weeks to come."

"Well, we had better start now, and lose no time," said Rivers. "Matamo, you have got the prisoner safe, I see. Why, I declare it is Van Ryk! a good job too!"

Chapter Twelve

"Up and bestir yourself, Redgy!" cried George, entering the tent, which Margetts shared with Wilhelm Baylen, a few days afterwards. "Cetewayo's time was up last night, and he has made no sign. The order to march has been given, and every one is already on the move. The mounted volunteers are to cross first, and our horses must be taken down to the Drift at once."

"I am sorry to say Wilhelm and I are to be left behind," said Margetts. "It's an awful nuisance, but there's no help for it."

"Left behind!" repeated George. "Why, what is that for?"

"I don't know, I'm sure; but last night, after you had left, there came an order that half a dozen of us would be required to stay on service here. Green didn't know how to settle it to any one's satisfaction, and it was determined at last to ballot for it. You are always in luck, George, and so are Ernest and Hardy, and the Dutchman Moritz. But Wilhelm and myself, and Vander Heyden—"

"Vander Heyden, eh?" interrupted George. "Has *he* got to stay behind? How did he take that?"

"Rather worse than we did," answered Margetts. "And we took it bad enough. Here we shall have to kick our heels, while you are having all the fun. By the way, what is to be done with Van Ryk? His trial took place yesterday, but I haven't heard the result."

"He is to be hanged," said George. "Not only you and I, but Vander Heyden and Moritz also swore positively to him. You'll have the pleasure of being his executioners after we are gone."

"I am not sure of that," said Redgy. "They allow a fellow three weeks now,—at least I suppose so,—and I should think you would have chawed up Cetewayo before three weeks are past."

"Hardly that," said George, "though I daresay it won't be very long. Well, I'm sorry for you, Redgy, but I can't stop here. You had better get up and see us off."

The banks of the Buffalo presented a busy and animated scene that morning. This river and the Tugela are often, in the later months of the year, so reduced in volume that a horse may cross them without the water rising higher than his knees. But in January, February, and March they are generally in deep and rapid flood, and difficult, and, except to experienced riders, impossible to ford. The mounted soldiers did contrive to cross, and so did one battalion of the Native Contingent, at a shallow spot a quarter of a mile or so up stream, and the 24th regiment was got over on ponts. When these were in position to repel any attack that might be made by the Zulus, the rest of the force was conveyed across, and lastly the waggons.

This was the heaviest part of the work, and occupied a long time. The waggons were dragged by the oxen to the edge of the bank; then the cattle were outspanned, and driven into the river to swim across, while the waggons were dragged on to the ponts by hand. This occupied the entire day; but by nightfall they had nearly all been got across, and on the following morning the march began.

"We are to move first on Sirayo's kraal," said George to Hardy, as they grasped hands. "He is the fellow, you know, that made the foray into Natal and carried off the women, whom he afterwards murdered. Cetewayo wouldn't give him up. He is in a strong position, I am told, by the Ingutu hill, about four miles from here."

"And he probably has a pretty large force with him," observed Hardy. "Cetewayo is said to have sent his prime troops against our column. Well, now, George, you'll see what these fellows fight like."

The order to move was presently given. The advance was necessarily slow through the broken and perfectly wild country on the north side of the Tugela; through which there was not so much as a path to be traced, except where the waggon of some trader had passed, and deep ruts had been left by the wheels. The ground was for the most part woodland, broken, however, continually by ravines, with deep and high fissures intersecting them — as difficult a country for a hostile force to traverse as could well be imagined.

After an hour or two of tedious advance, they came on the banks of the Bashee, a small mountain stream, running at the foot of the Ingutu mountain. Presently Sirayo's kraal came in sight.

"There is the kraal, George," exclaimed Hardy, "and there are a lot of Zulus ready to defend it. Now you may have a good sight of these fellows in fighting array."

George looked up at the crags above him, and saw a number of dark-skinned warriors, whose appearance was in the highest degree striking. On their heads they wore head-dresses, apparently of leopards' skin, surmounted by feathers, the dark plumes waving after a most picturesque fashion against the sky. Round their wrists and ankles they wore rings of ivory or burnished copper, while their waists were encircled by the tails of wild animals bound together. On their left arms they carried oval shields, large enough to protect the entire body from neck to ankle, proof against the sharp and dangerous assegay, but no protection from the rifle bullet. Their defensive weapons were rifles and assegays; the latter long spears cut from the wood of the tree which bears the same name, with an iron head and a barbed point, and which these savages hurl with great dexterity and force. As soon as the English soldiers came within hearing distance, they began to taunt and jeer them after their barbaric fashion, inquiring, "What were the white men riding there for?"

"What did they want in the land of the Zulus?"

"Were they looking out for some place to build a kraal in?"

"Would they ascend the rocks, and receive the greeting they were ready to bestow upon them?" and the like.

Presently the order to advance was given, and the men of the 24th began climbing the westward side of the hill, on which Sirayo's kraal stood. A fire was instantly opened upon them by the Zulus, from behind the various points of vantage where they had stationed themselves, by which a dozen men or so were struck down. But in a short time, in spite of an obstinate resistance, the enemy were driven out of the kraal, and fled in confusion along the hillside, followed, as soon as they reached tolerably level ground, by the cavalry, who cut down a considerable number in the pursuit.

"So much for the first brush with these rascals!" exclaimed Hardy as he sheathed his sabre. "Certainly these are gallant fellows, very different from either the Ashantees or the Abyssinians. But, nevertheless, savages, however brave, cannot stand against disciplined troops, and this is only one more proof of it. Well, I suppose we shall go no farther to-day."

Hardy's words were fully verified. Not only was the march not resumed that day, but more than a week passed before the troops were again in motion. It was found to be impossible for the waggons to make their way, without constructing for them what really was a new road; or rather, a road of some kind, the old waggon tracks being all but useless. In some places the rains or the overflow of the brooks had made the ground swampy, and here the wheels would suddenly sink up to the axles, and it was only after long and severe exertion that they could be extricated, to fall into a similar pitfall, perhaps, before another ten yards of the way had been surmounted. So slow was the progress, that it was not until the 20th of January that the column resumed its route, through a bare country, hardly exhibiting a tree or shrub, and reached on the evening of the same day, the base of the lofty eminence known as Isandhlwana, or "the Lion's Hill."

"This is to be our camping ground, then?" said Ernest Baylen as the order to halt was given. "Well, I have often heard of Isandhlwana hill, and have seen it from a distance. It doesn't look a bad sort of a place to pitch one's tent in."

"By no means," assented George, looking round him; "and it will be a strong position too, if it is properly secured from attack. What say you, Hardy?"

Hardy cast a scrutinising glance round him, and then expressed his assent. It was indeed a striking scene. On the west side the rock rose steep and rugged, and in some places precipitous, to a considerable height, sloping downwards towards the east until it reached the water-side. Ridges of rock and grassy mounds everywhere broke this descent, so that it was rendered very difficult to traverse. On the south there was a long platform of rock covered with grass overhanging an extensive valley. The whole ground chosen for the camp was a kind of sloping plateau, overlooked by an inaccessible eminence. The scene soon became lively and picturesque, as the white bell-tents were pitched in long rows, the fires lighted, and the men, in their scarlet jackets and white helmets, gathered in groups round them, or moved hither and thither on their various errands.

The companions, now reduced to four, for four had been left at Rorke's Drift, sat down to their meal in a somewhat dissatisfied humour. They were terribly tired of their long inaction, and it did not look as though matters were going to be any more expeditious as regarded the future. They had been more than ten days going five or six miles, and the waggon tracks, it was said, were to be no better. At this rate, when would they reach Ulundi? Not, at all events, until long after the other two columns under Evelyn Wood and Colonel Pearson had come into contact with the main force of the enemy, and probably reaped all the laurels that were to be gained. They were rejoiced when they were informed that Lord Chelmsford meant to send a force to reconnoitre on the following morning, and Ernest Baylen and Moritz were to accompany it.

"I envy you fellows," said Hardy. "Dartnell, who is to lead you, is a smart officer, and by all accounts the Zulus are mustering pretty thick in the neighbourhood, so that you will run the chance of some sharp fighting."

"Lonsdale is to make a reconnaissance with the Natal force in the same direction, I am told," said Ernest; "and Lord Chelmsford also means to take a party out, they say. There will be plenty of fighting to-morrow, I expect."

"Won't the withdrawal of all these detachments leave us rather a small force to defend the camp with?" suggested George.

"Oh, they will fortify it, of course, the first thing to-morrow," said Hardy. "I rather wondered that something of the kind wasn't done last night, seeing that the enemy are in force near us. But the men were very tired, and it was too dark to do much. But no doubt they will laager the waggons and throw up breastworks as soon as it is light."

With the break of day, Moritz and Ernest, attended by Matamo, rode off with Major Dartnell's force. And not long afterwards the Natal troops followed, taking the road, as they afterwards learnt, to Matejan's Kraal and Malatoko hill. But after this no further movement occurred during the day. The men busied themselves with the routine of camp duty, or were gathered in groups, talking, and smoking, and playing games. The scene was romantic and lively. In the foreground were the white bell-tents, making a forcible contrast to the scarlet of the uniforms scattered about; farther off were the waggons belonging to the different corps, each remaining in the place where it had been unpacked; and in the background was the wild uncultivated landscape—forest, and mountain ridge, and sandy ravine, and rocky boulder, mingled together in picturesque disorder.

"They don't seem inclined to fulfil your prediction," observed George to Hardy on the following morning, as they sat upon a large stone under the shadow of the great Isandhlwana hill. "No order seems to have been given for fortifying the camp. Look, there's Colonel Pulleine, who is now in command, and has been so since Lord Chelmsford and Colonel Glyn left. He is reading some letters, or papers of some kind. He does not seem to have an idea that the camp wants fortifying."

"He ought to know best," said Hardy, "and for the matter of that, I suppose he must have had the general's orders about it. And he, and we also, have nothing to do but to obey. All I can say is, that if the camp were to be attacked by any large force, as things now are, I don't see how it could be defended. What is there to stop the Zulus? The men might, of course, form into a square, if they had time to do it, with the ammunition in the middle; and as long as powder and shot lasted, I don't suppose the Zulus could break in. But look at them, scattered up and down and everywhere. Suppose there came a sudden rush of these black fellows from under cover, what time would the men have to form and collect the ammunition? The niggers might pour in by hundreds and by thousands, and cut our fellows up into small bodies, which might be destroyed in detail."

"It looks so, certainly," said George; "but our officers are men well used to campaigning, and, what is more, to campaigns with the natives. They can't have overlooked this, unless they knew that there was no risk."

"Well, all I can say is, no commanding officer under whom I have served before ever left a camp undefended, as this is," rejoined Hardy.

"Here comes Colonel Durnford," said George, as a fine soldierly-looking man rode up, attended by a force of mounted Basutos. "I knew he was expected about this time. He is senior to Colonel Pulleine; I daresay he will order the camp to be fortified. I suppose it would not be a very long job, would it?"

"No, not to put it into such a state as would be sufficient to repel an attack of these Zulus," assented Hardy. "Look at those waggons yonder. The oxen are already inspanned. If they were simply drawn together in a circle, the infantry and the ammunition collected and placed inside, the Zulus couldn't force their way in against one-half of the numbers that we have here. No, not if Cetewayo sent his whole army. Of course they might pillage the rest of the camp, and drive off the oxen. But they couldn't get inside,—not in a week,—and they would probably lose thousands in making the attempt. Look at those two guns there, too! If they were drawn in front of the waggons, they would shoot down any attacking force—whole heaps of men at every discharge. And they couldn't be taken under the fire of the laager. See there, Colonel Dumford is giving some orders. I hope he sees the danger, and is going to take some precautions against it. Let us move up nearer."

On approaching the spot, however, they found the colonel's thoughts were otherwise occupied. News had just come in that the Zulus were retreating in all directions, and would escape unhurt if they were not pursued. The colonel therefore was on the point of going after them, accompanied by his mounted Basutos and the rocket battery which he had brought with him, leaving the camp once more under Colonel Pulleine's command.

"I don't like it," said Hardy when this was reported to him. "I don't see what there has been to make these Zulus retreat. It is certain that they are in great force, and they can hardly be said to have been attacked. I hope this retreat is not a mere feint to draw more men out of the camp. I suppose, however, Lord Chelmsford must be returning to it, and Colonel Durnford knows that he is close at hand."

As he spoke, Colonel Durnford and his Basutos went past at a rapid pace, the rocket battery, under Captain Russell, following.

For some time after his departure there was no further movement in the camp. But presently the idea spread, and gained ground, that an attack from a large force of the enemy was to be looked for. The six companies of the 24th were drawn up—three of them in extended order on the left front, where the principal attack might be looked for, two more on the side where the waggons were posted, while one company (that of Captain Younghusband) was held in reserve. Close to the companies the artillery was stationed, and a little farther off a detachment of the Native Contingent.

About one o'clock heavy firing all round announced the approach of the struggle, and presently the Basutos, who had encountered an overwhelming force of the enemy, were seen falling back on all sides, pursued by large bodies of Zulus, who came rolling like a sable wave over the crest of the opposite hill. As soon as they came in sight, the artillery opened upon them, mowing them down with terrible havoc. But they continued to advance, hesitating now and then when the fire from the guns came among them, then rushing on more resolutely than ever. Presently they came near enough for the fire of the 24th to open, and this for the time checked their advance. Desperate as the courage of the blacks was, they could not face the storm of lead thus showered upon them.

"They won't stand this very long, Rivers," said Hardy, as they watched the battle from the flank, on which the volunteers were stationed. "They have wonderful pluck, certainly; but, unless the ammunition fails, it is impossible they can approach nearer. Even now I see signs of wavering among them. We shall soon be at their heels, I expect. Merciful Heaven!" he exclaimed a moment afterwards in an altered voice, as, chancing to turn round, he caught sight of some object behind him. "The Zulus have got into our rear! It is all over with us!"

Rivers glanced round, and a thrill of dismay shot through him, as he beheld the head of a Zulu column making its way round the precipitous hill in the rear of the camp, and pouring on in large and ever-increasing volumes to attack the English from behind. At the same moment the assailing force in front caught sight of their countrymen, and rushed forward with redoubled fury. Struck with terror, the native contingent broke its ranks and fled, leaving a wide gap in the fighting line, through which the black warriors burst like a raging torrent, and the whole camp in a moment became a scene of wild confusion. The various groups of white soldiers were cut off from their ammunition and from one another, presenting the appearance of an island here and there, encompassed by the overwhelming flood of the enemy. A fierce rush carried the guns, which had hitherto inflicted such deadly loss on their host. A desperate attempt was made by those in charge of them to force their way through the enemy. But the gunners were assegayed on the limbers, and the drivers in their seats. One gun was upset, the other was dragged off by the wounded horses. All was confusion, distraction, despair.

"Ride for it, George!" shouted Hardy. "The only hope is to reach Lord Chelmsford, if he is anywhere near at hand, as I hope he is, and bring him to the rescue. Some of our fellows may hold out long enough for him to come up. Ay, that is right!" he exclaimed, turning on his saddle as they galloped off; "there is Captain Younghusband retiring against the steep side of the hill. He, at all events, will hold out a long time there. All depends on how near Lord Chelmsford may be."

Urging their horses to the utmost speed, they broke their way through some scattered groups of combatants, and had got clear of the camp among some bushes, when they came upon two horsemen riding, at the top of their speed, in the opposite direction. George recognised them as Ernest Baylen and Matamo.

"Stop, Ernest!" he shouted; "do not make for the camp. The Zulus have broken in there. Where are our fellows? Where is Lord Chelmsford?"

Baylen reined in his horse. "Broken into the camp!" he exclaimed; "the Zulus! Then all is lost! Dartnell's men are dispersed or killed. Moritz has been assegayed. I was riding to bring help."

"Where is Lord Chelmsford?" interposed Hardy. "Is he anywhere near at hand?"

"No, miles off, I believe, but I can't say where."

"Then there is nothing for it but to make for Rorke's Drift. We may warn them in time to prepare for attack."

He was just turning his horse when half a dozen Zulus came rushing up, hurling their assegays as they advanced. One of these grazed George's cheek. Another pierced Ernest in the chest, who fell on the instant; while a third mortally wounded Matamo's horse. The Bechuana leaped from his saddle, and was instantly struck down by a blow from a club. George cut down the man whose assegay had narrowly missed him, and Hardy shot two more with his revolver. The others drew back for the moment; and the two Englishmen, taking advantage of their hesitation, galloped off.

"To the left, to the left!" shouted Hardy; "make for the thicket there. I know a path through it that runs down to the Buffalo. The pursuit is, fortunately, in another direction."

In a few minutes they reached the cover of the trees, followed only by the three or four Zulus from whom they had just escaped.

Once inside the wood they were tolerably secure. Elated by the signal success they had obtained, the news of which spread like wildfire in all directions, the Zulus were hurrying to witness the overthrow and slaughter of the white men, and get their share of the spoil, and the fugitives did not encounter a single enemy, while their pursuers were a long way in the rear. Hurrying along a path, which Hardy had often traversed when a resident of the country, in half an hour's time they found themselves on the banks of the Buffalo, at a part which was entirely out of sight of either friends or enemies.

"Will our horses carry us across?" asked Hardy as he looked at the swollen and roaring stream, which at that point ran with extraordinary speed.

"They must," said George. "Not our lives only, but those of our friends at Rorke's Drift depend upon it."

"You are right. We must cross at once."

The horses, which had somewhat recovered their wind during the passage through the wood, were extremely unwilling to enter the stream; and it was only by sharp use of the spur that they could be compelled to breast it. For about a third of the distance the water was comparatively smooth, and they made their way, though with difficulty. But as they approached the mid-current they found its force quite irresistible. Both horses were swept down the stream, and soon lost all power of resistance. George threw himself from the saddle, and, striking out with all his force, broke clear of the current and slowly made his way to the shore, while his horse, which had ceased to struggle, was carried down the torrent. George scrambled with difficulty up the bank, and, looking round for his companion, saw him a hundred yards lower down, clinging to the long, projecting branch of a large yellowwood. His horse too had disappeared, and he himself appeared to be quite exhausted. Shouting to him to hold on to the branch, George hurried to the spot, and, climbing into the tree, was able to approach him near enough to throw one end of his belt to him, while he drew him upwards by the other. After a quarter of an hour of great peril and exertion, they both stood safe on the farther shore of the Buffalo.

"We are saved, Rivers," said Hardy as soon as he had recovered his breath sufficiently to thank his preserver; "but I am afraid not in time to warn our friends at Rorke's Drift. We have come direct enough so far, no doubt. But Rorke's Drift lies some considerable distance off, and I am so much exhausted that it would take me a long time to reach it on foot. I am afraid you are not much better."

"Hush!" said George; "I hear some one moving close at hand. We have lost our revolvers, but we still have our sabres. Can these Zulus have followed us?"

They drew cautiously back under the cover of the reeds and rushes, and listened intently. Presently the tramp of horses' feet was distinctly heard, and two mounted volunteers came riding by at an easy trot, attended by two or three natives.

"It is some of our own fellows," exclaimed George; "how fortunate! By all that is lucky," he added a moment afterwards, "it is Redgy himself, and Wilhelm Baylen! Hullo, Redgy, what has brought you here? Stop a moment, and take us with you."

Margetts reined in his horse in great surprise. "I may return your question, I think," he said. "What brings you here? And, good heavens! what a condition you are in. You have swam the river, and are covered with blood besides! What has happened?"

"It will take a long time to tell that," answered George, "and we must not stop here to tell it. Every moment is of incalculable importance. Give me your horse, Redgy. I think I can contrive to sit in the saddle, and Wilhelm must ride by me. You and Hardy must make your way as well as you can on foot. He will tell you all about it."

He spurred the horse to its speed, and he and Baylen were soon lost to sight.

Chapter Thirteen

The morning of the 22nd of January broke calm and clear on the valley of the Buffalo. At one end of this, as the reader has heard, was situated the ford of Rorke's Drift, to which the occurrence of that day has given a world-wide celebrity. But for the fact that there are shallows close to it, by which cavalry may almost always cross, there is nothing that could cause it to be chosen as a military station. The valley indeed is open for some considerable distance above the Drift; but below it there rise rocky hills, which would enable an enemy completely to command it. On the north bank again, which is in Zululand, the ground is level; but on the Natal side there is high land, sloping abruptly down to the river at the point where the ford is shallowest. From this point, as well as from that before mentioned, the camp could be easily attacked, and probably with disastrous effect. It could therefore only be from that contempt of the most obvious dangers, which seems to be an inevitable feature in the English character, that a military storehouse and hospital could have been built in such a situation. It must have been evident to every one that, if a Zulu invasion—a thing which had already twice occurred, and which was now again apprehended with grave reason—were really to take place, and Cetewayo pour his dusky thousands across the Buffalo, the stores and the sick men must be, at once and without hope of deliverance, at his mercy.

In any case, one would have supposed that this consideration would cause some anxiety in the minds of the slender garrison left in it, when the three British columns had passed the frontier of Zululand to attack its renowned and dreaded king. All over Natal, if not all over Southern Africa, it was considered as, at all events, very doubtful, whether he would not prove too strong—not indeed for the power of England to cope with, but for the number of troops now sent against him. And if he obtained even a temporary triumph, and forced Glyn's column back over the river, what would all their lives be worth? Did not common prudence require the throwing up defences of some kind, which might keep the enemy off, for some time at least, until succour might arrive. The grand feat of arms, which averted a second disaster, has induced the world to disregard the strange imprudence exhibited here, as at Isandhlwana. But had the result been different, and had the garrison experienced the same fate as those who fell in the fatal battle on the morning of the same day, the outcry would in all likelihood have been quite as loud and quite as justifiable.

But no thought of danger disturbed the equanimity of the slender force left to garrison their untenable post. The men, when the necessary camp duties had been discharged, appeared to be sorely at a loss to know in what manner to employ their time. The day was warm and bright, and early in the forenoon it became oppressively hot. Some amused themselves by fishing in the adjoining river. Some strolled up and down, or sat smoking and chatting in the verandah, or under such shade as could be found.

At a little distance, in front of the Swedish pastor's house, Vander Heyden and his sister were walking up and down, engaged in earnest conversation.

"I wish you would think better of this, Annchen," he said. "Mr Bilderjik returns this morning to Colenso. He finds there is nothing to be done here, which the pastor himself cannot do, nor is there likely to be anything. He will take you with him to his house, and thence you will find easily enough the means of conveyance to Newcastle, where a temporary residence has been engaged. There all the waggons and the goods which were saved from the wreck at Bushman's Drift have been conveyed. There, too, you can make the necessary preparations for the journey across the Transvaal, which cannot be made here."

"You are resolved on settling at Pieter's Dorf, then?"

"Have I not told you so already? Bushman's Drift was completely destroyed by those fiends of Umbelini's. It would take a great deal of time and money to restore it; and even were that otherwise, I could never endure the sight of the place again."

"I know, I know," murmured Annchen, as she laid her hand pityingly on his arm.

"And Pieter's Dorf," resumed Vander Heyden, "is the place at which I have always wished to live, since it came into my possession. Additions to the house and farm buildings are needed, and these Hardy, the most competent man in these parts, has promised to undertake. We shall certainly set out as soon as I am free to travel."

"That is, as soon as Cetewayo has been put down, I suppose. But if you are to have no hand in putting him down, why wait for that?"

"I mean to have a hand in putting him down. As a soldier, I know I must obey orders, and therefore I have stayed here. But I have been promised that I shall take the place of the first officer that is killed or disabled. Every day I am expecting to hear that a battle has been fought and I am free to draw my sword. I must stay here."

"But, Henryk, may I not be as anxious to obtain the earliest information as yourself?"

"Of the safety of Frank Moritz?" suggested her brother, turning a scrutinising look on her; "or perhaps of some one else?"

Annchen coloured. "You have no right—no reason for asking me that," she said.

"I hope I have no reason," he answered. "As for right, that is a different matter. Let us understand one another. It was never supposed that there was any romantic affection between you and Frank, though you liked one another well enough to marry. But I have fancied once or twice that you were getting romantic about this young Englishman, Rivers. He is a fine fellow, I allow, and I admire and like him. But you shall never marry an Englishman with my consent. And though my control over you will cease after a time, you would no longer be a sister of mine if you were to marry one."

"I repeat you have neither right nor reason to speak thus to me," she rejoined. "Neither Mr Rivers nor myself have said or done anything that could justify it. And I really think it *would* be better for me to leave Rorke's Drift. I have no doubt Mr Bilderjik will give me permission to accompany him, and, as he means to set out very soon, I will go and prepare for my journey. Good-bye, Henryk; let us part friends."

They took leave of one another, and not long afterwards she was seen riding off in the Swedish pastor's company. Vander Heyden lounged up to the camp and joined some of the officers, who had gathered in a group near the storehouse, listening intently to some distant sounds borne by the wind from the eastern quarter.

"That is firing, I am sure," said Evetts, one of the volunteers; "but it is a long way off."

"Yes, that is firing," said the experienced Vander Heyden; "but it is not volley firing. It is only some skirmishing, I expect. How long has it been going on?"

"I should think it began about an hour ago," said Evetts, "but it was very faint and irregular then. It has been getting more distinct for the last twenty minutes. It is just half-past twelve now." He looked at his watch as he spoke. "But, ha! what is that?" he added a moment afterwards, as a deep, hollow boom came across the river. "That is cannon. There is a battle going on at Isandhlwana."

"A good job too," said Vander Heyden; "it is time there was some fighting. People had begun to think there never was to be any."

They continued to listen for a considerable time to the roar of the cannonade, which presently ceased, and the desultory firing was again heard.

"The action is over," observed Evetts. "The Zulus never can face the guns very long."

"Where is Margetts?" inquired another officer after another hour's conversation.

"He and Baylen have ridden out to the ford on the Lower Tugela," answered Evetts, "with some letters which were to be forwarded to Pearson's camp. I have been on the lookout for them for some time."

"And here they come," said Lieutenant Bromhead, the officer in command of the garrison; "I know Margetts' horse even at this distance."

"It is the horse, sure enough," said Vander Heyden, as they drew nearer, "but I don't think it is the man. No," he added a minute afterwards, "it is Rivers, not Margetts."

"Rivers!" repeated Bromhead. "And so it is! He must come from Isandhlwana. Depend upon it, he brings us the news of a victory. Well, Rivers, what is it?"

"I am sorry to say, Mr Bromhead," said George, saluting the officer in command, "we have suffered a terrible defeat. The Zulus have broken into our camp and massacred nearly the whole of the companies of the 24th, the police, and the volunteers. All the guns, ammunition, and waggons have been taken. I should fear that nearly a thousand men have been slaughtered."

"Good Heaven! you cannot mean it!" said Evetts. "Where is Lord Chelmsford? How can it have happened?"

"It is no use asking either question now," said George. "The Zulus are in immense force—ten or twelve thousand of them at the least. They are already, I expect, on the march to attack you. You must instantly retreat, or prepare to defend yourselves."

"We cannot retreat," said Bromhead. "It will be impossible to remove the wounded men, and we cannot let them fall into the hands of the Zulus.

Besides, it is of the utmost importance to maintain this post, if it be possible. We must throw up what defences we can, and, rather than surrender them, die behind them."

He was answered by a general cheer and a cry of determination to defend the place as long as there was a cartridge left, or a man to fire it.

As has already been intimated, a worse position for defence than Rorke's Drift can hardly be imagined. The two small frail buildings were more than a hundred feet apart from one another. The walls were thin, the doors weak, the roofs thatched, and easily set on fire. On two sides there was rising ground, from which they could be completely commanded. On a third they could be approached under cover within a few yards' distance. There was neither wall nor breastwork nor trench—nothing, in fact, to keep an enemy back. The attacking party would probably consist of some thousands of desperate and well-armed savages, flushed with victory. The defenders were one hundred and four in number (for the native contingent withdrew before the approach of the enemy), and they were cumbered with the care of thirty-five sick men.

They went to work, however, with a will, and for more than two hours employed themselves in loopholing the walls and constructing barricades between the two houses. These consisted of two waggons, which had fortunately been left at the station, and of piles of sacks filled with mealies and biscuit-boxes, the parapet thus formed being only a few feet high. It looked more like a mock fortification, put together for a schoolboy's game, than for the purposes of a real battle. The rude defences were still incomplete, when the dark masses of the enemy were seen crowding the rising ground to the south, and the foremost lines made a sudden charge down the hill, intending to carry the place by a *coup de main*. But when they had approached within fifty yards, they were met by a fire so heavy, as to check even their triumphant advance. Instead of continuing their rush, they withdrew into whatever cover they could find, and fired from behind hollows in the hillside, trees and shrubs and garden wall, every now and then rushing forward and trying to force their way in, until driven back by the weapon they dreaded most of all—the British bayonet.

"These fellows fight desperately," said George to Hardy, who had arrived an hour or two previously, as, aided by him and Vander Heyden, he drove back half a dozen Zulus, who had forced themselves half over the wall of mealie-bags; "yonder big fellow actually clutched the barrel of my musket as I fired it into him, and, though he was mortally wounded, attempted to tear it from me. If his strength hadn't failed him pretty quickly, he'd have got it, too!"

"Well, the fighting has gone on for four or five hours," said Redgy, who was close by, "and they have not gained an inch yet."

"Ay, but if they *were* to gain an inch, it would be all up with us," said Hardy. "Put those mealie-bags back again, Wilhelm. That last rush nearly had them down."

"Look out, here is another lot coming!" shouted George, as he indistinctly caught sight of a dark mass advancing towards them. A moment afterwards a dozen blacks vaulted nimbly on to the parapet, but were instantly hurled back by a volley of musketry, which carried death among the assailants. Three only had made their entrance good. George shot one with his revolver, Hardy bayoneted a second, and Vander Heyden, clubbing his rifle, brained the third, all falling dead within the enclosure.

"Safe once more!" exclaimed Hardy; "but how long is this to go on?"

At this moment a shout was raised that the enemy were forcing their way into the hospital, and the sick must be moved, or they would fall into the hands of the savages. With the utmost difficulty this task was accomplished, the soldiers fighting from room to room, and guarding the doors by turns, while their sick comrades were carried out under the very eyes of a crowd of swarthy savages, pressing on them with brandished weapons and yells of fury. Presently the hospital was set on fire, and the flames, rising high and catching the thatch, lit up the terrible scene with a lurid splendour. It guided the bullets of the defenders, who continued to pour volley after volley into the midst of the dense array of their assailants, heaping the ground everywhere round the entrenchments with their corpses.

Who can relate the achievements, who can recount the horrors, of that long night of trial? It was like a succession of hideous dreams, from which the sleepers were continually being awakened, only to renew them in sleep again. About midnight the little garrison, forced back on every side by overwhelming numbers, had to retire within an inner circle, formed, like the outer one, by mealie-sacks; and here the same scenes were, hour after hour, renewed in endless succession—of black warriors pouring in to the attack, and being driven back by volleys of musketry and charges with the bayonet.

At last the dawn broke. The Zulu fire ceased, and the dense array of the enemy was seen retiring over the heights by which they had approached. The garrison, diminished still further by the casualties of the night, stood triumphant in their citadel. The scene which the rising sun revealed was one of the most terrible and striking on which the eye of man has ever rested. There were the handful of defenders, with their faces blackened with powder or clotted blood, their uniforms ragged with bullet-marks and charred by fire, leaning exhausted against the walls, or stretched on the ground; and all round the camp the bodies of the assailants, scattered singly here and there, or piled on heaps upon one another, in some places six and seven deep. There they lay, in every conceivable attitude of repose or agony, some struck with sudden and almost painless death, others torn by gaping wounds or forced into hideous contortions by acute and protracted torture.

"What a night it has been, Vander Heyden!" exclaimed George, as he leaned on the stalwart Dutchman's arm, giddy with exhaustion. "A hundred times over I have given myself up for lost. I can hardly believe that it is over, and we are safe! It was like a horrible nightmare!—those interminable black faces and whirling spears and ferocious shouts! I think I shall never cease to hear them!"

"It has indeed been a tremendous struggle," said the Dutchman. "Ha! what is that shout? They are not returning to the attack, are they, Mr Bromhead?" he continued, addressing that officer, as, grim with dust and blood, he passed them on his way to the flagstaff.

"No, some of our fellows are in sight, and coming this way—escaped from Isandhlwana, I suppose. They raised a cheer when they saw that our flag was still flying, and our men returned it."

George and Vander Heyden followed him, just in time to see the remnant of Glyn's column coming up, headed by Lord Chelmsford himself. The commander-in-chief rode forward and looked with approval and admiration on the frail and slender defences, which a handful of brave men had converted into an impregnable fortress, on the vast multitude of black corpses heaped on every side, and on the gaunt and war-stained figures of the few defenders. Then he asked,—"Where is the officer in command?" Lieutenant Bromhead advanced and saluted. "You have done nobly, sir,— you and your gallant followers,—and England owes you her warmest thanks. Your brave defence has probably averted the mischief I had feared, and saved the colony from invasion."

The days which followed this fierce and protracted struggle were, as is usually the case, dull and inactive, the defenders being in truth too much exhausted to do more than lounge through the day and recover their strength and energies. It was some relief to George to find that Farmer Baylen had returned some time before to Horner's Kraal, so that it was impossible to send him immediate news of Ernest's death. Vander Heyden rode over to Colenso as soon as he was able, to break the news to Annchen that her lover had fallen at Isandhlwana. Walter Baylen was nearly convalescent, and it was agreed that as soon as he was sufficiently restored he should ride over to his father's house and inform him of their loss. There had been at first some apprehension that, notwithstanding the repulse at Rorke's Drift, Cetewayo might be so elated by his success at Isandhlwana as to send his dark-skinned warriors over the Tugela to overrun Natal. But the more the Zulu king learned of the event of the memorable 22nd of January, the less he felt inclined to be elated. He had killed a thousand of his enemies, no doubt, but they had probably killed nearly three times that number of his best soldiers. He had gained a battle at Isandhlwana, but he had lost one at the Inioni river; and presently he discovered that not only had another action been fought and lost at Rorke's Drift, but that his favourite regiment, the Tulwana, had been half destroyed in it. More red soldiers, he learned, were coming up "out of the sea" to supply the place of those lost. He had no means of filling the vacancies that had been caused in his own army. It was no time for sending troops out of Zululand. He would want all he had for its defence. Day after day did the garrison look across the waters of the Buffalo towards the fatal Lion Hill, but they beheld none coming that way, except now and then a wounded soldier, who had escaped by some marvel from the fatal field, crawling slowly and painfully over the broken ground to the friendly shelter where his wounds would be cared for.

It was one of the last days of January, when George and Redgy, who were sitting under shelter of the kraal wall, saw on the river bank what seemed to be a wounded Zulu, who was making his way with toil and pain to the camp.

"Do you see that darky there," said Margetts, "creeping up this way, and keeping out of sight as much as possible? He is up to no good, I expect."

"He seems to me to be wounded," said George, "or rather to be recovering from the effects of a wound. Perhaps he has been lying hurt by the river's bank, and has just recovered strength to crawl up here."

"Well, if so, we oughtn't to refuse to give the poor beggar shelter, I suppose," said Redgy. "But we had better not go near him until we have made sure. These black fellows take it for granted that you are going to assegay them, and generally try to anticipate the compliment. Here he comes, crab fashion! Hallo, darky, what may you please to want at Rorke's Drift?"

"I want your help, Mr Redgy," was the reply, — "yours and Mr Rivers'. You haven't forgotten Matamo, have you?"

"Hey, what!" exclaimed both the young men, starting up. "Matamo!" continued George. "Why, you don't mean it! I declare it is he! Why, we all thought you were dead, if not buried!"

"No, sir," returned the native, grinning and showing his white teeth. "I am not dead, nor buried. There is nobody buried yet at Isandhlwana. But I am almost dead with hunger. Please to give me some food, and I will tell you all about it."

Interested and astonished, the young men took Matamo to their tent and supplied him with food; after which he told his story.

"Mr George, you saw me knocked down by a blow from a knobkerry. I was stunned, not killed. I lay for some time, and then came to. I tried to get up, but the big Zulu you killed had fallen over me, and the dead horse lay on the other side of me. I was fast jammed in, but I could see under the Zulu's arm what was going on."

"What did you see? Tell us. No one seems to know the exact details," exclaimed Rivers eagerly. "Was the fighting still going on?"

"It was still going on; but there was no chance for the red soldiers. They were nearly all killed. There were half a dozen here, a dozen there, two dozen there, with hundreds of Zulus round them. Most of them were standing back to back, and stabbing with their bayonets. They were dropping one after another, but killing at least three men for every one. I saw one tall man kill five blacks without stopping, but the bayonet stuck for a moment in the ribs of the fifth, and then they assegayed him. The red soldiers died out, one by one, like the sparks in tinder. But none of of them ran away, and none called out for mercy."

"Could you distinguish who held out the longest?" asked Margetts.

"Yes, sir. One company had moved back against the steep rock and stood in three sides of a square. They were the last."

"Ay; that was Younghusband's company. I saw them retreating to the base of the precipice just as Hardy and I rode off the ground. They kept the Zulus *off* the longest, did they?"

"Yes, sir. They stood side by side, and couldn't be attacked from behind. They shot the blacks down by twenties at a time, till there were great heaps of dead in front of them. The Zulus kept back at last, and only threw at them from a distance. By and by all their cartridges were used up. Then the blacks rushed at them again. But the soldiers kept them off ever so long with their bayonets. At last the Zulus picked up the dead bodies and threw them on the bayonets, and so broke into the square and killed all."

"And how did you manage to get off yourself?" inquired Redgy.

"I contrived to pull off my uniform, bit by bit, and hid it under the horse's neck. Then I took the big Zulu's feathers and bracelets and put them on, and tied his cowtails round my waist. No one came near the part of the field where I was lying while I was doing it. Then I got up, took the Zulu's assegay, and nobody guessed that I was not a Zulu. I went first to Mr Ernest, meaning to bury his body. But he was alive, and did not want to be buried!"

"Ernest alive!" exclaimed George. "Why, I saw the assegay pierce him through and through?"

"No, it only grazed his ribs, and the handle remained in his side, so that the blood had stopped. As soon as it got dark, I carried him into the wood, to a cave which I found there. There he has been lying ever since, and I have nursed him. I got some supply of food from the camp before the Zulus took it all. But it was all done yesterday, and Mr Ernest would have died of hunger, so I came here."

"And you would have died of hunger too, you good fellow, though you never seem to think of that," said Redgy. "Where have you left Ernest now?"

"He is still in the cave, Mr Margetts. He is much better, but not able to walk yet. But he might be brought here quite safely."

"I'll go and speak to the lieutenant, or to Evetts, whichever of them I can find first," said George. "I have no doubt he will send out a party to fetch Ernest in. But tell me, Matamo, are the Zulus still in great numbers about there? Would they attack our fellows if they went out to bring him here?"

"The Zulus have been gone from Isandhlwana a long while ago," said Matamo. "If they had remained about there, they must have discovered Mr Ernest. No; they have carried off the cannon and the rifles and the revolvers, and everything they fancied. There are nothing but dead bodies there."

"Very well. As soon as you are rested, a party shall set out. I will go with it myself."

"Thank you, sir, I want no rest. I can go at once."

Chapter Fourteen

A long interval had passed since the occurrence of the events recorded in the last chapter. It was now July, the depth of the southern winter. Although Zululand is on the border of the tropics, there is often at that season damp and chilly weather, which is extremely trying to Europeans. When our story re-opens, George, Vander Heyden, and Redgy were lying on some tiger-skin karosses, under the shelter of a Cape waggon, enjoying the warm beams of the sun, which in the forenoon had considerable power.

The scene was very different from that surrounding Rorke's Drift, being extremely picturesque and beautiful. A rich undulating plain was spread out before them, terminating in woody heights. The green surface was varied by patches of mimosa scrub and groves of acacias and date palms. Under the hills to the right, which were mostly covered with thorns, the course of the noble Zulu river, the White Umvalosi, was distinctly to be traced, now lost between graceful masses of feathery foliage, now flashing out from behind its screen into the full sunlight.

"Do you know what that mound is yonder?" inquired Margetts, pointing to a vast green tumulus, conspicuous in the distance in the direction of the north-east. "Has a battle been fought there, or what?"

"That is King Panda's tomb!" said Vander Heyden,—"Cetewayo's father, you know. He was interred there in a sitting attitude, as is the custom of the country. The meaning of it, I suppose, is to signify that he is still ruling the land, as they have a sort of superstitious belief that he does. They are very particular about their funeral ceremonies. They have an idea that the spirits of the dead will punish severely any omission of them!"

"And they have an unpleasant custom of killing some hundreds of people to do honour to the dead, haven't they?" inquired Redgy.

"Yes, they have," assented Vander Heyden; "but to do your English Government justice, they would not allow that. One reason why I resolved to follow this out to the last, is because I know Cetewayo's barbarity has only been kept within any bounds by the power of the English. Were he to be able to defy that, the horrors of the past would be revived."

"Shall we pass Panda's tomb on our way to attack Ulundi to-morrow?" asked Margetts. "I am not sure that even now I know the exact position of the royal kraal!"

"It is there," said Vander Heyden, pointing with his hand, "in the centre of those masses of the mimosa scrub. It is as much as fifteen or sixteen miles from here. If we are to march to attack it to-morrow, as you say, Margetts, and as is generally believed in the camp, it will be a long day's work over a country like this."

"I agree with you," said George; "but, nevertheless, the attempt will be made. In a very few days, perhaps in a single day, the opportunity will be lost to Lord Chelmsford of recovering the laurels he lost at Isandhlwana. Sir Garnet Wolseley has already arrived from England, and may take the command over any day."

"I don't suppose we shall ever get very near Ulundi without having a brush with these black fellows," observed Margetts. "They are about in great numbers, and will never allow the royal kraal to be taken, if they can prevent it."

Much had happened during the last few months of public interest, as well as affecting the personal concerns of the characters of our story. In the first place, hostilities had altogether been broken off after the action at Rorke's Drift. Lord Chelmsford, over-estimating perhaps the gravity of the situation, as he had before certainly underrated it, resolved not to recommence operations until he was in command of a force sufficient to bear down all resistance. He argued, and perhaps rightly, that, after his experience at Isandhlwana, the native troops could not be relied upon in any action with the Zulus; and without them the forces at his command were insufficient to face the vast multitude still under Cetewayo's orders. Pearson had had to intrench himself at Ekowe, where he would be obliged to defend himself, until troops sufficient for his relief could be got together. Colonel Wood was in like manner under the necessity of fortifying a camp on Kambula Hill, unable to advance; though the terror in which his name was held, and his own extreme vigilance, rendered any attack upon him too dangerous to be attempted.

Lord Chelmsford's demands for powerful reinforcements were promptly granted. Two regiments of cavalry, five of infantry, two field batteries of artillery, and a company of engineers, were sent out in large and powerful steam-vessels, placing, with those already in Natal, not less than twenty-two thousand men at his disposal.

But, notwithstanding all the exertions made, a long delay ensued, during which the prestige of England seemed to be continually on the wane, and the terror inspired by Cetewayo continually on the increase. The general belief throughout Natal—it might be said throughout the whole of Southern Africa—was that if Cetewayo, leaving a sufficient force to keep Wood and Pearson within their camps, were to lead say thirty thousand of his braves into the colony, no resistance could be offered. The inhabitants would have to shut themselves up in the towns, which had been fortified in anticipation of such a danger, leaving their villages, their farm and country houses, their cattle and their crops, an undisputed prey to their invaders.

The anxiety was in a great measure relieved when, early in April, the battle of Ginghilovo was fought and the relief of Ekowe effected. But the disaster at Intombi, occurring at nearly the same time, which proved only too plainly how completely the blacks were masters of the country, and not long afterwards the melancholy death of the Prince Imperial, saddened all hearts. The universal feeling throughout the country was that, if the lustre of the British arms was to be vindicated, it must be by some brilliant achievement, which would throw all previous disasters into the shade.

All our friends, George and Redgy and Hardy and Vander Heyden, had been embarrassed by the untoward course of events. George had obtained leave of absence from camp duties. The Mounted Volunteers indeed had been reduced to a mere handful, and though he and Margetts and Vander Heyden all intended to accompany the British forces to the end of the campaign, they had to wait until they were drafted into some other corps. Rivers and Margetts proceeded to Dykeman's Hollow, where they learned that Mr Rogers was still detained in England by business connected with Cape politics. He had written, however, to George, of course in ignorance of Umbelini's raid and the disastrous issue of the invasion of Zululand, and George proceeded to carry out his instructions, as far as he was able. All the waggons and farm stock had been brought back, and nearly all the native servants had returned to their work. George commenced his duties as a Sunday school teacher, and though he felt somewhat strange and awkward in the discharge of them, he was not on the whole dissatisfied. His house was convenient enough, though curiously different in many respects from an English house. There was room enough for Redgy to be lodged in it also; and George took upon himself to engage him as an assistant at the farm, until he could hear from Mr Rogers, to whom he had written on the subject. The two young men had agreed that, although the present delay was extremely inconvenient to them,—Redgy being anxious to find some settled work, and George to set out in search of his mother,—their honour was pledged to accompany the British troops in accomplishing the overthrow of Cetewayo, and they must persevere. George had written to his mother, and a trader going up the country had promised to deliver his letter. But the weeks and months went by, and no reply was received, and he could not but be aware how slight the likelihood was that his letter had reached its destination.

The delay was equally embarrassing to Henryk Yander Heyden. He was not only weary of the enforced inactivity and anxious to set in order his new home, but his relations with his sister distressed him. He and Annchen had removed to Newcastle, to which town such of his goods and possessions as had escaped destruction at the hands of Umbelini had been conveyed. There he had found a tolerably comfortable abode, but there was nothing to employ his time, and inaction was particularly trying to him. If he had not felt himself bound by the vow he had made not to lay down his arms until Cetewayo had been deposed or slain, he would have set out for Zeerust without further concerning himself in the war. But he was a man who, when he had once taken a determination, persisted in it till the last. And when day after day passed, and the English troops, for reasons which it seemed impossible to understand, still delayed their march into Zululand, he only chafed and fretted, and made his comments on the English commander-in-chief in terms which were perhaps just, but not flattering.

As for Annchen, the present period of inactivity was even more trying to her. She had mourned sincerely for the loss of Frank Moritz, of whose good qualities she had been fully sensible. But along with this there was a sense of relief; for which she reproached herself, perhaps too severely. She had never been in love with him, in the real sense of that expression; and as time went on, the conviction stole upon her that she *was* falling in love, if she had not already done so, with some one else. The scenes during the wreck had brought Rivers before her in a very striking light; and she could not but be sensible (though nothing could be more respectful and reserved than his demeanour) of his devotion to herself. She saw that it was her brother's opposition alone which prevented his coming forward, and she rebelled against her brother's prejudices as unreasonable and even ungrateful. The mutual embarrassment that had for some time been felt increased during her residence at Newcastle. It was the nearest town of any size to Dykeman's Hollow, and George, who had temporarily assumed the management of Mr Rogers' property, had continual occasions of riding in thither on matters of business. Sometimes they met in the street and exchanged greetings, and some conversation passed. Sometimes it was the brother he encountered, and Vander Heyden was always cordial and courteous, though he never spoke of his sister or invited Rivers to his house. Considering that George must necessarily need refreshment after his long ride, and the hospitable habits of the Dutch, Annchen could not but feel that this was ungracious and marked. Once or twice she tried to express this to him, but stammered and hesitated so much over it that she was obliged to desist. If Vander Heyden had known much of feminine nature, he would have been aware that, if he wished to check the growth of an attachment on his sister's part for Rivers, he was taking the most likely means possible of defeating his object.

At last, one day about the middle of June, Henryk encountered his friend in the street at Newcastle, with an expression on his face which had long been absent from it.

"We are summoned to headquarters," he said, "at last. The march to Ulundi is to begin immediately. We are to set off to-morrow. We are to advance to Luneberg, where a junction will be effected with Sir Evelyn Wood; and then the whole army will proceed to Ulundi for what will be, I trust, the final struggle."

On the following morning, accordingly, the three adventurers set forth, and on reaching Lord Chelmsford's quarters, found Hardy already there. The three Baylens and Matamo, remained at Horner's Kraal, though the farmer adhered to the promise he had given of lending them Matamo for their expedition across the Transvaal.

In a few days more the march began. George was interested and almost amused at noticing the extreme caution which was now observed in securing the troops against the attacks of the enemy. Whenever any spot was approached where a ledge of rocks or a wooded hillside might afford protection to an assailing force, scouts were always sent forward to make the most careful examination of it. Immediately after a halt, the camps were always strongly fortified, and even surrounded by lines of galvanised wire, which the soldiers humorously called "Cetewayo catchers." The heliograph, too, was invariably set up, by which messages in cases of emergency could be despatched. The change from reckless indifference to danger, and unbounded contempt for the enemy, to the most extreme and jealous caution, was curious to notice.

On the 3rd of July, as the reader has heard, the English force had approached so near to Ulundi that an action was evidently imminent. The broad, open plain which extends between Nodwengu and Ulundi seemed to have been chosen by mutual consent to determine what might be called the decisive encounter between civilisation and barbarism. On the day following the conversation between George and his friends, the English army formed in square and marched on the royal kraal. It was an unusual order for a march, but one which rendered a surprise impossible. The infantry formed all four sides of a square; the cavalry, mounted infantry, and volunteers protected the front and flanks; the Basutos covered the rear. The cannon were placed at the angles; the ammunition and waggons in the centre.

The march proceeded past the green tomb of King Panda already mentioned, steadily moving onwards towards Ulundi. Presently there was visible in the distance a vast array of oval-shaped shields, above which rose multitudes of feathered head-dresses and the blades of glittering assegays, where the interminable host of Cetewayo's warriors were advancing to commence the battle.

The order was now given to halt, the ranks were formed in close order, four deep,—the two in front kneeling as though to repel a charge of cavalry, and the two behind firing steadily over their heads.

"They mean it," exclaimed George to Redgy, as they sat side by side on their horses, watching the movements of the enemy; "Ginghilovo hasn't frightened them after all."

"No," said Hardy, who was next to George on his other side. "I don't expect that any of these fellows were there, and it isn't an easy matter to cow them at any time."

"And look what multitudes of them there are!" said Redgy; "the whole plain seems full of them. They outnumber us, four or five to one, I should say."

"Quite," assented Hardy. "But if there were forty to one, it would not affect the result, if our fellows stand firm. It is impossible for them to approach the line of fire."

"They don't think so, though," observed Redgy. "Here they come."

As he spoke the dark columns were seen moving forward, the men advancing with a kind of springing step, holding their shields before them on their left arms. After firing their carbines, they did not stop to reload, but pressed forward, brandishing their assegays in their right hands. A stern silence was observed in the British line until they were within rifle fire. Then the word was given, and the fusillade began. The effect was terrific. The Gatling guns opened whole lanes in the advancing masses, and the leaden storm from the rifles struck down hundreds at every discharge. The ground was almost instantly heaped with bodies, so that the rearward file had to struggle over the piles of slain. They continued, however, to press forward with fierce shouts and undaunted valour to inevitable death, though the fire only grew heavier as they struggled nearer to it.

"What splendid fellows!" said George admiringly; "it really seems a shame to massacre them after this fashion, though no doubt there is no help for it."

"They are stopping now, though," said Hardy. "They have advanced nearer than any other troops in the world would, I think, have done, but they are wavering and recoiling now. Ha! there is the signal to charge," he added, as the bugle sounded. "Now for it, then, George?"

As he spoke, the cavalry darted forth from either flank, and swept down with the force of a hurricane on the disorganised and disheartened masses. In an instant the whole body of Zulus broke and fled in all directions, the horsemen with their sabres plunging among them and mercilessly hewing them down. Even in this extremity the gallant blacks turned again and again on their pursuers, pouring in desultory volleys or hurling assegays, which cost the conquerors many a life. Nor did resistance entirely cease till tracts of broken country were reached, where it was impossible for the cavalry to follow farther. Then they halted, recalled the stragglers, and slowly returned over the scene of the long encounter, the whole route being heaped with the dead and dying with a sad and terrible sameness.

"Well, Vander Heyden," said Rivers, as they lay on their karosses that evening, too much exhausted with their day's work to raise their heads from their pillows, "our vows are fulfilled at last. Cetewayo is completely crushed. His army is destroyed, or too widely scattered to be gathered together again. He will never fight another battle nor summon another council. Now at last we may think of our long-delayed journey to Zeerust."

"I do not know what the terms of *your* vow were, Rivers," answered the Dutchman, "but mine remains to be fulfilled Cetewayo is neither slain nor captive yet I grant his power is to all appearance broken. But he is a brave and resolute savage, and his people are still devotedly attached to him. So long as he is alive and at liberty, *my* vow is not accomplished. You of course can do as you will. But I am not free to depart at present."

George looked disappointed. "My own resolve," he said, "no doubt, was to see an end of Cetewayo before I left, and I should not like to set out without you,"—possibly George may have added inwardly, "or without Annchen." But if this was his thought, he kept it to himself. "I suppose," he added a moment afterwards, "Hardy also will wait to accompany you."

"No doubt," assented the Dutchman; "and besides, Rivers, I ought to tell you that, anxious as I am to set out, I should not like to do so at this season of the year. Even here the weather is extremely trying,—trying even to those who have lived as long in the country as I have. But in the camp here we have sufficiency of food and firing and shelter, as well as medical attendance close at hand, if we should want it. None of these things are to be had with any certainty in the Transvaal. It would be unwise, for you and Mr Margetts at all events, to make the attempt for five or six weeks to come. One of the things that vexed me most last April, when that extraordinary delay occurred, was that I knew that we could not then set out until the beginning of September. But by that time, I have no doubt, Cetewayo will have been killed or be a prisoner in our hands."

"I suppose you are right," said George reluctantly. "Well, if I must remain, I shall try to make part of the force that is sent to catch him. I only hope there will not be as long a delay about this part of the affair as there was about the march to Ulundi."

The feeling expressed by George was one generally entertained throughout the camp. But nevertheless the search after the Zulu king seemed to partake of the same inactivity which had prevailed from the first. Rumours were brought in that Cetewayo, who had refused all the offers made him, in deep distrust, no doubt, of the good faith of the English in making them, had fled into the recesses of a wild primeval forest on the borders of the Black Umvalosi, known as the Ngome Country. Here it was almost impossible to pursue him. The scenery was wild, broken, covered with rock and wood, presenting innumerable fastnesses, which could only be approached with the utmost caution, and great numbers of Zulus were still lurking in the neighbourhood, quite capable of exterminating any party which they might surprise unawares. A cordon was drawn round this district, and the circle gradually contracted; but for a long time, notwithstanding the rewards offered, and the fact that numbers of Cetewayo's bitterest enemies were on his trail, no certain intelligence of his lurking-place could be obtained. At last, on the 26th of August, information came in, which indicated exactly where the fugitive was to be found. Major Marter of the Dragoon Guards was ordered to take a squadron of his men, together with some of the native horse and a few mounted infantry, to effect the capture. With some difficulty, Rivers and Vander Heyden were included among the latter.

On the morning of the 27th they set out, the mounted infantry acting as scouts, and the others following. They made their way through wild and picturesque scenes, where the foot of civilisation seemed never to have trodden. Here and there the rude pathway was interrupted by mountain streams, leaping over rocky heights. The horsemen passed under groups of date palms, mimosas, and euphorbias, the giant trailers dropping from branch and crag in tropical luxuriance round them; overhead jays and parrots, exhibiting the brightest hues, screamed and croaked; and troops of monkeys chattered. Every now and then a watchful eye could see venomous snakes creeping off through the brushwood or making their way along the boughs of trees, scared by the sight of the scarlet tunics or the tramping of the horses' hoofs. It was a strange, bewildering journey.

At length they reached a mountain height, from which, at the distance of a mile or two at the most, a small kraal was to be seen, in which, as the spies confidently assured Major Marter, the royal fugitive had taken refuge.

It was a difficult point to approach. The wooded valley in which it was situated lay at a great depth, more than a thousand feet, it might be twice that distance, below; and if the party should be seen before they were close to the kraal, escape would be possible into a tangled wilderness, where pursuit would be extremely difficult.

The major made his arrangements accordingly. He caused the dragoons to lay aside their scabbards and all the rest of their accoutrements, which would make a rattling noise as they advanced. Then he sent some of the native contingent and volunteers, among whom George and Vander Heyden were included, to creep down the mountain-side, keeping carefully out of sight, and making no noise, until they reached the edge of the stream on the banks of which the kraal stood. Arrived there, they were to conceal themselves among the dense bushes which fringed the stream, until the major himself with his dragoons were seen coming up on the opposite side. Then they were to cross the stream, which a good leap would be sufficient to surmount, and surround the kraal. Marter himself led his Dragoon Guards to a point three miles distant, where the slope of the hills was sufficiently easy to allow of their riding down.

George and his companions accomplished the difficult descent successfully, clinging to the baboon ropes,—as a species of long trailer is called, and swarming down the date palms, all in profound silence. The chief danger arose from the incessant screaming of the monkeys, which rose in such a chorus that the adventurers were afraid that the attention of the occupants of the kraal might be attracted by it. But Cetewayo and his followers either felt confident in the security of the place of their retreat or were over-wearied by their recent exertions. George and his companions succeeded in reaching the bank of the stream unobserved. They could see a Zulu soldier or two moving about, and now and then a woman coming out and going back into the kraal. But all was listless and dispirited. The alert and watchful activity of the Zulus seemed completely to have deserted them. Presently the sound of hoofs was heard, and the Dragoons, sabre in hand, came galloping up. At the same moment George and his comrades rushed from their concealment and cleared the little stream at a bound.

The Zulus offered no resistance. It might be that they felt that the struggle would be hopeless, but it seemed as though all heart and hope had deserted them. They raised a feeble cry. "The white soldiers are here, my father! You are their prisoner."

There was a moment's pause, then the door opened, and the huge and sinewy figure of Cetewayo came forth. He looked worn and over-wearied, but he still retained something of his native dignity. George and Vander Heyden stepped up on either side, as if to arrest him, but he waved them off.

"Lay no hands on me," he said, "white men. I am a king; I surrender not to you, but only to your chief."

Chapter Fifteen

The waggons had stopped for the night, the oxen were outspanned, and the native servants were engaged in knee-haltering their masters' horses, which were then turned into the veldt to graze. They had not yet advanced far enough into the Transvaal country for any danger to be apprehended from wild animals. George and Margetts, assisted by Hardy, were engaged in lighting two large fires, partly to cook the supper, partly to dispel the chill which they felt creeping over them; for, though winter was now past, and the early spring was usually mild and balmy, yet after nightfall it is apt to become extremely cold. There is no country in the world, it may be remarked, more liable to sudden and rapid changes from cold to heat, and again from heat to cold, than that which they were now traversing.

They had left Zululand—that is, Vander Heyden, George, and Redgy had left it—a day or two after the capture of Cetewayo, and proceeded straight to Luneberg, whither the waggons had been despatched from Newcastle to join them. Annchen had travelled under the charge of her brother's two chief Hottentot servants, Koboo and Utango. Matamo and Haxo had been despatched by their respective masters to join the party at Newcastle, and Hardy arrived the following day from Landman's Drift. The whole party being assembled, they set off about the end of the first week of September.

There were two waggons, each with its full team of oxen and four servants attached to each. All these belonged to Vander Heyden, and contained valuables of all kinds, household furniture, farm implements, guns and ammunition, and a considerable supply of provisions, it being difficult and sometimes impossible to procure even the commonest articles at various places on their route. They were to proceed first to Heidelberg, by Elandsberg and Standerton; afterwards journeying north of Potchefstroom to Lichtenberg, and so to Zeerust. Supposing them to be able to travel every day, and no casualties to delay them, it would probably be five or six weeks before they would reach their destination. But there might be obstacles of all descriptions to encounter. Heavy rains might oblige them to remain inactive for days together. Disease might attack the cattle, especially the lung disease, of which mention has already been made, to which horses were so liable in that country. There was also a risk from wild animals. The more dangerous beasts, the lion, the rhinoceros, and the like, had become very scarce of late years in all the southern portion of the Transvaal, unable to endure the vicinity of the white man and his rifle. Still they might be met with at various points of their route, and the tiger (that is, the African leopard, which is so-called in that country) and the hyena were still numerous. Annchen and her attendant were accommodated in the best waggon. Vander Heyden and Hardy usually slept in the other, as did the others indeed also, Vander Heyden having courteously offered sleeping berths to George and Margetts. The native servants usually made their bed on the ground outside.

It was now the end of the second day of their journey, and they were beginning to make their way into the wilder country of the Transvaal, leaving the more civilised parts behind them. The road during the greater part of the day had lain across lonely tracts of country—such kraals and farmhouses as they had fallen in with being few and far between. The main features of the scenery had been long undulating downs, over which the tall coarse grass was growing up in abundance, diversified now and then by masses of rock rising abruptly into sharp eminences, and crossed occasionally by deep watercourses overgrown with weeds. These were, in general, difficult and sometimes dangerous to pass. Every now and then herds of springboks came by, bounding straight up into the air, as they caught sight of the travellers, like Jacks-in-the-box, to an astonishing height, and then rushing away with the fleetness of the wind. More rarely elands and hartebeests appeared, and once a number of gnus—these strange animals, which seem to be something half-way between the horse and the ox—went by at their awkward gallop. George and Matamo rode in pursuit and succeeded in killing a hartebeest and two springboks, the more dainty parts of which were cooked for the evening meal.

Annchen took her supper with the rest of the party, but soon afterwards retired to her waggon; and the four Europeans, sitting round the largest fire, for the night was unusually cold, began to converse together.

"This is near the place where that disaster occurred—Intombe—isn't it?" asked Margetts, knocking the ashes out of his pipe.

"Yes," answered Hardy; "the spot where the massacre took place is down on the bank of the river, only a little way from this. One would have thought that Isandhlwana would have been enough to teach even our countrymen common prudence. But I suppose nothing ever will."

"It looks like it, certainly," said George. "But it does not often happen that three such instances of carelessness, followed by such terrible results, follow in the course of one single campaign, as Isandhlwana, Intombe, and the death of the Prince Imperial."

"That last was rather cowardice than carelessness, wasn't it?" asked Margetts.

"I don't think so," said George. "The Prince Imperial was an entirely raw and inexperienced officer. The country was known to be in a most dangerous state, full of armed Zulus, who are among the most stealthy and cunning of all enemies; and he was allowed to go out in command of a party with no one competent to advise him. They tried to make out that he was not in command of the party, but nothing could be plainer than that he was; and that it was his total ignorance of the Zulus and the Zulu country that caused the disaster."

"The troopers might have stopped to help him," suggested Margetts.

"They were told to mount and ride," said George, "and they did what they were told. How can you blame them for obeying their officer's orders? Don't you think so, Hardy?"

"Most certainly," assented Hardy. "It does not appear that any of them, except his own French attendant, knew that the Prince was in any more danger than the rest of the party, until it was too late to do anything for him. The attempt to make out that that unfortunate Lieutenant Carey had the command of the party and was answerable for the loss of the Prince, was one of the most dishonest things I ever remember. The person really to blame was the officer who sent out the party under the Prince Imperial's charge. But I suppose it was necessary to have a scapegoat, and this poor young Carey was the most convenient person to select."

"What will become of Cetewayo?" suggested Vander Heyden. "Will they send him to Robben Island, along with Langalabalele and a lot of others?"

"Most likely," said Hardy; "and there he will enjoy himself along with his wives, and grow fat, and die an old man most likely."

"Yes, if a party in England don't take him up," said Rivers. "I am told there are persons in England who are raising a great clamour and making out that he has been shamefully used."

"I wish they could be made to come out and live under his rule in Zululand," suggested Hardy. "What is that?" he exclaimed a moment afterwards, starting up. "There is something in the bush there, creeping near us. Take your rifles. We must see to this." He caught up a long burning stick from the fire and threw it down among a number of dry canes and reeds which lay at a short distance. A bright flame sprang up and showed some dark figures moving off into the scrub at a little distance; but the shadows fell so confusedly that it was difficult to make out whether they were men or animals. A minute afterwards Matamo passed them on horseback, cantering off in the direction of the scrub.

"That's all right," said Vander Heyden; "he's sure to truck them, if any one can. We may sit down again. I suppose you couldn't see what they were, Hardy?"

"It was something crawling on four legs," said Hardy, "and I caught a momentary glimpse of a spotted skin, but whether it was the kaross of a Zulu, or a real tiger, I can't say."

"The tigers are very bold," said Vander Heyden, "in this country. I suppose they are not such formidable beasts as the tigers of Bengal, though."

"No, indeed," said Hardy. "If you had ever come into contact with them, you would know the difference."

"Did you ever kill a tiger in Bengal?" asked Margetts.

"Why, no, Mr Margetts, but one very near killed me."

"Did he? Tell us about it," said Redgy.

"Well, it was very soon after I went to India, when I was quite a young man. There was a letter of importance to be taken to the officer in command at Meerut; there was no one at hand who could take it, and they were obliged to entrust it to me. I was to travel by what they call dak, — travelling all night in a palanquin on men's shoulders, and resting during the hot hours of the day. We were travelling in the wildest part of the country, when one of the bearers put his head in between the curtains. 'Would massa like to see a tiger?' he said.

"I had been dozing, but I started up. 'No,' I said; 'there are few things I should like to see less.'

"'Massa see one if he like it. Very big tiger yonder!'

"I looked out, and there, sure enough, about two hundred yards ahead of us there was a big tiger, trotting along in advance; I could see his striped skin clearly in the moonlight.

"'Won't you stop?' I inquired of the bearers.

"'No good stop!' was the comforting reply; 'tiger see us before we see him. If he mean to eat us, he eat us; if he don't, he leave us alone.'

"I looked carefully to the loading of my gun, and lay back in the litter, watching our fellow-traveller, who jogged on, apparently entirely regardless of us. Presently he turned into the jungle and disappeared.

"'Well!' I said, 'to be sure you are not going to pass the spot where he very likely is laying wait for us?'

"'If he mean to have us, he have us,' was the only answer I got.

"I had a strong presentiment that he *did* mean to have us, and I was half inclined to get out of the litter and leave them to make the experiment in their own persons. But at this moment there was a ringing noise heard in the distance, and a troop of native horsemen, who had been sent on some errand, came riding up. I informed the officer in command of our predicament, and he gave us an escort of his men to the nearest station. We heard afterwards that the tiger in question had been for many weeks past the terror of the neighbourhood, having killed great numbers of men. I was exceedingly glad to hear, when I returned that way a week or two afterwards, that he had been tracked out and shot."

"I know they are formidable beasts," said Vander Heyden. "I saw some of them when I was in England, and also at the Cape. The so-called tiger of this country is an awkward beast to come into contact with, though. But I consider the buffalo, if he is wounded, a much more dangerous animal."

"I agree with you," said Hardy. "A full-grown buffalo is pretty nearly a match for a lion, and a herd of them can put a lion to flight at any time."

"Yes, I have seen that myself," said Vander Heyden. "I remember once, when I was out hunting in the country near the Crocodile river, I came upon a lion who had just seized a buffalo calf, which had strayed, I suppose, for none of the herd were in sight. He was carrying it off to his lair probably. I fired, and my bullet struck one of his legs. It was a bad shot, and only inflicted a flesh wound. The lion turned, and I suppose would have rushed upon me. But at that moment a trampling was heard, and a troop of buffalo came in sight, headed probably by the mother. The lion left the calf and galloped off as fast as he could to the jungle, which lay a mile or so off. He would have got clear of them, I have no doubt, if it hadn't been for the wound I had given him. But that crippled him so much, that the herd presently overtook and charged him. He turned and sprang upon one of them. But they had him down in a minute, and gored him to death with their horns, without his being able to make any resistance."

The sound of horses' feet was now heard, and Matamo came up. "Well, Matamo," cried Redgy, "what was it then? was it a tiger, or a hyena, or a wild dog, or what?"

"I am not sure," said Matamo, "but I think it was a bush thief?"

"A bush thief?" repeated Hardy; "do you mean a native or a white man?"

"A white thief, Mr Hardy," answered the Bechuana,—"the same who attacked us before."

"What! on the banks of the Blood river, you mean—before Isandhlwana, eh?" said George.

"Yes, Mr Rivers,—the man you rode after and did not catch."

"What makes you suppose that? Colonel Wood is believed to have cleared the country of the gang by whom we were attacked," observed Margetts.

"The colonel did not drive him off," said Matamo. "I remember him quite well; I saw him in Luneberg the day before we left. He was looking at the waggons and asking questions. He thought I did not know him, but I did."

"Then you think he is dogging us?" suggested Rivers.

"He is certainly after us, and means us harm," rejoined the Bechuana. "I saw him long way off to-day. I knew his horse."

"Horse! was he on horseback when you saw him just now—that is, if you did see him?"

"He was creeping through the bush on his hands and knees when I first saw him," was the answer. "When I first got on my horse and rode after him, I saw him a long way off, on the edge of the wood, he and one or two more. They got on their horses and rode off before I could come up."

"Well, they won't come back to-night, anyhow," observed Rivers; "and to-morrow we must devise some means of circumventing them."

No more was said, and presently the party turned in to their sleeping-places for the night.

Rivers tapped Vander Heyden on the shoulder, and the two moved off a short distance out of hearing.

"What do you think of this, Mr Vander Heyden?" inquired George when they were out of hearing distance.

"I am afraid Matamo is right," answered the Dutchman. "I know more of this man Cargill, or, as he chooses to call himself, Bostock, than I have cared to say. He was once in the Dutch service, and was received in society as a gentleman. At the Hague he fell in with my sister, to whom he offered very marked attentions—indeed, once made her an offer of marriage."

"But she repelled him?" said George.

"Yes, so decidedly that he had no pretext for intruding further on her. But he would not desist, and my sister appealed to me for protection. I called at his quarters, and the result was a quarrel and a challenge, which I accepted. But the same night, at the burgomaster's ball, he was so insolent in his demeanour to Annchen, that I insisted on his leaving the ballroom. A fracas with the police ensued, and he was lodged in prison, from which he made his escape. I never heard what had become of him until I saw him on board the *Zulu Queen*. But he had sent a notice to me, while in prison, that the defiance which had been exchanged between us still held good, if I dared to meet him. I answered that I stood prepared to do so when and where he might demand it. I could not then foresee that he would fall to his present level. He reminded me of my words when we met that day near the Blood river. I daresay you wondered that I should condescend to a duel with such a fellow. But my word had been given, though at that time I did not like to tell you all."

"I see," said George; "but you are not bound to meet him again."

"No, nor have I any intention of doing so. Indeed, I told him so. But you heard what he said,—'he would find his opportunity of returning my fire,' or some such words. He is quite ruffian enough to shoot at me without further warning."

"If I thought that," exclaimed George, "I declare I would fire upon him without ceremony! What, do you think he was creeping up through the reeds with that intention when Matamo saw him?"

"I cannot say. But if it was really he that Matamo saw, I don't think it unlikely."

"Well, we must be on our guard of course. It is a pity we haven't a good dog with us. We must see if we can't get one at one of the houses we pass. There is nothing for it but to go to sleep now. I think we are safe for to-night."

The night passed as had been anticipated, without further disturbance. In the morning the route was resumed, the place appointed for that evening's halt being Elandsberg. They were able to proceed with greater speed than on the previous day, the long, level plain being rarely interrupted by watercourses. The only drawback was that the veldt, though to all appearance level and firm, was in many places undermined by the burrows of the ant-bears which abound in this district, and which the long grass renders invisible. The horses were continually plunging into these fetlock deep, and sometimes almost to the knee. The greatest care was necessary to prevent a dangerous accident. This formation of ground lasted through the whole of the morning's ride, so that Vander Heyden had no opportunity of resuming the conversation with George which he had held on the previous evening. But when the mid-day halt had been made, the Dutchman, who had been seated near him under the shade of a large oomehahma, asked him to take a turn with him into the wood, while the drivers were engaged in inspanning the cattle.

"Mr Rivers," he said, "I think I ought to tell you what I have heard from my sister about this man Cargill, of whom we were speaking last night. I suppose she had overheard something from the Hottentots, which induced her to suppose that he had been seen in the neighbourhood. But it certainly is necessary that some steps should be taken to prevent the mischief which may otherwise not improbably follow. You will perhaps think it strange that I should speak to you, of all men, about her. I know the light in which you regard her. You have never, indeed, made any secret of it." He paused and hesitated, looking at George in an embarrassed manner.

Rivers bowed rather distantly. "You are right, Mr Vander Heyden," he said; "I have said and done nothing secretly. But I am aware of your feeling on the subject. You must allow me to say that you have made no secret of *your* feeling either."

"That is true, Mr Rivers, and is one reason why I wish to speak to you now. I will not deny that when we first met, on board the *Zulu Queen*, my feeling was one of simple dislike to your countrymen. That may be an unreasonable prejudice; but if you knew my family history, you would not wonder at it. But the events which ensued on board the ship, and afterwards during the campaign in Zululand, have, permit me to say, completely altered my feeling. I have learned your true character, and honour and esteem you."

George again bowed, and put out his hand, which the other took frankly. "I, too, Mr Vander Heyden, have had prejudices to get over," he said, "and may say with truth that I have surmounted them."

"I am glad that you can say so," resumed Henryk. "To proceed—I would now willingly accept you as a suitor for my sister's hand, and, to be perfectly frank, do not much doubt that she would receive you favourably, but for a circumstance which is perhaps to be regretted, but cannot be set aside. My father entertained a still stronger resentment against the English than ever I have felt. The idea of being connected with them in any manner was odious to him. Above all, the notion that either I should ever marry an Englishwoman, or an Englishman become the husband of Annchen, was one against which he was determined to guard by every means in his power. She is seven or eight years younger than I am, and was indeed not more than twelve years old at the time of his death. He thought her too young to be spoken to on the subject. But he put a clause into his will, by which she forfeited her whole inheritance if she married an Englishman, and he also laid his solemn commands on me never to allow such a marriage. I gave him my promise, and nothing can ever release me from it."

He again paused. But George only once more bowed, and Henryk went on. "I have never told Annchen of my interview with my father, which took place only a few days before his death; nor is she aware of the clause in his will of which I have told you. When I perceived your attentions to her, I warned her against entertaining any reciprocal feelings, but only on the ground that I could never consent to such an union. I did not wish to bring in my father's name, if I could help it. Nor shall I do so, unless it becomes absolutely necessary. May I not hope, Mr Rivers, that you, seeing what the consequences of a marriage with her would be, will prevent the occurrence of this necessity by abstaining from any further persistence in your suit?"

George was silent for a minute or two, and then replied, "You have spoken frankly, Mr Vander Heyden, and in a manner that does you honour. I do not fear poverty myself, but I ought not to reduce her to it, unless at her own expressed wish. We should not, in England, think it right for a parent to exercise so extreme an authority over a daughter as a prohibition to marry a person of any particular nation, be he who or what he might, would amount to. But under the circumstances of the case, I am willing to respect your joint wishes, and will not, unless with your permission, ask Annchen to be my wife."

"I thank you, Mr Rivers. You will observe that my father's command was not addressed to her, forbidding her to marry an Englishman, but to me, requiring me to forbid it. If I could think it right to set my father's injunction aside, she doubtless would feel no scruple. But that, I fear, can never be the case."

There was a further pause, and then Vander Heyden again spoke. "Having told you this, I have no hesitation in asking your help in the present condition of things. This man Cargill, or Bostock, or whatever he may choose to call himself, does not pursue us in this manner only because he bears me a deadly hate. He has an equally deadly passion for Annchen. I had no idea till last night of the length to which he had gone. Even on board the ship, he had the insolence to speak to her. On the day when we left the Cape he contrived to find her alone, and warn her that there would probably be mutiny and danger to the captain and officers and passengers, but she might trust to him to preserve her from all harm."

"Why did not Miss Vander Heyden warn you?" exclaimed Rivers, greatly startled.

"He timed it well. It was only just before the ship struck. Moritz and I were asleep in our cabin, and the captain was asleep in his also. He knew that there would be no possibility of warning us. Again, as I learn, while she was at the Swedish pastor's house, just after our encounter on the banks of the Blood river, she received a letter which he contrived to have handed to her, telling her of his unaltered affection, and that he was still resolved she should be his. I learn that he was seen in Luneberg making inquiries as to the route we were to pursue, accompanied by some of the mutineers and one or two other notorious ruffians. There is, I am afraid, no doubt that some attempt will be made to carry her off during this journey to Zeerust."

"It sounds like it, I fear," said Rivers. "Well, Mr Vander Heyden, you may command my services to the utmost in averting so dreadful a calamity."

"I thank you; I knew I might reckon on your generous help. I think, if we can reach Standerton in safety, as with great exertion may be done to-morrow, we may engage more men to accompany us. Our party may be made so numerous, that Cargill will not venture on any violence. We are at present ten in number, but two or three of them cannot be relied on. If we could engage five or six stout fellows, and arm them well with rifles and revolvers, they would not dare to attack us. I propose to have a watch kept throughout the night, as well as two or three men riding always in advance, and they may follow in our rear by day."

"I think you could not do more wisely," said George; "and until we reach Standerton we will undertake the duty ourselves. Margetts and I will keep one watch, you and Hardy another, and Matamo and Haxo the third. And the same with the parties in advance and in the rear."

"I thank you heartily," said Vander Heyden. "I will speak to Mr Hardy and the two servants, if you will do so to Mr Margetts."

Chapter Sixteen

The dawn was only just beginning to dapple the skies, when the voice of Henryk Vander Heyden was heard rousing his Hottentots and superintending the inspanning of the oxen and the saddling of the horses. The sun was hardly above the horizon before the party had set out, Vander Heyden and Hardy riding two or three hundred yards in advance with their guns and revolvers loaded, keeping a keen lookout as they advanced, and two of the Hottentot servants following in the same manner in the rear. In this manner they advanced for three hours or so, through a country resembling in character that which they had passed yesterday, with the difference that the ground was harder and drier, so that the progress of the waggons was less interrupted. About nine o'clock they halted for the first meal of the day on the edge of a dense mass of shrubs and underwood, through which nothing but the woodman's axe or a herd of elephants could have forced their way. Here occurred an incident which was remembered by one of the party, at all events, long afterwards. Redgy Margetts had alighted, and was about to take his place at the breakfast table, if the rough boards taken from the cart, on which the viands were spread, could be so designated, when he saw what he took to be the end of a long green plantain among the stems of the cacti. They are very delicious eating; and, thinking to add to the attractions of the meal, he took hold of one end to draw it out. To his surprise and alarm, he felt it move and writhe in his grasp, and the next moment a hideous green head made its appearance from the bushes, and would have sprung on him, if Matamo, who was calling out to Margetts to warn him, had not dexterously flung the large knife which he was holding in his hand, wounding the snake in the neck and disconcerting its aim. It missed Redgy's face, at which it had darted, and fell on the ground close to him, and Haxo, who had caught up an axe, struck its head off.

"A lucky escape, Mr Margetts," said Matamo. "A big mamba, that; he is seven or eight feet long. I never saw a bigger."

"The brute?" exclaimed Redgy. "I took him for a big cucumber, or something of that kind. Is he poisonous, Matamo?"

"Yes, Mr Redgy, very poisonous. A man, if he was bit by him, would die in an hour, perhaps in less. I've known one die in three-quarters of an hour."

"You must be careful, Mr Margetts," said Annchen, who had witnessed what had passed with a shudder of horror. "I have been learning a good deal about the African snakes. They are the worst things in the country. We newcomers cannot be too careful."

"You are right, miss," said Matamo. "Some of them look like sticks or green stalks or stems of trees lying on the ground. Strangers sometimes don't find out that they are snakes, till they are bitten."

"But, as a rule, they won't harm you unless you provoke them," said Vander Heyden. "They have the cobra in India as well as here. In which country do you think it is the most venomous, Hardy?"

"It is bad enough anywhere," answered Hardy; "but I think it is worst in India. Its venom is very rapid in its action there. I remember Captain Winter's Hindoo cook being bitten by one. She used to keep her money in a hen's nest near the kitchen door. One night she heard a noise in the nest, and thought some one was stealing her money. She crept down in the dark and put her hand into the nest to feel if the money was safe. The noise had been caused by a cobra which had crept in to eat the chickens. It bit her, and she was dead in less than half an hour."

"Yes, no doubt it was in a state of great irritation, and the bite unusually venomous," observed Vander Heyden; "but I consider both the puff-adder and the cerastes to be quite as dangerous as the cobra, and the mamba yonder is almost as bad as any. But with proper care there is not much danger. If they do bite you, as a rule, the only thing to be done is to cut or burn the flesh out."

The meal was now eaten, and the waggons were soon once more in motion, the same precautions being observed during the remainder of the day. No enemies, however, were sighted, or, indeed, any living creatures at all, except some koodoos, which Haxo and George pursued and were fortunate enough to overtake, killing one and bringing the prime parts home for supper.

About five o'clock they reached Elandsberg; which had never been more than a tolerable-sized village, and had been sacked and burned by the Zulus some months before in one of their incursions. It was now deserted; and it was fortunate that the koodoo had been killed, or the party might have had but a slender supper to partake of. But as it was, they soon made themselves comfortable. All the cottages had been wrecked, and the furniture broken to pieces or carried off; but the walls of some were still standing, and one of the largest—a farmhouse apparently—had suffered less than the others. The roof, of corrugated iron, over two of the rooms was still almost whole, and even the windows of one, the principal bedroom, had escaped. This room was got ready for Annchen and her Hottentot. Her bed and box were brought in, and a rug spread on the floor for the servant. In the other room, which had been the kitchen, the men of the party took up their quarters. A fire was lighted on the hearth, at which the koodoo's flesh was roasted; a half shattered table was rescued from the débris outside and propped up with boxes, and the party presently sat down to an appetising supper. Two of the servants were left to keep guard outside, their places being taken by others at midnight. Then the rest of the company wrapped themselves in their rugs and lay down round the fire.

The night was undisturbed, and the route resumed with the first glimmer of daylight, Vander Heyden being particularly anxious to reach Standerton that night; where, he believed, his anxieties would be at an end. It was a most delicious day, and everything went smoothly until after the halt for the mid-day meal. Then it was arranged that Margetts and Haxo should form the advanced guard, while Matamo and Hardy followed in the rear.

Redgy rode on, thoroughly enjoying the delicious afternoon. The sky was beautifully blue, and for a long time not flecked by a single cloud.

"How lovely the afternoon is!" he exclaimed half to himself, as they paced leisurely along. "I wish our halting-place was farther off. I shall be quite sorry when this comes to an end."

"It is quite far enough off, sir," replied Haxo, to whom this remark appeared to be addressed. "It is about half a mile on, and I wish it wasn't a quarter."

"Why do you wish that, Haxo?" asked Redgy, turning in surprise to his companion, whose presence he had almost forgotten.

"Because the river is between us and Dolly's Kop, sir," answered Haxo; "and I am not sure whether the waggon will get across."

"Get across! Why not? I suppose it is like the other rivers we have passed to-day,—so I understand at least. We have had no difficulty about crossing them."

"Just so, Mr Margetts. The rivers about here are nearly all sand, with just a little water. But after an hour's rain they look different."

"Rain! Yes, but we've had no rain."

"We are going to have it, though, and that pretty soon. Do you see those clouds?" He pointed as he spoke to a thick bank of black vapour which was creeping over the sky. "See, they're hurrying on the oxen as fast as they can. They may get across, but I don't think it."

They turned round and rode up to the waggon, where, indeed, the giraffe-hide whips were in full requisition, and the waggons proceeded at a pace which would soon have brought them up to the river-side had it continued. But they were presently obliged to moderate their pace, and before long it became difficult to proceed. The sky grew so dark as almost to obscure the track—indeed, but for the lightning, which repeatedly burst forth with a vividness which illuminated the whole scene, they would not have been able to distinguish their way at all. Then there came a cold, biting rush of wind, and suddenly the rain burst forth in torrents, which soon drenched every one to the skin, while the animals became almost unmanageable. It was well they had experienced drivers, or some serious disaster must have ensued.

At length, after a fierce struggle with the elements, the banks of the river were reached. But it became evident at a glance that all hope of crossing it must for a long time to come be abandoned. The narrow streamlet had risen to a roaring torrent, not only filling its sandy bed, but expanding into wide lagoons on either side, and filling up hollows which in some places were fifteen or twenty feet deep. Fortunately for the belated wanderers, the ground at the point which they had reached was high and rocky; and they were glad to avail themselves of Matamo's local knowledge, who ordered the oxen to be turned aside from the track, and presently drew the waggons into a cavern, running far enough back into the rock to afford a shelter from both wind and rain. The horses were now stabled in an adjoining cavern, and the oxen turned out to find what food they could. The condition of the party was in some degree improved. But they were sufficiently miserable nevertheless. The deluge of rain had not only soaked the men to the skin, but had forced its way into the waggons, and Annchen and her maid, and the beds and wraps and every other article inside, except the solid chests, were as completely drenched as though they had been plunged into the river. Some wood, with which the floor of the cave had been strewn, was heaped together and a fire lighted, but it would evidently be hours before anything like warmth or comfort could be restored. Our travellers were greatly relieved when they saw a horseman, wearing a heavily flapped hat and leggings and boots of untanned leather, together with a thick cloak wrapped round his person, suddenly draw up at the mouth of the cave and ask in intelligible English who they were, and whether they required any help.

"We are mostly English travellers," replied George. "We have been caught in the storm, and are almost wet to the skin. The lady who is with us, in particular, may suffer from the effects of the exposure. We should be thankful to you to show us any place where we can obtain warmth and food and shelter."

"English!" repeated the stranger; "my countrymen. I do not often come across them in these regions, and shall be pleased to offer them such hospitality as I can. You have horses, I think; you had better mount and ride with me. My house lies at the distance of about a mile from here, though the wood lies between it and us."

All complied without hesitation; even Vander Heyden, though unwilling to be indebted for any services to an Englishman, felt that, for his sister's sake, it would be impossible for him to refuse. The servants were left behind under Matamo's and Haxo's charge, there being plenty of food for their wants, as well as accommodation quite as good as they were used to.

The party rode off, following a path evidently well known to their conductor, though indistinguishable by them. The rain had now entirely ceased, though the sky was still clouded. After a quarter of an hour's ride they reached the house; which stood, as well as they could discern, on the edge of a wide, deep hollow, which the floods had converted for the time into an inland lake. There was light enough to distinguish clearly the outlines of the building. It was externally like the houses of the Dutch; but the internal arrangements were different. The kitchen was at one end, and there was a sitting-room adjoining it, and two or three separate bedrooms at the other end. The furniture, too, was different, the articles being less massive and solid than is usually the case with the Boers. There was even a bookcase in the parlour, containing it might be thirty or forty books, articles rarely to be seen in the houses of the Dutch.

Annchen was immediately shown to one of the spare bedrooms, and some clothes brought her by one of the Hottentot women, while her own were taken out to be dried. The males of the party were similarly accommodated, and in an hour's time all the travellers were assembled round the stranger's board, with the exception of Vander Heyden, who, having seen his sister made comfortable, took a courteous farewell of his host, and expressed his intention of returning to the cavern, not considering it safe, he said, to leave the waggons and cattle entirely in charge of the natives.

"You may be right, sir," said the Englishman. "Natives, unless you have had long experience of them, cannot safely be left in charge of valuable property. More particularly is that the case at the present time."

"Indeed!" said Vander Heyden, delaying his departure as he heard his host's words. "To what do you more particularly refer?"

"The whole country has been for a long time past overrun with ruffians and outlaws of every description," was the answer. "Zulus and Kaffirs, whom the recent war has driven out of their own country; Hottentots, who will not work, and live by pillage and pilfering; rogues from the diamond fields, who have been expelled for their knavish tricks, as well as convicts, who have broken loose from their confinement, have for years past formed a sort of banditti, against which one has perpetually to be on one's guard. After the annexation, our Government almost entirely put them down; but the events of the last half-year have renewed the mischief almost as bad as ever. I have no doubt, however, that now that the struggle has come to an end, quiet and security of life and property will be reestablished. But you need not be afraid, I think, for your waggons. You do not seem to be aware that a bridge over the river has been recently made, and there is a good road from it all the way to Standerton. I shall be pleased to show it to you to-morrow. It is one of the boons for which we have to thank the English Government."

Vander Heyden made no reply, but once more bowed and took his leave.

Rivers and Hardy looked at one another and smiled.

"What a pity it is that he dislikes the English so!" said the latter. "He really is a fine fellow—brave and generous and honest, and full of kindness to every one, except an Englishman."

"We ought to feel it all the more a compliment that he is so civil to us. I suppose there must have been some very great wrong done to his father by our countrymen," said George.

"To his grandfather first, and then to his father," said Hardy. "His grandfather was one of those who rebelled when they found that the country had been permanently handed over to the English after the fall of Napoleon.

He was taken prisoner with arms in his hands, and was hanged like any highwayman. His son migrated to Natal, and was again driven out by the English, when they annexed the colony. Proceedings were taken against him which were extremely harsh, and he died, as I have heard, of a broken heart. His son, our friend Henryk, got together all he could of his father's property, and withdrew into the Transvaal; where he bought a farm, but left it in charge of an agent, while he himself served in the Dutch army for several years. The annexation of the country by the English, three or four years ago, was the last drop in the cup of his indignation. He had returned to the Transvaal, having become wealthy again, partly by his deputy's successful farming, partly through money left him by his uncle, Van Courtlandt. He went again to Europe, to try if he could not procure the repeal of the Act of Annexation. He has come back now, bitterly disappointed at his failure. It is no wonder, I must say, that he cannot endure the English."

The host now informed them that supper was ready, and they took their places at the table. After the meal Annchen withdrew for the night, and the rest of the party, gathering round the hearth, for the rain and wind had made the air chilly, smoked their pipes and drank their host's Schiedam at their ease.

"If you would excuse my curiosity, sir," said Hardy after a while, "I should like to know what brought you into these parts. You are, I think you said, an Englishman. But—"

"But I don't look as though I had lived in England,—that is what you mean, I think? Well, I'll tell you my history. It illustrates what we were talking of at dinner,—as to what is the truth respecting the treatment of the natives by the Boers. My father and mother were English. They came out to the Cape Colony somewhere about 1830, and they settled on a farm in Namaqualand. It didn't pay. Their cattle were continually driven off by the bushmen, and their fruit plundered and their guns and hoes and the like stolen by the Hottentots. Nothing they could do would prevent it. The native servants were often as not in league with the thieves. Every now and then they would run off and take anything of value with them."

"As for the cattle-stealing," remarked George, "that is an old story. A man must be a good deal wiser than I am who can say how it is to be prevented. But I wonder, I must say, if you treated the Hottentots well, as I have no doubt you did, that they didn't stay with you."

"Perhaps they might," said Prestcott, which they afterwards found to be their host's name, — "perhaps they might, if they had been left to themselves. But there were always a lot of Hottentots going loose about the country; and they threatened our servants with their vengeance if they didn't give them food and drink. They didn't dare refuse, and then they expected to be severely punished, and ran off. Anyhow, they couldn't keep any servants, and their property was continually pillaged. They must have left the country if they had lived. But one day my father was speared by a party of bushmen, whom he had caught driving off a bull. My mother, who had seen the transaction, ran screaming out, and they speared her too. They then entered and pillaged the house. I was a child of eight years old, and they no doubt would have killed me along with my parents, if it hadn't occurred to them that old Potgieter, a Boer farmer a few miles off, would give them something handsome for me. They took me to him, and he did buy me."

"You don't mean that he bought you of them, knowing how they had come by you?" exclaimed Redgy, horror-stricken.

"No, sir. They were too clever to tell him that, and he was too clever to ask. They merely said they had found me, and they believed my father and mother were dead."

"And they had excellent reasons for believing so," remarked Redgy.

"True, sir. Well, old Herman Potgieter took pity on me, as he was pleased to express it. He took me over to the field-cornet's house, and apprenticed me, after their fashion, to himself, until I should be one-and-twenty years old."

"Ay, I have heard of that before I left England," remarked Margetts. "But I thought the age was five-and-twenty, and it was further remarked that it was astonishing how long these apprentices are in reaching their five-and-twentieth year."

"Just so, sir. The natives seldom know how old they are; indeed, they are seldom able to keep any account of time; and they are obliged to prove that they are five-and-twenty before they can claim their freedom. I have known a native kept in service until he was nearly forty. But though I was not nine years old before I was taken before the field-cornet, I knew something of their ways, having heard my father talk about it. I produced a Prayer-Book he had given me on my eighth birthday, insisting upon it that in a little more than twelve years' time I should be free. I suppose when they found out I was really an English boy, on my father's side at all events, they were a little frightened, and thought it best to be cautious."

"I have no doubt of it," assented Hardy. "I suppose you took good care of your Prayer-Book?"

"Old Potgieter contrived to get hold of that," said Prestcott; "but I was not to be beaten. The house where my father had lived stood only a few miles off, or rather had once stood, for no one had lived there since it had been wrecked by the Hottentots, and it was a mere ruin. But I knew my father had buried a box under the stone paving in one corner of the room, and that it contained among other articles my baptismal certificate. One day, when I wanted but a few weeks of becoming one-and-twenty, I took a pick-axe with me, went over to my old home, and dug up the box. There was my baptismal certificate, sure enough, and a good bit of money besides, as well as shares in an English company at Cape Town. I put these back into the box, which I buried again, but I took the certificate with me, and on my twenty-first birthday went over to the field-cornet's again. Old Potgieter thought he had destroyed the evidence of my age, and was dumb-foundered when he saw the signatures to the papers, and durst say no more.

"I repossessed myself of my money and shares, and sold the latter at Cape Town, where they fetched a good price. Then I bought this land here and built this house, where I have lived ever since. I married, but never had any children. A few years ago my wife died, and I have never cared to marry again."

"What became of old Potgieter, the old wretch?" inquired Redgy.

"Poor old Potgieter!" said Prestcott. "He wasn't unkind to me after all; and when I heard how barbarously he had been murdered, I was as hot as any one to punish his slayers."

"How was he murdered?" inquired Hardy.

"He was making a journey somewhere, I forget where. It was only for trading purposes, but I suppose the Kaffir chief, near whose kraal he halted for the night, thought otherwise. And it can't be denied that there was some reason for his thinking so. Old Potgieter had been on a great many commandos, and had killed more natives than he would find easy to reckon up. Makapan, as the chief was called, attacked the camp by night and killed them all. I have been told that they flayed him alive, and the story was generally believed, though I have great doubts whether it was true. The Dutch, when they heard of it, ordered a general commando, which was joined by a large party of Potgieter's relatives and friends, and I, as I told you, went with them. We were several hundreds in number, with waggons containing military stores, and a cannon or two. Makapan and his tribe were quite unable to resist. They retired into the broken country adjoining the kraal, and there assailed us with arrows and assegays from behind their rocky fastnesses. But we continually forced them back; and at last they retired into a cavern, which was some hundred yards in depth, and so dark that it was impossible to see anything, except close at hand."

"It wouldn't have done to have followed them there," said George. "You would have been an easy mark for their poisoned arrows."

"No doubt, and we might have fired as many rounds of ammunition as we pleased and hit nothing but the rocks. Praetorius and the others knew better than to try that."

"What did they do?" asked George.

"They first tried to blast the rocks, but that had no effect but that of wasting powder. Then a sort of blockade was established. Guards were set at every opening, and nothing allowed to come out or go in. But either the Kaffirs had collected large stores of food, or they had some way of going out and getting in which we could not detect. At last the Dutchmen came to the conclusion that the only thing to be done was to build them in."

"Build them in! What, build a wall in front of the cave, do you mean?"

"Build up the mouth of the cave itself. They had pretty clearly determined that there was but one mouth, — the fact that the cave ran deeper and deeper into the hillside seemed to prove that, — and if so, there could be no way out."

"Why, that is very much what I remember reading in my history of Scotland," said Margetts, "that a very barbarous Highland tribe did to another. It was in prehistoric times, so that there was only a legend about it."

"As for barbarity, Redgy," observed George, "I don't fancy the Boers of the nineteenth century are much behind the McLeods of whom that story is told. And the French performed nearly the same feat in Algeria forty years or so ago. Only they, I believe, smoked the Arabs like bees in a hive."

"That would have been much more merciful," observed Prestcott. "These Kaffirs died of hunger, the most dreadful of all deaths, and no quarter was given them. Whenever any of them made their appearance at the mouth of the cave, they were shot down. More than a thousand were killed in that way. The blockade was maintained for nearly a month. After that no Kaffirs appeared, and there came so dreadful a stench from the cave that the Dutch could endure it no longer, and made their way in. I had gone away some time before that, not being able to endure the horror of it. But I am told that they found no living thing. The whole tribe had been destroyed."

"Then, I suppose, they went home and celebrated their victory," said George.

"Yes, and boast that peace has been maintained in that district ever since," replied Mr Prestcott.

"Solitudinem faciunt pacem appellant," said George, who had not forgotten his classics. "I did not know the Boers were as bad as that!"

Chapter Seventeen

"I should like to ask you, sir," said Margetts after a pause, "the rights about the presence of the larger animals—wild animals, I mean—in these parts. In Zululand, which is very nearly on the same parallel as this, they were certainly to be found. Some of the horses were attacked by lions while we were actually in the country. We had been informed that it was very much the same state of things in the Transvaal. But here we have been journeying several days, and we have not come upon the slightest trace of elephant, or lion, or giraffe, or rhinoceros. We did hear a roaring one day, which we thought was that of a lion, but it turned out to be only an ostrich,—so Matamo said, at all events."

"If you heard the roaring by day, Mr Margetts," said Prestcott, "it was pretty sure to be that of an ostrich. As a rule, the lion only roars by night. The two roars are certainly very much alike, though a practised hunter could distinguish between them easily enough. As for the great game of which you speak, it has certainly left the lower parts of the Transvaal. If a solitary specimen here and there is to be met with, the animal in question has been driven southward by some accident. It is a different thing in Zululand from what it is here. The natives do not hunt the lion or the rhinoceros, as the European settlers do. After they have once begun to people a land, the big game soon disappears. We have, however, still herds of antelopes of all kinds, springboks, gemsboks, elands, koodoos, hartebeests, and gnus. The lion preys upon all these, and where they are to be found in great numbers he might be looked for also. But the white hunter is too much for him, I expect."

"They are old acquaintances of yours, I perceive, sir," suggested George. "Have you ever had any perilous encounters with them?"

"Well, sir, I have had one or two brushes—narrow escapes they may be called. I had one in Namaqualand some years ago—no one ever had a narrower, I may say."

"Please let us hear it, sir," said Redgy. "If one can't see the lions themselves, as I had hoped, at all events one may hear about them."

"Well, I'll tell you my adventure, sir, if you like it," said Mr Prestcott, who had evidently no disinclination to relate his personal experience. "I had gone to Walfisch Bay, where some English traders had settled, with whom I wished to establish business relations. I had to pass through the Hottentot country. At that time there were a good many villages scattered about, and there I could procure food and lodging. There were few or no white men at that time in the country, and the lions had never been disturbed in their occupation. One evening I reached a kraal on the Fish river, and there I found all the Hottentots in a terrible state of alarm about a very big lion, which was lurking somewhere in their neighbourhood and had taken to man-eating. I daresay you may have heard that when a lion once does that, the only chance is to kill him at once. He gets so fond of human flesh that he won't eat any other, and he will lie in wait near one of the villages for days and weeks together, hiding himself in one place or another, and springing suddenly out on some unwary traveller."

"Isn't that fact disputed, Mr Prestcott?" asked Hardy. "I have met with old hunters who say that the man-eating lion is merely an old animal, who has become too stiff in the joints to run his victims down, and that he only preys on men in the way you have described, because they can't run away from him in the way that an antelope or a gnu would."

"Yes, I have heard that," assented Mr Prestcott, "and think it may very possibly be true. Certainly such man-eating lions as I have seen killed were very wretched, mangy-looking creatures. That was attributed to the fact of their living on human flesh, but I don't know why that should cause such a result. Their appearance is certainly consistent with their being old, worn-out animals. Any way, the Hottentots were in a state of great disquietude about this lion. No less than five victims—two men and three children—had been killed and carried off into the long jungle grass, where he principally took up his abode, within the last week or two. Several times the whole of the men had gone out to spear him. But though they had seen him at a distance, they could not get near enough to wound him with their shots or arrows. They implored me so earnestly to deliver them from this terrible pest, that I agreed to remain for a day or two and see what I could do for them. Well, I stayed with them a week, and made several excursions, but could see nothing of him. At last it was supposed that he had been killed or had left the neighbourhood. I had delayed there longer than I liked, so I took my leave one morning, and, having loaded both barrels of my gun, I set off on my way for Walfisch Bay. About a mile from the Hottentot village there was a clear spring of water. As the day was very hot, I resolved to bathe my hands and feet and take a good draught before going farther. I took off my coat and shoes and stockings and laid them at the foot of a large mootjeeri that almost overhung the pool, but I retained my gun in my hand. I was just stooping to take a draught of water, when I heard a stealthy movement in the long tambookie grass, like that of a large animal creeping towards me, and at the same moment my horse, which I had fastened to the bough of a small tree, broke away and rushed off at full speed I sprang up and swung myself round the mootjeeri, only just in time to escape the spring of a large lion, which struck against the tree and was thrown by the shock on its side. Before it could regain its legs I had dropped my gun and skimmed up into the tree, the lower limbs of which were only six feet or so from the ground. I seated myself on a branch, and took a good look at my assailant, who was now standing only a few feet below me, eyeing me with a hungry look, and every now and then giving vent to his impatience at being kept from his supper in short, angry roars. There could be no doubt that it was the man-eater, and that he had tracked me, waiting his opportunity. It was a good job for me that the mootjeeri was so close at hand, and that lions cannot climb, or he would have made short work with me. But though I thanked Heaven for my escape so far, I was by no means out of the scrape. If I had been able to take my gun up into the tree with me, I could soon have rid myself of him, but it was lying on the brink of the spring. Nor could I even recover my coat and shoes, which I had placed at the foot of the tree, a couple of yards below the branch. I could only reach them by hooking them up with a long stick. I did try this. I cut a long wand with a crook at the end, and let this down. But the lion instantly seized my coat in its teeth and tore it away. It was the same with my shoes, and I was presently obliged to give up the attempt. He instantly clutched anything which I attempted to move.

"I was obliged to remain quite passive, but my condition was getting very uncomfortable. My arms and feet were bare, and the leaves of the mootjeeri afforded me a very insufficient shade from the blazing heat of the sun overhead. I also became very hungry as the evening came on. What food I had had with me was all in the bags attached to my saddle. My only chance, I felt, was that the lion might get tired of waiting for me and go off to seek food elsewhere. But I was sensible that this was not worth much. It was clear that he wanted me, or he would have sprung on my horse when he first made his attack; and I knew how eager the craving of the man-eater is for human flesh. He would wait as long as nature would allow him to hold out, in the hope of making his meal on me, and he would probably be able to last out much longer than I could.

"Presently he left the foot of the tree and went back to the spring, where he took a long draught, and then lay down on the grass under the shrubs, keeping his red and angry eye still fixed on me, and every now and then displaying his terrible teeth. The whole afternoon passed thus. I was in hopes that some of the Hottentots might pass that way, and repeatedly shouted at the top of my voice for help.

"By and by it grew dark, and some of the smaller animals which were accustomed to resort to the fountain to drink made their appearance in the distance, and again I hoped that he would pursue and make his supper on one of them. But no, it was quite plain that he had made up his mind to have me and nothing else. At last it grew quite dark, only a few stars being visible in the sky, and the lion, so far as I could make out, was sound asleep. I attempted to creep stealthily down from the branch, but the moment I moved he started up with a short roar, and rushed up to the tree so quickly that I had only just time to regain my former position.

"Daybreak came at last. I was worn out for want of sleep and ravenous with hunger. I foresaw that I should soon get weak and dizzy and drop from my perch into the jaws of my enemy. Suddenly it occurred to me, that although my supply of tobacco, was in my saddle-bags, I might have a small quantity in my belt, which would for the moment relieve my hunger. I felt accordingly, and drew out—not, alas! any tobacco, but my match-box. I usually carried this in my coat pocket, but by good luck I had thrust it into my belt at starting. The matches were of an unusually good kind, and when once ignited would burn for two or three minutes quite to the very end. The moment I saw them, I felt I had found a mode of deliverance if I could only accomplish it. I took my powder-flask, which was fortunately quite full, and dropped some loose powder on the ground. I then took one of the matches and fastened it to the end of the long stick by which I had endeavoured to hook up my coat and shoes. Having firmly secured it, I lighted it, and then dropped the flask on the heap of powder which I had scattered below. The lion, as before, rushed instantly up and put his head down to lay hold of the flask. Quick as lightning I thrust the stick down and applied it to the powder. The flask exploded directly in the lion's face, setting his mane and whiskers on fire and severely scorching his mouth and nose. With a yell of terror and pain, he galloped off at the top of his speed, while I crawled down so exhausted that a long draught from the fountain and a feast of some wild medlars, which I fortunately found growing by the fountain, only restored me so far as to enable me with a great effort to get back to the Hottentot village, where I had to rest several days before I was fit to resume my journey."

"What became of the lion?" asked Redgy.

"Nothing more was, I believe, ever heard of him. I inquired about him on my way back, but the Hottentots said he had entirely disappeared from the neighbourhood. They fancied that the fright he had had prevented his returning to his old haunts. But my opinion is that his eyesight had been completely destroyed by the explosion, and that, being rendered unable to provide himself with food, he had soon died of hunger."

"Well, sir, that was a near touch, certainly," said Hardy. "But I think what happened to my old comrade Robson may match it. He and I were in the same regiment in the war with the Ashantees. He told me the story, I remember, one night on our march to Coomassie, when the mosquitoes and the heat made it impossible to sleep. Robson had been servant to an officer who was very fond of field sports. He and two or three others who had got a short leave were resolved to pass it in some genuine African hunting, as they called it, going quite beyond the usual resorts of white men. They started from Graham's Town, and travelled northwards across what is now the Orange Free State and the Transvaal, till they came within a short distance of the Limpopo. The country was wild enough even for them. They fell in with a number of savage tribes, and here and there a Dutch settler. But there had been nothing to scare away the wild beasts. When they encamped for the night, Robson said they could hear the lions roaring about them to their heart's content. They were obliged at night to light two large fires, one on each side of the space enclosed by their waggons. The oxen were all placed in the middle, so that they couldn't get out, or the lions get in, otherwise they would certainly have been seized and devoured. Sometimes the lions were so bold, that they were obliged to cut long stout poles and lash them to the spokes of the wheels to prevent the animals creeping in under the waggons. One or two always kept watch, and the others slept with their loaded rifles by their sides. Robson said that if any of the oxen had contrived to slip out, they would have been seized and devoured in no time. By the light of the moon, he had sometimes seen three or four lions stalking about, trying to find some way in. Till he got used to it, their roaring was the most terrible sound to him that could be imagined, and he used to lie quaking with terror. It seemed to fill the whole air in all directions, he said."

"Ay," remarked Prestcott; "that is because the lion when he roars puts his head close to the earth, so that his voice rolls along the ground and echoes among the rocks. Go on with your story."

"Well," resumed Hardy, "what the party wanted above all things was to fall in with a herd of elephants. They had been told how they went about everywhere in that country in large herds, breaking their way through the thick forests like a fleet of men-of-war through the waves. They were a good deal disappointed that several weeks passed without their meeting so much as a single elephant. Robson said that he was as much disappointed as the rest. But one day he had his wish, and something over, as the saying is. There had been a great hunt among the Matabeles to the north, and a large herd had been driven some way south of the Limpopo. One evening the scouts came hurrying in with the information that the whole forest a few miles to the north of them was full of elephants. They were resting for the night, the blackies said, but in the morning they would be pretty sure to make for a piece of water which lay about a mile to the south of us. They would pass through the very glade where we now were, in which there were some very large trees. If we climbed up into these, we should get some capital shots as they passed. But not a moment was to be lost in placing the waggons and oxen in some secure spot. The elephants would pass down the middle of the glade, trampling everything to powder that came in their way.

"The oxen were inspanned accordingly, there being just daylight enough for the purpose. Fortunately one of the party had seen some high steep cliffs about half a mile off, which the elephants could not get down if they tried. Thither the waggons and oxen were conveyed, and were placed in a shady nook immediately under the precipice, leaving some of the men in charge of them. The rest returned to the glade, and, after taking their supper, climbed up into the largest trees they could find, taking care to be fully eighteen or twenty feet from the ground. Robson made himself as comfortable as he could, but he could not sleep. The air was full of insects of one kind or another, and their bite was very annoying. Besides this, he kept continually fancying that he heard noises of one kind or another in the distance. Now it was a low rumbling, which he presently discovered to be the wind, now a shrill cry for help, which, after intense listening, he recognised to be the call of some bird. Repeatedly, too, he imagined he was falling out of the tree, in a fork of which he had fixed himself. At last he resolved to descend and lie down to rest on a heap of long grass which lay near the foot of the tree. He was convinced that his slumbers would be but light. Anyhow the crash of the advancing herd would be enough, he argued, to wake the dead. Two minutes would be enough to enable him to regain his station on the branch.

"He descended accordingly, and having made a careful examination of the grass, to make sure there were no snakes in it, he lay down with his rifle in his hand, and almost instantly dropped asleep. He did not know how long he slept, but it was probably several hours, for it was broad day when he awoke. The crash and din he had anticipated were fully realised. Babel itself seemed to have broken loose, but it was not the herd of elephants that created it. They were no doubt in motion. He could see, indeed, from the excited gestures of his companions in the great nowana above him, that the leaders were already in sight. But it was a crowd of frightened animals of all descriptions that had awakened him. They had been driven from their lairs by the approach of the monsters, and were flying in confusion from them. There were herds of buffaloes crowded so close together that it was with difficulty they could advance, whole legions of boks of every variety, a few jackals, hyenas, wild pigs, even here and there a lion or a rhinoceros, hurrying through the forest paths, in terror of being trampled under the feet of the elephants, which would have crushed them into atoms, scarcely aware of their presence. Among the runaways were crowds of monkeys, which did not join the crowd below, but sprang from branch to branch, along the lower parts of the trees immediately over his head, making it impossible for him to climb to his former perch. He would have been knocked off, gun and all, before he had mounted a dozen feet.

"It was evident to Robson that he must find some other place of refuge, and that without loss of time, for even he could now see, about a hundred yards off, the heads of the great bull-elephants which always marched in advance of the others, tearing and forcing their way through the dense forest as a man would through a field of standing corn. In a few minutes more they would be close upon him, and the crowd of animals still prevented him from escaping. The only chance that presented itself to him was creeping into the hollow of a huge nowana, close to which he was standing. The roots of this were above ground, and there was a huge cleft in them which was at all events large enough to hide him from sight. He forced his way through the opening in the bark accordingly, though with great difficulty, and found the hole inside larger than he had expected, though he could not distinguish how far it extended, for the climbing plants outside almost covered the entrance. But he had not been in his hiding-place five minutes before the leading elephants came up. On strode the giants, some of them appearing to Robson to be fully fourteen feet high, the large trees giving way before them and the very ground trembling under their feet. Just as the leaders came in front of the hole in which he was lying, a shot from above struck one of the largest behind the ear and passed into his brain. It was instantly fatal. With a loud roar the huge beast fell dead, and his head blocked up the lower part of the opening through which Robson had entered. It was impossible for him now to make his way out; but then, on the other hand, he was now safe from intrusion—so, at least, he fancied.

"He resolved to wait until the herd had passed, and then to shout to his companions for help. The tremendous noise for the present prevented the possibility of being heard, if he had shouted ever so loudly. There was nothing for it but to remain quiet. By and by the light became better, or rather, I should say, Robson's eyes became used to the darkness, and he perceived that he was not the only occupant of the cave. There was something indistinct and shapeless in the farthest corner, a slight quivering motion showing that it was alive. It was probably some wild animal which in its terror had taken refuge in the hollow of the tree, as he had done. It might be something quite harmless, a stray goat, perhaps, from a herd,—there were plenty kept in the neighbourhood, and underground caves and hollow trees were favourite places of retreat for them. It was as well, however, for him to be on his guard. He took up his rifle and brought it to his shoulder. As he did so, there came a rustling sound from the dark corner, and two fiery eyes were visible against the light. Instinctively, rather than with any settled purpose, he drew the trigger, there was a loud hissing noise, the light from the eyes disappeared, a writhing motion which lasted for several minutes followed, and then the dark mass, whatever it was, lay motionless. Robson told me that a sickening sensation came over him, and he supposed that he must have fainted. When he came to, some time afterwards, he was in the hands of his friends. They had been engaged in cutting out the tusks of the great bull elephant, and had heard a shot fired inside the tree. In great surprise they searched the hollow, and dragged Robson out, to all appearance more dead than alive."

"And did they pull out his companion too?" inquired Redgy eagerly.

"Yes, sir, they had pulled it out, and it was the first thing he saw lying on the ground near him when he came to his senses, and it didn't improve his spirits."

"What was it?" exclaimed several of the party together.

"A cobra, seven feet long, sir," answered Hardy. "It had crept in there out of the noise, I suppose, and had been as much frightened as the other creatures were; that was no doubt the reason why it did not fly at Robson the first moment he entered. When he levelled his gun, the creature's instinct probably warned it of its danger, and it had spread its hood and raised itself for a spring, when the bullet struck it between the eyes and killed it on the spot. If the shot had gone anywhere else, Robson would never have told me the story."

"That was enough to shake a fellow's nerves, certainly," said George.

"Yes, sir; Robson could never endure the sight of even harmless snakes, and used to shake all over when he saw one, like a man with the ague. I used to joke him about it, and I think he told me his adventure to prevent me from doing so any more. Well, I suppose it is time that we go and lie down, isn't it? We are to set off, I believe, as early, or rather earlier than usual to-morrow."

"Are you going on to Standerton the first thing in the morning?" inquired Mr Prestcott; "and does the Dutch gentleman intend to accept my escort? He didn't say positively."

"I have no doubt he will," replied George with some hesitation. "And you must accept," he added more confidently, "our thanks for your kind and hospitable reception of us. Mr Vander Heyden is, as you have noticed, a Boer, and, like some of his countrymen, does not love the English."

Mr Prestcott smiled. "We English settlers here," he said, "understand all about that. This annexation of the Transvaal, though they were glad enough of it at the time, when their country was in the greatest danger of invasion, to which they could have offered no resistance, is not at all to their mind now. I hear they are trying to induce the new governor to get it rescinded; and if they are rebuffed, as probably they will be, they will get more and more discontented. But it has occurred to me, since speaking to Mr Vander Heyden, that there is an opportunity for him to travel in safety as far as Heidelberg, at all events. There are a number of waggons containing Government stores on their way to the town which are resting for the night a few miles from this. I have no doubt he might obtain leave to travel in their company. There is a military escort, which of course would make the journey quite secure. I have some acquaintance with Lieutenant Evetts, and would give Mr Vander Heyden an introduction to him, if he would condescend to make the acquaintance of a British officer."

"Lieutenant Evetts," repeated Rivers. "What, of the Mounted Volunteers, do you mean, who was present at the attack at Rorke's Drift?"

"Yes, the same, only he now holds a commission in the Natal Mounted Police."

"There is no need of any introduction to him," said George, — "not for me, at all events. We knew one another for some weeks, before the advance into Zululand. And even if we had had no previous introduction, that night at Rorke's Drift would have been introduction enough."

"Were you there, Mr Rivers?" asked Prestcott eagerly. "And do I understand you that Mr Vander Heyden was there too?"

"Yes, he and I and Evetts were all three there, and saved each other's lives at least half a dozen times during those nine or ten hours of fighting."

"I am glad to have had you under my roof, Mr Rivers, and I must forgive Mr Vander Heyden his dislike to the English. No, sir, no introduction to Lieutenant Evetts can be required. I should as soon think of introducing one twin brother to another."

"I say, Hardy," said George, as they went off to bed, "that was a pretty good one about the cobra in the hollow tree, wasn't it?"

"I wasn't going to be beaten by him," answered Hardy; "though his wasn't a bad one about the lion, I must admit that."

Chapter Eighteen

Nearly a week had passed, and the cortège was again setting out from Heidelberg, where it had arrived three days previously. Lieutenant Evetts greeted his old companions in arms with much cordiality, and they had travelled in great comfort as well as safety under his escort. He had expressed his great regret that he could not accompany them with his men to Lichtenberg. The distance between these two towns was much longer than between Luneberg and Standerton, or between Standerton and Heidelberg. The country, too, was wilder and more sparsely inhabited. His presence, and that of half a dozen of his men, would have made everything smooth. But he was under orders to leave immediately for Newcastle, as soon as he had performed his errand. All efforts to engage trustworthy men at Heidelberg had proved vain; and they were obliged to set out at last with the same party which had started from Luneberg. It was with equal surprise and satisfaction that they overtook, a few hours after leaving Heidelberg, some soldiers belonging apparently to the Natal Contingent, with a corporal at their head, who were escorting some prisoners, chiefly natives. These were handcuffed, as well as linked together by lashings round their arms. The soldiers were all white men. George, who was riding in advance of his party, moved up and spoke to the corporal. He introduced himself as Mr Rivers, late of the Mounted Infantry, and stated that his companions had belonged to the same corps.

The man answered civilly enough, though with rather a confused manner, that he remembered Lieutenant Rivers and his friends quite well, having been present at the action at Ulundi. George then inquired whither he was conveying his prisoners, and heard with much satisfaction that it was to Lichtenberg. It appeared that there had been a riot there. Houses had been plundered and murders committed, and these men, who were believed to have been concerned in the riot, had been arrested on the frontiers, and were on their way to Lichtenberg to be identified and tried. George again expressed his satisfaction, and proposed that the two parties should travel together for mutual convenience and security. To this the corporal rejoined that he should be quite satisfied with such an arrangement; and George rode off well pleased to give the information to Vander Heyden and

Margetts, who were acting as rearguard. The Dutchman at once expressed his satisfaction, as did Margetts, though in a more guarded manner, and George noticed, with some surprise, that he scrutinised very closely the corporal and his men when he rode up to speak to them. He made no remark, however, and George, riding back, resumed his place by Margetts' side. It was still quite early. Desirous of avoiding the mid-day heat, which for the last day or two had been very great, they had started two hours before daybreak, and the whole landscape had hitherto been wrapped in a gloom through which they could not do much more than distinguish their way. But the dawn now began to dapple the skies, and with the first light appeared a scene so startling, that our two travellers drew rein to gaze with wonder on it.

As they had approached Heidelberg a few days previously, they had noticed how dull and uninteresting the landscape appeared. The ground had been rising continually for a long time past, until it had attained the height of some hundreds of feet, and then a long undulating level had succeeded, extending as far as the eye could reach, without rock or forest or scrub to break the monotony. Nor were there, for vast distances together, traces to be found of the hand of man. There were few enclosures or habitations, and even flocks of sheep were of rare occurrence. They had expected to find the country on the other side of Heidelberg very nearly the same in appearance as that which they had encountered before reaching it. But the landscape which they now beheld formed the most striking contrast to it. In place of the sparse and barren plain, varied only by dried clumps of dull vegetation and bare heaps of sand or stone, there appeared a scene which might have vied with that of fairyland. Rich forests, with a most picturesque variety of outline, were seen environing the shores of a lake whose deep blue surface was studded with verdant islets. In the foreground rose castles and abbeys and picturesque ruins, grouped with a skill that no landscape painter could have surpassed, and the distant view was closed by mountain ridges, presenting the most striking effects of light and shade.

"Pretty to look at," remarked Matamo, who had just ridden up, as he noticed George's admiring gaze. "Pity it is not real."

"Not real!" returned George. "What do you mean?"

"You'll soon see," was the brief reply; and, sure enough, almost immediately afterwards the brilliant landscape melted away like a dissolving view in a magic lantern, and a long stretch of barren down and rock and scrub was all that could be discerned.

"A mirage!" exclaimed George. "Well, I have often heard of them, but I could not have believed the delusion was so perfect."

"Wonderful country for cheats of that sort," remarked Matamo; "it often looks like that before sunrise."

The mid-day halt was made under some high cliffs, which threw a long shadow and afforded some protection from the heat. Here Vander Heyden had some conversation with the corporal, and agreed with him that, as his party could not proceed beyond a certain distance every day, all of them, except the corporal himself, being on foot, the soldiers should be allowed occasionally to change with the mounted men of Vander Heyden's party, while the prisoners were permitted to take their seats in the waggon. Margetts uttered a hasty exclamation when this arrangement was reported to him, but he said nothing more, and everything went on prosperously till the halt took place. They sat down in three parties—the corporal and his men by the side of one waggon, Matamo, Haxo, and the Hottentots by the other, while the third, consisting of what might be termed the gentry of the party, took their places under some mimosas, on the brink of a small fountain, almost immediately under a high and steep rock.

The meal was half over, when suddenly there was heard a loud jabbering noise above, and the party, looking up, saw several hideous faces peering over the ridges of the rocks.

"Bushmen!" exclaimed Redgy. "I have been expecting to fall in with them for some time. We are not so very far from their country, I believe. Hallo up there?" he continued, as a number of large stones came rattling down from above. "Stop that, do you hear, or you'll find two can play at it." He raised his gun as he spoke, and pointed it at the rocks.

"It is no use talking to them," observed Hardy, laughing; "I don't suppose they would understand you if they *were* Bushmen. But they are not. They are baboons—mandrils, I believe, is their exact name. There are great numbers of them in this part of the country. I wonder we haven't fallen in with them before."

"Baboons, hey!" cried Redgy. "The mischievous brutes!" he added a minute or two afterwards, as another large stone passed over his head, which it very narrowly missed. "I say, I am not going to stand this sort of thing! I'll just give them a shot or two to improve their manners."

"Stop, Mr Margetts, don't fire!" cried Vander Heyden. "They are the most revengeful and malicious creatures in the world, and as strong and fierce as tigers. There are hundreds of them, and they'll attack us in a body if you provoke them."

His warning came too late. Redgy had already fired, and a yell of pain from above announced that his aim had been successful. The next moment a dozen huge mandrils had sprung over the rocks and began to descend the cliffs, leaping from point to point as nimbly as squirrels.

"Run for it!" shouted Hardy. "Take shelter in the waggons. We may keep them off there, but it is about our only chance."

There was no need of further warning. Matamo, Haxo, and the Hottentots, the corporal, his men, and his prisoners, though they had been too far off to hear what was passing, no sooner saw the baboons coming down the rocks, screaming and gesticulating with fury, than they became aware of the danger of the situation, and made straight for the waggons as the only haven of shelter. Nor were they a moment too soon. The front and back boards of the waggons were only just secured, when they were surrounded by a multitude of infuriated brutes, endeavouring to pull down the tilt and boards of the waggons. Others climbed on to the top and tore away the tarpaulin covering from the ribs, endeavouring to wrench out the ribs themselves with their strong, sharp claws. They became, however, in this manner an easy mark for the party inside. These at first only loaded their guns with powder, hoping to scare their assailants without further rousing their fury. But they were soon obliged to try sterner measures. The brutes, some of which were nearly five feet high and extremely strong and agile, succeeded in loosening more than one of the ribs of the waggon, and would soon have forced their way in, if the bullets which followed one another in rapid succession had not laid assailant after assailant in the dust. But undeterred apparently by the deadly shower, they continued their attack, gibbering and screaming with fury. The whole of the covering of the waggon was now torn away, and the baboons, thrusting down their long sharp claws, endeavoured to clutch their enemies within, rendering it almost impossible for them to continue to load.

"I say, George," exclaimed Redgy, as he rid himself with difficulty from a huge baboon which had seized him by the hair, firing his revolver directly into his chest, "these brutes are worse than the Zulus. I wish I had my bayonet here. That would have been the thing for them."

"You are right, Redgy," answered George. "I am just going to use my wood-knife. My revolver is empty, and I have no time to reload. The knife isn't as good as the bayonet, but it is the next best thing."

The others followed his example—all excepting Hardy, who, with the coolness of an old campaigner, had lain himself down on the floor of the waggon out of the reach of the assailants, and from thence took aim with his revolver, bringing down one baboon after another, and always singling out those which seemed to be the most likely to break in. But, notwithstanding the vigorous resistance offered, it seemed as if the strong ribs of the roof must speedily give way, when suddenly there burst forth a volume of flame which enveloped for a minute or two the whole waggon. Screaming, not with rage now, but with fright, the mandrils leaped down and rushed away, scrambling up the sides of the rocks more quickly than they had come down. At least twenty were left on the ground, either dead or too severely wounded to effect their retreat; while several others limped in the rear of their companions, scarcely able to accomplish the ascent.

"Stop, Mr Margetts," cried Hardy, as he saw Redgy raise his rifle; "don't fire at them. You may provoke them to come back. Well, that was as near a thing as I remember to have seen. How did you manage it, Matamo?"

"Koboo and Utango and I had been piling a big heap of reeds to make fires of," answered the Bechuana. "It was lucky we made the heap so large. When we saw Mr Margetts fire at the baboons, we knew what would happen, and we heaped the reeds round the waggon while the brutes were coming down the rocks. I dropped a match among the reeds as soon as they began the attack, but for a long time it wouldn't catch. Lucky it did catch at last, or we should have been torn to pieces!"

"Well, you managed famously, Matamo," said Hardy, "and we all owe our lives to you."

"Yes, sir, and your dinners too. Very good eating is baboon, and there is enough for a great many dinners."

"Eating!" repeated Redgy in great disgust. "You don't suppose any one would eat these brutes, do you?"

"Wall, Redgy, I agree with you,—the idea isn't pleasant," said George. "But they can be eaten, I believe. An old messmate told me that when his ship was at Gibraltar, many years before, the colonel of one of the regiments there sent Captain Waters the haunch of a large ape, which had been shot a few days before. The captain didn't see the haunch, but invited all the officers of the ship to dine off it. The colonel, who had only intended a joke, sent a note explaining it. But somehow it wasn't delivered until just as the haunch was being removed from the table, having been declared to be excellent. The captain put the note into the fire, and said nothing about the matter."

"He was a wise man," said Hardy, "and we shall be wise to follow his example, and make a good dinner off our late enemies."

His advice was at once followed. Fresh fuel was collected and fires lighted, and presently the cooks were busily engaged over their roasting and frying.

"Come and take a look at the soldiers," suggested Margetts to Vander Heyden and Rivers. "I wonder how they came off in their waggon."

"They were much luckier than we were," said Rivers. "Either the baboons didn't take any notice of their waggon, or they were bent, like Hardy's elephant, on punishing the culprit who fired on them. The soldiers were not attacked at all."

"I am very sorry, I am sure," said Redgy; "I'll promise to be good another time, that is all I can say. But they made their preparations against attack, I suppose."

"Yes," said Vander Heyden, "they took off the prisoners' handcuffs of course. They couldn't have left them in that helpless state to the mercy of those ferocious brutes. But I see they are going to put the handcuffs on again now."

They moved nearer to the prisoners, and stood for a while watching the replacing of the handcuffs. Then Rivers called out to Margetts, who was standing at a short distance, and asked him and Vander Heyden to ride a little way on the road by which they had come that morning, to search for his revolver, which he must have dropped. The other two assented, and they went away together.

About half an hour afterwards, when the dinners were nearly ready, Vander Heyden and Rivers returned, looking a good deal put out.

"Corporal Sims," said the Dutchman, riding up to the person named, "this is vexatious, but I am afraid we must stay here to-night. Mr Rivers cannot find his revolver, and thinks he must have dropped it a long way back—at the first stream which we crossed. Mr Margetts has offered to ride back, and look for it, and I am afraid we shall, in consequence, be obliged to remain here all night. As some repairs must be made to our waggon, perhaps it is not of so much consequence. But are you able to stay?"

The corporal hesitated a moment, apparently a good deal surprised. Then he answered civilly that he saw no reason why they should not remain, as there was plenty of food and a good spring of water, and there was no particular need for haste.

"Very well, then," said Vander Heyden, riding on, "we will stay here till to-morrow."

Nothing was said until the two horsemen were out of hearing. Then one of the prisoners said in a guarded tone,—"Do they suspect anything, do you think, Andrewes?"

"No," answered Andrews, "I am pretty sure they do not. Why do you ask that, Bostock?"

"I have been uneasy all day," was the answer, "lest either Rivers or Vander Heyden should recognise us. It is quite true that I am stained as dark as any Zulu in the country, and so are Gott and Sullivan. And our beards and whiskers have been shaved, and our hair frizzled and dyed black, so that we could hardly recognise ourselves in the glass. But they are both of them wide-awake fellows, and I shouldn't like this kind of thing to go on long. I suppose our intention holds good, to make the attack to-night, doesn't it?"

"I don't see why not," answered the pseudo-corporal. "It was agreed that we should, all of us, approach the waggon together as soon as the moon sets, and that will be before twelve o'clock. They keep a watch all night, I know. One of them stands sentinel at the fire near the waggon. But a rifle bullet will quiet him. Then we rush up and shoot the others. We shall have only four to deal with instead of five now. The Hottentots are sure to run off at the first shot."

"Margetts may return," remarked Gott.

"If he does, he'll hardly reach the camp," returned Bostock. "Some one had better be on the look-out for him a mile or so on the Heidelberg road. There will still be twelve of us left. That will be enough to settle four men, won't it, even if they should not be asleep."

"You forget the women," said the corporal with a smirk.

"No, I don't forget them, Andrewes," answered Bostock angrily. "But you had better do so—forget Miss Vander Heyden, at all events. You will remember that she is to become my wife as soon as we can reach Doomberg, where the missionary has promised to marry us. You had better all keep that in your heads, or you may chance to find an ounce of lead there."

"Well, you needn't be so cranky about it, John Bostock," said Sullivan. "Will Andrewes and the others have been your pals ever since we came into the country, nigh upon a twelvemonth ago, and Jem Gott and I was your pals long before. And we've never done nothing but please you, and we ain't going to now."

"Well, that's as it should be, Sullivan. We need have no more words about that. And now dinner's ready, I see, so we had better fall to at that."

Meanwhile Vander Heyden and his two friends had no sooner completed their meal than they hastened to the waggon, and summoned Matamo and Haxo to assist in repairing the damage sustained. Their first step was to renew the canvas covering, which had been torn down. Then they nailed thick boards all round the lower part of the waggon, and constructed a kind of citadel in the middle, consisting of four strong boxes, about three feet high, inside which two persons might take refuge.

"I wish you would not think so much of me," urged Annchen, from whom it had been impossible to conceal the approaching danger. "My life is of no more value than any one of yours. And you are neglecting, I am sure, your own safely. Henryk, will you not listen to me? Mr Rivers, will not you?" She blushed deeply as she spoke.

"Say no more, Annchen," returned her brother sternly, though with evident tenderness of feeling. "We shall all do our best for ourselves as well as for you. And there is every hope that Margetts will return before these scoundrels even begin their attack. It cannot be more than a two hours' ride to Heidelberg. I could myself do it in little more than one; but then, unfortunately, I was only on terms of distant civility with Lieutenant Evetts."

"It will take Margetts at least two hours," observed Hardy; "and then there may be difficulty in finding Mr Evetts and in getting his men together. It was three o'clock when Margetts rode off. If he is back by ten, it is as early as can reasonably be hoped."

"Ten will be time enough," remarked Rivers. "They will wait for the moon to set, or they would be an easy mark for our bullets."

"And the moon does not set till eleven," said Vander Heyden. "Besides, even if they do make their attack, it remains to be seen whether we cannot keep them off. It can hardly be worse than it was at Rorke's Drift, when we three stood side by side together. But I think we have now been as long at work in the waggon as it is safe for us to be. We might awaken suspicion if it was thought that we were fortifying it. We must get out, and not return to it until after the moon has set. Annchen, I shall wish you good-bye now. You must be in your place of shelter when we return."

He folded her in a warm embrace, and then leaped from the waggon, forgetting that George still remained, or unwilling perhaps to witness his adieux.

George took her hand and looked earnestly into her face. "This may be the last time we shall meet," he said. "I know I can never have my wish, but I should like you to know how fondly I love you."

The tears rose in her eyes and streamed down her face. "I do know it," she murmured, — "I do know it, George; I prize and I return it."

Their lips met for a moment, as if by a mutual impulse, and then Rivers leaped down and joined his companions, who had taken their places by the fire.

The night came on clear and bright, as is the night of those regions,—the moon, a dazzling globe of crystal; the stars studding the sky with brilliant specks of light. The three friends affected to converse carelessly together, intermingling their talk with bursts of merriment. But every ear was in reality strained to catch the distant tramp of horses' feet—the more keenly because the hour had now indeed come when Margetts' return was not only possible, but might be reasonably looked for. Anxiously they watched the moon as it sank slowly down the heaven, disappearing at last behind the distant mountain range, and comparative darkness succeeded, which under the shadow of the cliffs rendered objects even at a little distance scarcely distinguishable. Then they rose, and somewhat noisily bade the Hottentots good-night, desiring them to keep a careful watch. Moving off to their own waggon, they crept stealthily behind and round under its cover to the other which was reserved for Annchen and her attendant, and got inside, joining Matamo and Haxo, who were anxiously expecting them. They had lighted a lantern, whose light just showed the interior of the waggon.

"Hark! what was that?" exclaimed Hardy, as a sound resembling that of the discharge of a gun was heard at some distance. "Can that be Margetts' signal?"

"It is most unlikely that he would discharge his gun," said Rivers. "It would have the effect of putting these ruffians on their guard. He knows that we have no need to be warned."

"True," said Hardy; "but if he is coming at all it ought to be soon. It is nearly half-past eleven. These fellows will make their attack almost immediately now. Ha! listen! Yes, I hear them coming!"

Even as he spoke, a hand was laid on the shutter by which the back of the cart was closed, and attempt made to pull it open.

Vander Heyden put his head out. "What are you doing here?" he asked. "This is my sister's sleeping-place."

"I know that, Mr Vander Heyden, and I know you, and you too know me. I am Langley Cargill, of the Nassau Regiment—your equal by birth and station. I design your sister no harm, but to make her my wife. Give her up to me, and I will ensure her safety and the most honourable treatment."

"*I* would as soon give her into the hands of Satan!" cried Vander Heyden fiercely. "You and your ruffians will do wisely to move off at once, or we will fire on you without mercy."

"Then take the consequences of your own folly. Fire into the waggon, boys!" he shouted; "we'll soon make an end of this."

A dozen guns were discharged, and the leaden hail came rattling between the ribs of the tilt above them. It did not produce much effect, as all those within had thrown themselves on the floor, where the solid sides of the waggon, strengthened by the recent defences, prevented the bullets from penetrating. The next moment the fire was returned with more effect. Two of the pretended soldiers were shot dead on the spot, Bostock and one of his men were severely wounded.

"Rush up and smash the shutters in before they can load again?" shouted Bostock, regardless of his wound. He caught up a heavy piece of timber, which shattered the stout boards at a blow, and was about to mount to the attack, followed by his comrades, when a volley of musketry was suddenly poured in, which stretched two or three more of the banditti on the ground, and a voice was heard calling them to surrender, or no quarter would be shown.

Vander Heyden and his companions leaped from the waggon to shake hands with Margetts and Evetts, who, with a couple of dozen of his men, had now completely surrounded the robbers, nearly all of whom indeed were either killed or wounded. But the danger was not entirely at an end, as they had supposed. Bostock had been pierced by a second bullet, and it was plain that he had received his death-wound. But his fierce spirit still bore him up. He heard Evetts' challenge with a scornful laugh.

"Surrender?" he cried. "Not I, at all events. I believe I am done for this time, but there is still some fight left in me. Henryk Vander Heyden, I told you I should one day return your fire; there is time to do so yet."

He raised himself with difficulty, and, levelling his revolver, fired at his antagonist, who was only a few feet from him. With fell satisfaction he noted that the shot had taken effect. Then he fell back and expired without a groan.

Chapter Nineteen

"Are you much hurt?" cried Rivers, rushing up to Vander Heyden and raising him, while Hardy supported him on the other side.

"I don't know, I hardly felt it," he answered. "I don't think it struck the ribs."

"We must get his coat off and stop the bleeding," said Hardy. "If you will hold him, I will unfasten the coat. Bring the lantern closer."

"Leave him to me, sir," said a voice behind. "I know something of surgery, as a man has need to do who lives in this country."

Both Rivers and Hardy turned round in great surprise. The speaker was Mr Prestcott.

"Ah, you wonder to see me here! I had no intention of leaving home when we parted, but I was summoned to Heidelberg two days afterwards, and was on my way to Mr Evetts when Mr Margetts met me. We must cut the coat away. If the wound is where I suspect, it would give him great pain to take it off his shoulders. Ah, I thought so," he continued when the sleeve had been cut away and the shoulder had been laid bare. "You have had a narrow escape, sir. The bullet struck the cartridge-belt which was hanging round your neck, and glanced off, passing out through the fleshy part under the arm-pit, just missing the rib. But it is a nasty wound too. You will have to lie quite quiet for some time, and be careful that the bleeding does not burst out again. There must be some proper person to nurse him."

"His sister, Miss Vander Heyden, is here, sir," said Rivers. "She is in the waggon yonder. She does not know anything about this yet."

"You had better go and warn her," said Mr Prestcott; "then we will carry him to the waggon."

His instructions were obeyed. Annchen was of course terribly distressed, but repressed her emotion, and instantly set about the necessary preparations. The boxes were removed from the waggon, and as soft a bed as possible made upon the floor of dried grass and reeds, over which several rugs were laid. The waggon fortunately stood in a sheltered place under two large trees, whither it had been moved to render it as secure from attack as possible. Annchen and Rose undertook the nursing; and Mr Prestcott engaged to send over the necessary medicines from Heidelberg.

"He must be kept as quiet as possible, remember. I suppose there are enough here," glancing round as he spoke at the Hottentot servants, as well as at Matamo and Haxo, "to secure him against disturbance or attack."

"There will be no further fear of attack," said George, to whom this remark appeared to be addressed. "This wretched Bostock is dead, and all the rest of the gang have either been killed or are prisoners. Stay, though," he added; "I see Gott is prisoner, and Van Ryk was hanged at Rorke's Drift; but I am afraid Sullivan has escaped."

"It will be a pity if he has," remarked Lieutenant Evetts. "I hear at Heidelberg that the whole gang has been for months past the pest of the neighbourhood."

"Sullivan has not escaped," said Margetts; "I can account for him. He had been set to watch for me as I returned to the camp, and pick me off, I suppose; but he fell into his own trap."

"Ha, that must have been the shot, then, that we heard," said Rivers. "What made you so long in returning, Redgy? We were getting alarmed."

"Well, I missed the track," said Margetts, "and had ridden past Heidelberg. By good luck I met Mr Prestcott, who was riding in to see Mr Evetts, and he took me with him. It was after all no loss of time, I believe, for he knew where to find Evetts, which I did not. And during our ride to Heidelberg, he told me something, George, which you will be interested to hear. But first I will tell you about Sullivan. Evetts got his men together, and Mr Prestcott volunteered to come with us, wanting to identify some of the gang, who had more than once stolen his property. When we got within a mile or two Evetts scattered his men, and told them to move up with as little noise as possible. One of them in this manner got past Sullivan without being seen by him. He chanced to look back, and saw Sullivan just levelling his gun at me, and he anticipated the shot by sending a bullet through the back of his skull. He was lying dead by the roadside when I passed, and I recognised him as Sullivan, notwithstanding his disguise."

"Talking of his disguise," observed Rivers, "I wonder where they got the soldiers' uniforms from. I know there are fellows among them who are clever enough at staining Europeans so as to look like natives; but how did they come by the uniforms?"

"That is a question easily enough answered," remarked Lieutenant Evetts, who had now joined the party. "The Zulus stripped soldiers enough at Isandhlwana to fit out a regiment or two, and for months afterwards they were to be had for anything the Zulus could get for them. But I must say the get-up, on the whole, was not bad."

"No," assented Hardy; "and the fellows who wore the uniforms had all, I fancy, been really in the army at one time or another. Certainly the corporal had."

"Yes," said Rivers. "When I first spoke with the man I thought I knew his face, and probably I had seen him in the ranks. That was one of the circumstances that for a long time prevented me from entertaining any suspicion."

"By-the-bye, George," said Margetts, "I have forgotten to ask you how you discovered Bostock. I thought, as I told you, there was something strange about the party, but did not suspect Bostock was among them, and his disguise was so perfect that I can hardly believe he is the fellow lying dead yonder. There was no time to ask you when you sent me off to Heidelberg; but I should like to ask you how you recognised him."

"It was your remark and his limp that first made me suspect him," said George. "He has always limped since he received the wound on board the *Zulu Queen*. I happened to know he had received another wound a few months since—a bullet-wound on the wrist. I went and stood close at hand while the pretended corporal was putting the handcuffs again on the prisoners' wrists; and there was the scar of the wound plain enough. I saw Bostock glance suspiciously at me, as he saw I was scrutinising his wrist, and I had some trouble to keep myself from showing that I had discovered him. But you were saying, Redgy, that Mr Prestcott had told you something which I should be interested to hear. May I ask what it was?"

"Well, Mr Rivers," said Prestcott, "it was simply that I am well acquainted with your mother. In the course of my business I make frequent journeys to Zeerust, and know old Ludwig Mansen and his family quite well. I was there not many weeks ago. It is odd that his name did not come up in the course of our conversation about Zeerust. I did not particularly notice yours, or it would certainly have done so. You wrote to her some time ago, did you not?"

"Yes," said George, "eight or nine months ago; but I have never received any reply to my letter."

"Ah, I supposed so. The man to whom you gave it was several months in getting to Umtongo, which was the name of Mansen's farm. Then she could get no messenger to carry her reply for several weeks, and it must have reached Rorke's Drift somewhere about the beginning of June. But it appeared you had left the Natal Volunteers, and it was thought you were going to join some other corps; but that was not known for certain. She is in a terrible state of alarm now, that you have been killed at Ginghilovo, or Ulundi, or one of the smaller battles."

"Well, her anxiety will soon be relieved now," observed Margetts.

"I trust so. But in that case Mr Rivers must not wait to accompany Mr Vander Heyden to Zeerust Mr Vander Heyden cannot be moved for three weeks, and then he must travel very slowly. I do not suppose he can get to his destination under a month, at the very earliest."

"Of course I shall not wait for that," said Rivers. "I shall ride across country, if I can find a guide. I suppose it will not occupy very long, Mr Prestcott?"

"No, sir. Your horse, if that is your horse yonder, would take you there in four days—probably in three, but certainly in four."

"And as for a guide," interposed Hardy, "you will not find a better in all the Transvaal than Matamo. He knows the whole of this country as well as I know the paths about my own farm. I am sorry that I myself cannot remain here; I have another engagement to fulfil at Newcastle. But I will undertake to return before Mr Vander Heyden can reach Zeerust. Meanwhile Mr Margetts will stay here and look after the party."

"Must that be so?" asked George. "I should have liked Redgy to accompany me."

"It must be, I am afraid," said Hardy. "I am sorry that my engagement must be kept."

"I am sorry too," said Margetts; "but of course we cannot leave Vander Heyden here alone. When shall you set out, George?"

"To-morrow, if Matamo is prepared," was the answer. "But we must lie down now and take some rest. The dawn must be close at hand."

"I shall return with my party and the prisoners at once," said Lieutenant Evetts; "and I suppose you also, Mr Prestcott, will accompany me."

"Yes," said Mr Prestcott. "The medicines and lint ought to be sent out at once."

They parted, and our travellers, lying down, took some hours' repose. Then George summoned Matamo, and inquired of him whether he knew the way to Umtongo, and would undertake to guide him thither.

"The way to Umtongo," repeated Matamo. "I know it quite well. I have been there two, three times. I could ride it in the dark."

"That's all right, then," said George.

"Yes, sir; we can get there in three days,—Koodoo's Vley one day, Malapo's Kloof two days, Umtongo three days. But they will be long days."

"Then had we not better start at once?"

"Yes, sir, or we shall not reach Koodoo's Vley to-night. I will go and get everything ready."

In two hours they set off, the Bechuana appearing to be in high spirits. The track he pursued led through a country wilder than any George had yet seen. It ran for some miles along the banks of a small but most picturesque stream, the banks of which were clothed with trees of every variety. The mimosa predominated, but it was intermingled with date-trees and Kaffir plums and huge cacti, with their swordlike leaves, and acacias already coming into flower. Overhead hoopoes and parrots kept up a never-ending chorus, while countless tribes of monkeys and squirrels leaped and chattered among the branches. Occasionally there sprang up, with the whirring noise so familiar to the sportsman, a covey of red-brown partridges. Notwithstanding that they were well supplied with provisions, George's instinct could not forego the opportunity. He let fly right and left with both barrels. Two partridges dropped dead just in front of them, while others flew off wounded. Matamo dismounted and secured them, and they proved a most appetising addition to their supper when they halted a few hours after.

"How far are we from Koodoo's Vley?" said Rivers, as he leaned back against the sloping bank, after having made a delicious meal.

"Koodoo's Vley? About three hours' ride. Give the horses a long rest, and we shall get there before the moon goes down."

George relapsed into thought. The excitement of the last few hours had left no time for reflection, but now the recollection of what had passed between himself and Annchen came vividly back. He had long felt assured that, notwithstanding the distance at which he had always been kept from her, she was not indifferent to him, but now he had had a distinct assurance to that effect from her lips. For a moment the doubt crossed him whether, in the few hurried words he spoke to her before the attack, he had not in some measure broken his promise to Vander Heyden. There had been little time for reflection, and his had been dictated by a sudden impulse. But no. He felt sure it had not been so. His promise to Vander Heyden had been that he would not ask her to be his wife, and he had not asked her. Doubtless she would expect him to follow up his declaration by a formal offer, but it must rest with her brother whether that must be made. On the whole, he had good hope, when he recalled the particulars of Vander Heyden's interview with him, that he would withdraw his opposition. At all events, there was no need to be down-hearted about it, and perhaps the less his thoughts rested upon it the better.

He turned to Matamo, who was sitting on the other side of the fire, sorely disturbed, apparently, at the long silence to which George's reverie had consigned him. He responded at once to George's advances, who inquired of him whether he had known Mr Prestcott before he met him a few days previously.

"Do I know Mr Prestcott? Yes, sir, I have known him a long time. Very good Baas, is Mr Prestcott. He tells pretty stories."

"More pretty than true, hey, Matamo?" suggested George. "Did you hear his story about the lion and the powder-flask?"

"Yes, sir; I have heard that more than once. It gets nicer every time it is told. Mr Hardy, too, he tells a nice story about the cobra in the tree, but not so nice as my story about the big boa."

"Your story—an adventure of your own, like the leap off the hippopotamus's head, eh? Let us hear it by all means, Matamo."

"Yes, sir. It happened a great many years ago. I had been sent on an errand to the Kasal Mountains. A fat old Dutchman seized me, and would not believe my story, but made a slave of me. If I said a word, he tied me up to the cart-wheel and flogged me with the jambok. One day he sent me after an ox that had strayed. He was always afraid that I should run away, and if I was any time out, came to meet me with the jambok ready in his hand. I couldn't find the ox anywhere, but I thought I saw something moving in a thick bush, and I fancied it might be the stray beast. I forced my way inside, and trod on what I thought was the end of a log. But it was a great boa, not a log. The boa put up its head and was going to spring; but I ran like a springbok, and the boa after me. I never went so fast in my life, but the boa went faster. Just on the edge of the wood, I saw the fat Dutchman coming with the whip. When the Dutchman saw the boa, he too turned and ran. But I ran faster than the Dutchman anyhow. The boa thought he was better eating than a lean Bechuana boy, and he caught him round the waist and twisted himself all about him. The Dutchman was so big that the boa only went twice round him. He bellowed for help so loud that every one could hear him, so there was no need for me to tell them."

"What did you do then, Matamo?"

"I ran away as fast as I could, and went home to Mr Baylen."

"I suppose the Dutchman was killed, wasn't he?"

"Yes, sir. The big snake ground him up like corn in a mill,—jambok and all," added Matamo significantly.

"Well, you must tell that story to Mr Prestcott and Mr Hardy. I don't think either of them could beat it."

"Ah, but I had another escape, from a rhinoceros, closer than that," said the Bechuana, evidently much gratified at George's approval.

"Closer than that!" said George. "It must have been a near one, then, indeed. Let us hear it, by all means."

"It was in the rocky country above Standerton," said Matamo. "I was hunting, and had to climb some steep crags two or three hundred feet high, and in some places as steep as a wall. I got to the top, and sat down to rest under a small tree that grew close to the edge of the precipice. Presently I got up and went on to the wood, where there were plenty of elands and antelopes. All of a moment a big female rhinoceros broke out and ran at me. I put up my gun and hit her just in the right place, and she dropped. I was going to load again, when I saw close behind her the male rhinoceros, and he made a rush at me. There was no time to load. I threw my gun away, and ran for it as hard as I could. But the precipice was right in front, and no room to turn to the right or the left. The rhinoceros is very swift of foot. He was close behind me as I approached the edge. I thought we should both go over together, but just at the last moment I seized the bole of the tree and swung myself round. The rhinoceros couldn't catch hold of the tree, and couldn't stop himself. Over he went in a moment, and I heard him strike the ground three hundred feet down. I went below and took a look at him. He was smashed to atoms."

"That was a close shave too," said George. "But come, Matamo, it is time we were off again. The horses must be fully rested."

They remounted, and proceeded for several hours. But for some reason they did not make good progress. The horse ridden by the Bechuana appeared to be completely tired out, and could with difficulty be urged to an easy trot. The moon had set while they were still fully three miles from Koodoo's Vley, and Matamo declared it would not be safe to proceed further that night.

He off-saddled his horse with more care than usual, and, instead of knee-haltering and turning him out to graze as usual, secured him by a headstall under the shelter of some trees, and brought him some grass and water. But the animal, though it drank thirstily, seemed unable to eat, and presently lay down, too much exhausted, apparently, by its day's journey to stand.

"Bad job this, Mr Rivers," said Matamo, after carefully noting the horse's condition.

"What do you think is the matter with him?" inquired Rivers.

"The horse-sickness, sir. I've been afraid of it for an hour or two, but there is no doubt of it now. It is less common at this time of the year, but it happens sometimes."

"Can't anything be done?" asked George. "I know this horse-sickness is a strange malady, which no one seems to understand. But is there really no cure for it?"

"None that I have ever heard of," was the answer. "Yes, he's getting worse. He'll die; nothing can cure him."

"Has he been bitten by the tsetse, do you think?" asked George.

"The tsetse? no, sir. The tsetse is not found here; there is no mistake about it, where it is found. I know it well, and its buzz too. It is certain to kill any horse it attacks, or ox either."

"Doesn't it hurt a man, then?" inquired George.

"It never bites a man, or a donkey, or a mule. But what this poor brute has is the horse-sickness, and nobody knows either the cause or the cure of that."

An hour or two afterwards Matamo's predictions were verified. As the darkness came on, the poor brute's malady got worse. Its flanks heaved; it drew its breath with ever-increasing difficulty; its tongue lolled from the jaws, which were tightly clenched on it. Then violent convulsions came on, and it expired.

"What is to be done now, Matamo? Can you go on with me on foot?" asked George. "We could ride alternately, you know; of course we should not go nearly as fast, but we should get there in time."

"I am very sorry, Mr Rivers, but I can't go. Mr Baylen wants me back. I must have returned to Horner's Kraal the very day after the party reached Lichtenberg."

George remembered that Mr Baylen, while they were at Colenso, had told him that the time of the year when he could never spare Matamo was the spring. At the time when he made George the offer of the Bechuana's services, there had been no idea of the journey to Zeerust being delayed so long. He felt, therefore, that he ought not to urge Matamo to remain longer with him. But, on the other hand, if he returned to Heidelberg with Matamo, and obtained another guide, at least a week would be lost. Knowing his mother's anxiety and distress, he was most unwilling to protract them. Besides, he could remain only a certain time at Umtongo, and he would not cut that any shorter, if he could help it.

"Do you think I could find my way by myself, Matamo, if you gave me full directions?" he asked.

"I am not able to say that, sir. I will tell you the way as well as I can. But if you go on to Koodoo's Vley, you will find the Kaffirs' kraal, which is close to it, and they will show you the way to Mansen's farm, if you pay them money. The Kaffirs will go anywhere for money, and they know the place well."

With this George was obliged to be contented, and, having obtained the most minute directions as regarded the road to Koodoo's Vley, which lay only two miles off, he said goodbye to the Bechuana on the following morning and rode off alone. There was no difficulty in finding his way, Matamo's directions having been very clear, and the landmarks easy to find. He proceeded, however, cautiously, and in about two hours reached the Vley, which he clearly enough recognised, as well as the Kaffir kraal, standing, as Matamo had described it, on the banks of a small stream and in an open glade surrounded by a wood. But, to his great disappointment, it was wrecked and deserted. Either there had been a quarrel with some hostile tribe, or a Dutch commando had been sent against it. But, whichever may have been the case, all its inhabitants were gone. George searched all round, but could nowhere find one single Kaffir.

He was now greatly troubled. Relying on Matamo's assurance of meeting with a guide, he had not even taken any instructions from him as to the way to his mother's house. He only knew in a general way that it lay to the north-west. He would at once have ridden back and endeavoured to overtake Matamo, but he reflected that the Bechuana, being now on foot, would probably take a shorter way to Heidelberg, which he had been unable to follow while on horseback. There was only, in fact, the alternative of going on, in what he knew must be at least the right direction, or return to the town. After a long debate, he determined on the former course. He took out his pocket compass, and turned his horse's head directly to the north-west.

He rode on for seven or eight hours, and presently the aspect of the country changed. An open stretch of veldt succeeded to the mingled forest and scrub and jungle through which he had been passing. The grass grew up to his horse's hocks, and in some places up to its shoulder. Suddenly there came a rush through the grass, and a hartebeest, closely pursued by a pack of wild dogs, rushed by him George had not hitherto come much into contact with these creatures, which, however, are to be found in large numbers in these regions. They are curious animals, more resembling hyenas than dogs, though the specially distinctive mark of the hyena, the drooping off at the hind-quarters, is not to be found in them. But in the stripe, and the bushy tail, and the peculiar-shaped ear, they closely resemble the hyena. They are not so cowardly as the last-named creatures, and are in consequence more dangerous to encounter.

The hartebeest was evidently almost exhausted. It was not likely that it could run another mile; and George, who had omitted to take any provision with him, expecting to get his dinner at the Kaffir kraal, resolved to follow and rescue the carcase from the wild dogs, whom a shot from his rifle would probably disperse, or, at all events, keep at a distance, while he cut off the meat he required. He spurred his horse accordingly, and started in pursuit. But the ground was soft, and for some time he gained but little on his quarry. The hartebeest held on with more vigour than he had expected, and at last, when he had got within distance, a sudden stumble of his horse caused him altogether to miss his mark. He was obliged to stop and reload, and the ground thus lost was difficult to regain. It was not until after a full hour's pursuit that he saw the hartebeest, unable to go any further, at last turn round in despair and face his enemies. Rivers had now sufficient time to take aim at the leader of the pack with his first barrel, and the hartebeest with the second. Both shots were successful. The hartebeest dropped instantly, with a ball through its heart, and the dog rushed off with a yell of pain, falling dead before it had gone a hundred yards. But the rest of the troop did not take to flight, as George had expected. Probably the pursuit of the prey had been stimulated by hunger, which now rendered them insensible to danger. After a moment's hesitation they rushed on the carcase, while one or two, bolder than the rest, sprang on his horse, from which he had alighted to drive off the dogs with his hunting-knife. Terrified at the attack, the steed broke loose from George's hold, galloping off at full speed, and pursued by the greater part of the pack. George shouted and endeavoured to follow, but became instantly aware of the hopelessness of the attempt. The horse was already a hundred yards off, galloping at the utmost of its speed, in the hope of distancing its pursuers. The darkness, too, was rapidly coming on. It would plainly be impossible for him to recover his horse that night, as it would presently be too dark to discern any objects at a distance. He must provide himself as well as he was able with food and shelter for the night. Hastily reloading, he first rid himself of the two or three dogs that were busily engaged in mangling the body of the hartebeest. Next with his hunting-knife he cut down a quantity of bushes, part of which he piled up as a shelter against the wind, which began to blow with some sharpness as the dusk came on. The rest of the wood he set alight by the help of the matches in his belt, and presently succeeded in kindling a tolerable fire. Then he cut off some meat from the carcase of the hartebeest, of which there was a good deal left, notwithstanding the ravages of the dogs. By these means, and by obtaining water from a clear rivulet, which he found flowing at a little distance, he contrived to satisfy his hunger and thirst. He sat down in the shelter which he had provided for himself, and looked up at the sky above him. It was a delicious night. The constellations of the Southern Hemisphere are not in themselves as beautiful, as those with which we of the northern regions are familiar. But their liquid brilliancy, seen against the background of the deepest blue, renders the general aspect of the heavens far more lovely and imposing. The sense also of entire loneliness came upon him with profound solemnity. He was here far—he knew not how far— from all human help and sympathy. Whatever good or evil fortune might befall him was his concern and his only. The utter helplessness of man so situated impressed him painfully. We seldom realise the full meaning of passages of Holy Writ until some striking circumstance of our lives bring them home to us, and George felt for the first time how profound a meaning was contained in these words: "It is not good for man to be alone."

Chapter Twenty

George awoke chilled and cramped with the night air, and was preparing leisurely to get up and commence the search after his missing steed, when his eye lit on an object a few feet of him, which caused him instantly to leap to his feet. A snake, which had probably been attracted to the spot during the night by the warmth of his fire, was just raising its head, as if preparing to dart upon him, spitting venom at the same time from its open jaws. His rapid backward spring just enabled him to avoid its fangs. But some of the poison had been spurted on to his face, and he instantly felt a sharp sting of pain. His first act was to crush the head of the reptile with his heel, and then to sever its neck with his knife. It was of a dark brown, almost a black colour, and six or seven feet long. George had never seen one of the kind before, but recognised it from the descriptions that had been given him as the picakholu, the most venomous, it was said, of any known serpent, and called by the natives the "spitting snake." George noticed that the fangs were still distilling poison in a considerable quantity, notwithstanding that the neck had been completely severed. He felt a good deal of pain in the places where the poison had fallen, and especially in the white of the left eye. He hurried to the spring, which was fortunately only at a short distance, and, kneeling down, plunged his head again and again into the water, hoping in that manner to get rid of the painful smart. This gave him some slight relief, and he hoped that, as no poison could have mixed with his blood, the pain would gradually wear itself out.

The first thing, of course, was to find his horse. He had hoped that if it had succeeded in shaking off the wild dogs, it would return to the spring to drink. But though he did not doubt that it would soon outstrip them, they having been evidently completely exhausted by the long previous chase, there might be water nearer to the point at which the animal found itself after its escape, and in that case of course it would make for it. Taking up his gun, he began following the track of the animal's hoofs, which were clear enough to be traced in the soft grass of the veldt. After an hour's search, the grass was exchanged for a long arid stretch of sand, diversified by scrub and stone. Here the hoofs of the horse and the lighter prints of the dogs' feet were still more plainly to be distinguished. The sand became looser and looser as he advanced. It was evident that the horse must have grown rapidly more exhausted, as its feet plunged almost to the fetlock at every step. At last he came upon the carcase of the animal itself, which had evidently been torn down by the pack and devoured. There had plainly been a furious struggle, one or two of the dogs having been killed by the dying efforts of the horse.

Rivers was now seriously alarmed. He must retrace his steps as well as he was able to the spring, and seek again to relieve the burning pains in his face, which under the scorching heat of the sun stung him more sharply than even at first. Then he must make his way on foot, keeping as before to the north-west, and hope to fall in with some traveller, or reach the shelter of some friendly habitation. He was well aware that, if all these chances failed him, his life on earth would soon be ended. He began his return across the sandy waste, and, after several hours of painful exertion, succeeded in reaching the spring, by the side of which he sank down completely exhausted. Long and copious draughts somewhat restored him; and as the cool of the evening came on, he got up and resumed his journey, making another meal before he started on what remained of his morning's repast. He walked on for a mile or two, leaning on his gun, and hardly sensible of the objects round him. At last he got to a part of the wood where the trees seemed to have been cut away, and a broader path, almost approaching to a road, cut out. He staggered for some distance along this track, and then his senses completely deserted him, and he dropped to the ground, his gun going off as he fell, though happily without injury to himself.

When he opened his eyes again, he looked around him with great surprise. He was lying on a comfortable bed, in a tolerable-sized room; which, though different in many respects from any chamber he had hitherto occupied, was nevertheless evidently of European construction. There was a sash window, looking out, so far as George could distinguish, upon a garden. The walls were of plank, planed and fitted together with some neatness; the floor of mud, beaten hard and smeared with cow-dung. There were no tables or chairs, no chests of drawers, or washing apparatus, but there was a bench and one or two solid chests. The bed itself was tolerably clean, and there were sheets, but of coarse material. By his side, on a shelf, were a tea-cup and spoon and several bottles.

With some difficulty he recalled the incidents which had taken place previously to his fainting fit, — the poison spirted on his face by the snake, his search after his horse, and his subsequent journey through the wood. But all seemed dim and confused, and as if it had taken place a long while ago. He lay thinking for a long time, or rather in a state of half consciousness, in which dream and reality were blended together. Then he closed his eyes and again fell asleep, waking up a second time, also to his confused fancy after a long period of inaction. He found himself lying on the same bed and in the same room, but this time he was not alone. There was an old man sitting by his bedside and watching him apparently with some curiosity. He was a Dutchman,—that was plain from his physiognomy alike and his dress,—and probably a man of some substance. His clothes were of the usual material, but of a good quality, and had not been much worn. His features were rather harsh, but not repulsive, and his demeanour quiet and self-possessed. He noticed the change in George's appearance, and proceeded to express his satisfaction in English, which was not quite idiomatic, but nevertheless was intelligible.

"The Englishman is better; is he able to talk?"

"Thank you, I feel much better," said George. "Will you please to tell me where I am, and how I came here?"

"I heard your gun, and found you in a swoon. This is my house; it is called Malopo's Kloof."

"I am very thankful," said George. "How long have I been ill?"

"It is more than five weeks since I found you—five weeks last Monday."

"Five weeks!" repeated George, becoming dimly conscious of strange, wild scenes, among which he seemed to have passed an immeasurable period of time,—gallops over interminable plains, struggles with armed assassins, writhings of wounded snakes, and the like phantasmagoria of a sick fancy, succeeding and intermingling with one another. "Five weeks! Have I had a fever?"

"A marsh fever, and a very bad one. I thought several times the Englishman would die," said the old man.

"And who has been my doctor?" inquired Rivers, only able to recall two figures that were not quite shadowy and unreal,—the figure of the man before him, and another younger than he. "Who have been my doctor and my nurse?"

"You have had no doctor: there is none in these parts. Rudolf and I nursed you," was the answer. "We put on cool bandages and gave you cool drinks—nothing else."

"And I have to thank you for my life then!" exclaimed George, feebly stretching out his hand, and becoming aware for the first time how thin and wasted it had become.

"We could not let the Englishman die," said the old man simply. "But you must be quiet—you are not strong enough to talk." Putting a glass containing some mixture which tasted deliciously cool and refreshing to his lips, the Dutchman now withdrew, and Rivers was soon once more buried in slumber.

He woke again after a long interval, feeling stronger, and so went on for a week or two more, gaining strength continually, until at last he was permitted to get up and sit for an hour in the garden, which was now in the prime of its beauty and luxuriance. Mynheer Kransberg—that he presently discovered to be his host's name—had been one of the earliest settlers in the Transvaal, long before the country bore that name, and when it was only inhabited by the native tribes. He had been quite a young man, though possessed of good means, when the Dutch first broke out into resistance to the English rule. Aware of the hopelessness of rebellion, and unwilling to take part against his countrymen, he had withdrawn with a considerable following of his own dependants into the then unknown regions lying to the north of the Orange river. Here he had purchased land of one of the native chiefs, built his house, and enclosed his farm, and here he had lived ever since, through all the numerous changes which the country had undergone, paying as little heed to them as if he had belonged to another planet. He had never married, or felt any inclination to do so. He had ridden about his fields, and reared his cattle and sent them to market, and brewed his Dutch beer, year after year, with a placid contentment which is rarely witnessed, even in a Dutchman. If he was indolent he was at all events extremely good-tempered, and his oldest servants scarcely ever remembered to have seen him ruffled.

He had lived alone until within the last few years, never seeming to experience the want of a companion. But about two years since his solitude had been broken in upon by the arrival of his nephew, Rudolf Kransberg, a tall, gawky youth of two-and-twenty, who came to claim his help and protection. His father, a merchant in Graham's Town, had died insolvent, and his son, calling to mind for the first for a great many years his uncle in the Transvaal, had made a journey hither, in the hope of gaining a kind reception. In that he had not been disappointed. The old man heard of his arrival, and of the misfortunes which had befallen his brother, without exhibiting the smallest emotion, but at the same time he gave the young man shelter and maintenance, allowed him, in fact, to live in his house, treating him in all respects as though he had been his own son. Rudolf, who in many respects resembled his relative, accepted the situation with equal complaisance, and they had now lived together two years in perfect contentment, not a word having been exchanged between them as to the older man's disposal of his property or the younger one's prospects in life, till within the last few weeks, when Rudolf had consulted his uncle on the subject of a marriage which he was anxious to contract.

The two were sitting in the garden in a Dutch summer-house which old Kransberg had run up with his own hands some forty years before. It was generally thought that the old man liked the society of his nephew, and especially during the smoking of the evening pipe, though he never expressed any feeling to that effect, or, indeed, to any effect whatsoever, unless compelled by absolute necessity. He was therefore somewhat surprised when one evening Rudolf took his pipe from his lips, and after rolling out a long puff of smoke, addressed his uncle.

"My uncle, there is something I would ask you. May I speak?"

The old man similarly removed his pipe, emitting a corresponding puff, and then answered briefly, "Ya."

"My uncle, I am four-and-twenty."

He paused, but his uncle not considering this to require a verbal acknowledgment, only nodded.

"My uncle, it is time I was married."

This apparently was regarded as calling for a reply. The pipe accordingly was again removed, and Mynheer inquired "Whom?"

"Thyrza Rivers."

Another long silence followed this communication, after which the old man remarked, "Englishwoman."

"True," assented the nephew, roused by his feelings to unusual prolixity of speech; "but she has always been bred up in our ways. And her father-in-law is a good man."

Old Kransberg again gave an affirmative nod. "Go over and ask her," he said.

Rudolf nodded in his turn, and so the conversation ended.

It was on the day following this that Mynheer Kransberg, as he was proceeding after supper to smoke his usual pipe in the summer-house, was startled by the discharge of a gun at a short distance. As the reader has heard, the country had been for some time infested by bands of ruffians, who committed great depredations in the neighbourhood. The old man's first idea was to summon his servants and send them out to see after the marauder, but, casting his eyes along the road, he saw the figure of a man lying prostrate, having apparently been shot. Straightway he summoned two of his Hottentots and desired them to bring the wounded man or his body, as the case might be, into the house. It was soon discovered that there was no wound, but the stranger had a dangerous attack of fever of some kind, and was in imminent danger of his life. Without more words he had him consigned to the bed in his guest-chamber, where he and his nephew nursed him with all possible kindness, until he had recovered his consciousness, as the reader has heard, and appeared to be in a fair way of recovery. George soon made acquaintance with both uncle and nephew. No great effort, indeed, was necessary to form such an acquaintance. All that was required was to sit still and smoke, exchanging, it might be, two words in the course of every hour. During all this time Rudolf's courtship had been held in abeyance. As it was necessary for him to stop at home and assist his uncle in nursing, it was not possible he could be spared to ride over twenty miles to Umtongo. If the swain had been a Frenchman or an Italian, or even an Englishman, it might have been argued that his attachment to the lady was not a very ardent one. But that would have been to mistake the case. Rudolf was very sincere in his devotion, and was anxious that his visit should not be delayed any longer, and he had ordained in his own mind that he would set forth on his errand the following day, when he was greatly startled by a question which his guest put to him.

George had been sitting, as the reader has heard, in his host's garden, enjoying the scent of the delicious flowers, when he saw Rudolf Kransberg advancing towards him. The young Dutchman bestowed a nod upon him, his usual greeting, and then, sitting down on the bench beside him, lighted his pipe and began to smoke. Presently George inquired whether Rudolf could tell him of a farmhouse in that neighbourhood called Umtongo, the residence of a farmer named Ludwig Mansen.

Rudolf was so startled that he actually dropped his pipe. He stooped, however, to pick it up again, before he repeated the words, "Umtongo! Ludwig Mansen!"

"Yes," said George, supposing that his companion did not understand him. "I was on my way to his house when I was taken ill. The farm must lie at no very great distance. Perhaps you may be able to tell me where it is."

"You going there!" ejaculated Rudolf with more animation.

"Yes, I was going there, and I want to go there now."

"It will not be fit for you to go for a long time yet," returned the Dutchman, relapsing into silence, from which he could only be roused to make monosyllabic replies. A minute or two afterwards, indeed, chancing to see his uncle in the distance, he got up and went to join him.

George was perplexed, but the demeanour of his hosts had puzzled him from the first. He saw, however, that they meant kindly by him, and supposed that Rudolf was simply afraid that he might bring on a relapse by venturing on a long ride in his present weak condition. He knew, indeed, he was not fit to make the attempt yet. Impatient, therefore, as he was to rejoin his mother and sister, he resolved to remain quiet for a few days more. He was more ready to do this, because he felt his strength returning to him every day, and it was evident from Rudolf's manner that his stepfather's house lay at no great distance.

He was a good deal surprised when, on the following evening, Rudolf Kransberg, who had been absent all day, returned to Malopo's Kloof, but with a companion. He was sitting alone in the arbour, the time for old Kransberg's pipe having not yet arrived, when a well-known figure suddenly presented itself, and the voice of Redgy Margetts greeted him.

"Hooray, old fellow! this is glorious indeed! Why, here have we been scouring the country for you for weeks past, and your mother and Thyrza— your mother and your sister," added Redgy, correcting himself, "have put off going into mourning for you day after day, only because they couldn't bear to think you were dead. And here have you been alive all the time, only twenty miles from us. Old Kransberg, they say, never holds any intercourse with his neighbours, and it must be so, or he must have heard of the hue and cry that has been raised. Matamo had gone back to Horner's Kraal, and we only heard from some people in Heidelberg of his having parted company with you somewhere near Koodoo's Vley. We searched the whole country, Hardy and Haxo and I, and some of Ludwig Mansen's men, and we found at last the skeleton of your horse; we knew it by your saddle. And by the spring, where it was quite clear you had camped for the night, there were the remains of one of the most venomous snakes in the country. We were afraid you had been bitten by it, and had staggered somewhere into the bush and died. There would have been small chance for you, they said, if it had bitten you. But it doesn't matter, happily, what we thought, only I should like to know if you are able to tell me the true history of the matter."

"You shall hear presently," said George. "But first of all I want to know about my mother. Is she looking well?"

"Well, I never saw her before, you know," said Redgy, "and of course she has been in great distress about you; but as regards looks, I'm sure she's an extremely handsome woman, and she will soon now be at her best again. You should have seen what a difference there was in her when we found out all about you from young Kransberg."

"Young Kransberg," repeated George. "I supposed he guessed the truth, then, from what I told him yesterday, and rode over to tell you about me."

"Hem! no," said Margetts shortly; "that wasn't the object of his visit. He didn't know that you were in any way connected with Mrs Mansen—didn't know what your name was indeed. He only mentioned quite casually at dinner that a young Englishman had been found close to his uncle's house, nearly two months ago, who had been seized with a bad attack of marsh fever. We all caught at it at once, and felt almost sure, from his description, that the person of whom he had been speaking must be you. But Mrs Mansen couldn't bear to be kept in suspense a moment, and I offered to ride over here the moment dinner was over; and Rudolf Kransberg," added Redgy with something of a chuckle, "was obliged to accompany me."

"Well!" said Rivers. "But there's plenty more I want to know. I haven't seen my sister since she was quite a child. She must be grown up now."

"Yes, she is grown up," assented Redgy shortly. "And she promised to be pretty?"

"That's a matter of opinion," said Redgy with evident embarrassment. "Some people, I believe, do think her so."

"But you don't, eh?" said George, glancing at him in some surprise. "But never mind that, I shall soon be able to judge for myself. There are other things I want to know about. What has become of—of the Vander Heydens?"

"Oh, they are all right," said Margetts. "Vander Heyden recovered rapidly, and got home in three weeks after the time you left us. Their place is only a few miles from Umtongo. They have been continually over there to see your mother and sister. Miss Vander Heyden and Miss Rivers have struck up a very close friendship, and I must do Vander Heyden the justice to say that nobody has been more active in the search after you than he was."

"He's a good fellow," said George, "though he is a Dutchman, and hates the English, and is as proud as Lucifer into the bargain. Well, and Hardy—what of him?"

"Hardy is at Pieter's Dorf—that's the name of Vander Heyden's place. He has designed a capital house, which they have already begun building. It will go on all the faster now that the search for you is happily over. Well now, it's my turn, George, to ask questions. Do you think you are strong enough to be moved? Mr Mansen proposes to send over his light bullock waggon for you. Of course you couldn't sit in the saddle for twenty miles, and won't be fit to do so for some time yet. But you might be able to bear the motion of the waggon. You look quite as strong as Vander Heyden did, and you haven't so far to go."

"I should think I certainly might," said George. "I don't know whether it is in consequence of seeing you and hearing your good news, but I feel ever so much better than I did this morning."

"Very good," said Margetts. "Then I will ride back at once and tell them to send the waggon. It will take one day to come here, then you can go back the next. That will be the day after to-morrow, you know."

"Very good. I must of course consult my kind host. But I don't fancy he will make any difficulty. We shall have to arrange, also, what I am to pay him for my lodging and nursing. I must have been a considerable expense, as well as trouble to him."

Margetts took his leave, and George went in quest of Mynheer Kransberg, whom he found in his usual seat in his summer-house. He listened in silence to George's proposed arrangements, as well as to his thanks for the great kindness shown him. But when his guest inquired how much money was due for the lodging and attendance he had received. Mynheer Kransberg answered quietly,—

"There is nothing due. This is not an inn."

"I am aware of that," returned Rivers, colouring a little, for he had entertained the idea that all Dutchmen were eager to make any profit in their power, and had spoken accordingly. "But I must have occasioned some considerable outlay, and besides have given your servants and yourself and nephew, a great deal of trouble," he pursued.

"We do not, any of us, grudge it," said the old man in the same tone as before. "We do not want money for doing a simple act of Christian charity. You have rendered me your thanks—that is enough."

"I do indeed render them most heartily," said Rivers, "and I shall never lose the recollection of your generous kindness."

During the journey in Farmer Mansen's ox-waggon, which occupied nearly the whole of the day, he had time to reconsider the opinion which he had formed respecting the Boers, and which had been very much the same that is entertained by Englishmen generally. There is undoubtedly a strong prejudice felt against them. They are believed to be selfish, cold-blooded, and cowardly,—harshly oppressive to the helpless, but descending to falsehood and trickery in their dealings with those whom they dare not openly defy. A good deal of disgust also is felt at the strictness of their religious profession, which is thought to be inconsistent with their harsh and worldly conduct.

That there is some truth in these censures is not to be denied. They have been for many generations slaveholders, and no nation ever yet escaped the degradation which that most odious of all customs entails. Slaveholders become inevitably selfish, unjust, and brutal, and incline to become cowardly also. It is the coward only that oppresses the weak, and they who habitually oppress the weak cannot but become cowards. But the Boers have virtues to which justice has not been done. They are kind-hearted and generous to all except the blacks. No nation exceeds them in industry, in simplicity of life, and in the practice of domestic virtues. The profound respect rendered to parents, the faithful affection subsisting between husband and wife, the anxious care bestowed on their children, the loyal attachment and devotion to their country, might put to shame many who are their severest censors. And their religious profession is sincere enough, however blinded their eyes may have become as regards some obvious Christian duties.

Prayer is offered in almost every Dutch household morning and evening to Almighty God. The Sunday is given up to the strictest religious observances; the periodical communions are punctually and reverently attended. If the curse of slavery could be torn out by the roots, and the natives recognised by them as of equal value with themselves in the sight of Heaven, there would be few worthier races to be found on the face of the earth than they.

Chapter Twenty One

"Here is a letter for you, George," said Mrs Mansen, as the former entered the parlour at Umtongo, about three months after his arrival at his mother's house. "It looks like Mr Rogers' handwriting. But I believe Mr Rogers is still in England."

"It is from him, though," said George when he had finished reading the letter. "He has returned to Dykeman's Hollow—has been there about a fortnight, he says."

"What has made him come back so much sooner than he had intended? He wrote us word that his business in England was prospering, but he would be obliged, he thought, to remain another twelvemonth."

"Ah, but there is, it appears, a total change of things in England. Another Government has come in, and is likely to reverse altogether the policy of the old one. He says, too, that a lot of people have taken up Cetewayo's cause, and declare that he is a very ill-used man, that he never hurt or wronged anybody, and if we had left him alone, he would have left us."

"Do they?" said Mrs Mansen. "I wish some of them had been Cetewayo's neighbours, as we were."

"Well, the upshot is, that Mr Rogers thought it was of no use for him to stay any longer in England, so he has come back. And now he wants me to go back to Dykeman's Hollow, and take up my old work as schoolmaster and teacher."

"Well, I hoped you were going to settle here," said Mrs Mansen. "There is as much need for your services here as there could be at Dykeman's Hollow. And my husband would be willing, as you know, to give you a part of this farm to look after,—quite as large as you could manage,—and to build you a house to live in, or rather, I should say, enlarge the small house at Droopsdorf. Two more rooms would make it a comfortable house."

"He and you are very kind, mother. But, you see, I engaged myself to Mr Rogers, and I ought to keep to my engagement."

"Yes, but that was a year and a half ago, and things have happened since then which make all the difference. Mr Rogers didn't know that we had removed from Spielman's Vley, and that you, by engaging yourself to him, would be, not half an hour's ride from us, but a good week's journey at least, and you didn't know it, and couldn't guess it, either."

"No doubt that is true, mother; and I must allow that if I had known that there would be all the width of the Transvaal between you and me, I shouldn't have made the agreement. But, you see, I did make it."

"Yes, but I don't think Mr Rogers could refuse to cancel it. It would be very unhandsome of him if he did. Then again, I don't suppose he has heard of your long illness. He thinks you have been living with us nearly six months, as Mr Margetts has; whereas for three months, or for two at all events, you didn't come here at all, and for a good month more you were quite an invalid. I haven't had more than two real months of you yet, my dear boy, and after so long a separation,—I may say after what seemed like a recovery of you from the grave—I can't afford to part with you. Isn't that reason, Thyrza?"

"Yes," answered Thyrza. "I think Mr Rogers would at least give you a longer holiday, if he didn't consent to your staying here altogether. I know father thinks so too."

"I am sure I don't want to leave you," said George, looking affectionately at his mother and sister. "I have never been made so happy by anything as by finding you."

Mrs Mansen and her daughter were indeed two relatives of whom any one might be proud. The mother was a little past middle age, but was still strikingly handsome, and though her dress differed in some particulars from that of an English lady, she would have passed muster, both as regards appearance and manners, in good English society. Her daughter nearly resembled her in height and feature; and if the reader could have seen her, he would not have been surprised that even the ponderous Rudolf Kransberg should have been captivated by her charms. She was a lively girl in her nineteenth year, and, as yet, fancy-free. It had never occurred to her that Mynheer Rudolf had viewed her with any sentiment of admiration; and we are afraid that, if the idea had entered her head, it would have had no other effect than that of affording her unmixed amusement.

"And it isn't father only," pursued Thyrza, "who wants you to remain at Umtongo. There's another person—"

"Redgy Margetts, I suppose," interrupted George. "I have no doubt he likes his quarters well enough—"

"Mr Margetts!" broke in Thyrza hastily, and with a little accession of colour; "I wasn't thinking about him. I don't suppose he knows his mind on that subject or any other. No, it is a different person altogether—"

"My dear Thyrza," interposed Mrs Mansen, "there is your father out in the garden, beckoning. He wants you, I am pretty sure. Go out and speak to him."

Thyrza departed, and Mrs Mansen, after a pause of a minute or two, addressed her son in a tone of some embarrassment.

"I am sorry you said that about Mr Margetts," she said—"sorry for two reasons. In the first place, I fancy—if indeed it is only fancy—that he is attracted by Thyrza."

"Redgy is as easily attracted by a handsome girl as a bee is by a honeysuckle," said George; "but his attachment does not generally last much longer."

"I hope you may be right," returned his mother; "but I own I think otherwise. I grant Thyrza either does not see, or does not much care for, his preference. But how long that might continue, I do not know."

"Well, mother, even if it were so, what objection is there to Redgy Margetts? He is a gentleman by birth, well educated, and a capital fellow every way. Thyrza might do much worse."

"No doubt. But he is, I understand, in no position to marry. He is a younger son, with no fortune, only a precarious allowance, and his family would probably be opposed to such a marriage."

"That is true," assented George; "but then Redgy is too honourable a fellow to engage Thyrza's affections, if he did not see his way to marrying her."

"Very likely. He would not intentionally make her fond of him. But he might do so, nevertheless. No, George, it is certainly better that *he* should leave Umtongo; and my idea is that he should go and take your place at Dykeman's Hollow."

"We had both better go," said George. "There is a reason—"

"Yes, I think I understand it," interrupted Mrs Mansen. "And I was going to say I was sorry you introduced Mr Margetts' name, because it led to Thyrza's remark. You would not like her to speak to you on the subject. But may not I do so?"

George again coloured and walked once or twice across the room. Then he spoke.

"I do not affect to misunderstand you, mother. I know to whom Thyrza meant to refer. But—"

"But hear me for a moment, George. I can understand your unwillingness to address Miss Vander Heyden, knowing, as you do, her brother's rooted dislike to the English. But you do not know all that I know. When the brother and sister reached their home, several months ago, we were just beginning to be seriously anxious about you. Rumours reached us, first, that you had been one of a party attacked near Heidelberg, and secondly, that you had left your friends on the day after the attack, and had set out for Umtongo. What had become of you during the last month? Of course we were anxious and alarmed, and the alarm soon spread. Miss Vander Heyden herself came over here to inquire. Her distress had completely broken down all the barriers of reserve. She did not, indeed, tell us of her attachment to you, but it was impossible for us not to see it. After another month of continual inquiry, we were all convinced that you must have perished in the bush. Then Annchen spoke to me—she could not, in fact, keep it to herself. Considering you as no longer belonging to this world, she told me of the vows of affection which had been interchanged between you."

"They never ought to have been," said George. "I was to blame. But I should be still more culpable if I allowed myself to be influenced by what you have told me. It cannot be, and that is all I have to say.

"Yet," he resumed a few minutes afterwards, "I am not sorry that we have had this conversation, painful as it has been. You know now my main reason for wishing to return to Dykeman's Hollow. It has been very nice being with you and Thyrza. But Umtongo is too near Pieter's Dorf for me to fix my residence there. Perhaps, by and by, when she has married and gone away—"

"There is but little chance of her marrying any one, unless it is yourself, George," interposed Mrs Mansen.

"That may be so—I cannot say. But as our wishes can never be fulfilled, it is unwise—indeed, it would be cruel in me, were I to reside where my continual presence must needs be continually thrust upon her."

"Only one word more, George. Is your scruple founded on your want of money? Do you know that Umtongo is my property, not my husband's, and that it will of course one day come to you? I have already said that we would provide you with a house and an income at once. But the future also would be provided for. Mr Vander Heyden could not allege—"

"My scruples, as you term them, have no connection with money. You must urge me no more. I must go, and at once. I shall speak to Margetts without delay," he continued. "He, too, will be sorry to leave Umtongo. But I shall be much surprised if he does not fall in with my suggestion at once."

Meanwhile Thyrza, who had joined her stepfather in the garden, was having an interview with him which altogether took her by surprise. Old Ludwig Mansen—he was always called *old* Ludwig, though he wanted a year or two of fifty—was a man very generally respected and beloved. To the shrewdness of the Dutchman and his placid temper, he added a generosity and unselfishness which are not so common with that people. He was particularly fond of his stepdaughter, and was just now greatly pleased at a piece of information imparted to him a few days before, which he considered to be the best possible thing for her, and of which he was now going to apprise her.

On the previous Monday he had ridden into Zeerust, to attend a meeting convened for the purpose of protesting against the annexation of the Transvaal, which had taken place several years previously, but which had become every year more odious in the eyes of the Boers. At Zeerust, to his great surprise, he had met old Kransberg, who also had ridden in from Malopo's Kloof. Mansen knew that his neighbour cared no more about the annexation than he did himself. Influenced probably by his English connections, he did not regard the rule of Queen Victoria with any aversion, and knew that, although the English might administer the law with little regard to Boer prejudices, they would at least administer it justly. As for old Kransberg, he had seen too many changes of government to care much who governed the country, so long as they maintained law and order. This was so well known to Ludwig, that he could hardly believe his eyes, when, on turning from a bridle path into the road near Zeerust, he fell in with Kransberg leisurely riding along in the same direction.

Zeerust is one of the loveliest spots in the whole of the Transvaal. It lies in a valley nearly surrounded by hills, which rise to a considerable height on the north, east, and south, while towards the west the level plain extends into the far distance, beyond the range of human vision. It differs from many other valleys of the same country in being supplied abundantly with water throughout the entire year. The vegetation is in consequence always of the freshest green, and every kind of tropical fruit and grain is cultivated, and yields a rich return.

The town, into which the neighbours rode, is not large, but consists of solid, substantial houses, with the great Dutch Presbyterian meeting-house towering in its centre. In the market place adjoining, the horses and waggons of the Boers from the neighbourhood were grouped together, while their owners were flocking in to take part in the meeting. Mansen and Kransberg did not join them. At the request of the latter they betook themselves to the principal inn, where, with much solemnity, but no unnecessary expenditure of words, he made his communication to his neighbour. His nephew Rudolf, it appeared, had arrived at the conclusion that a marriage between himself and Ludwig's stepdaughter would be a desirable arrangement, if it could be arrived at, and he desired permission to pay formal addresses to her if agreeable to her parents. Old Ludwig replied, with equal gravity, that he would inform his wife of the proposal, and answer to it should be sent in due season. The two Gerontes then adjourned to the Town Hall, and listened with imperturbable stolidity to the speeches delivered.

Ludwig rode home, as has been intimated, much pleased with what he had heard; but he did not proceed, immediately on his arrival at Umtongo, to pass on the news, as an English parent would probably have done. He took an opportunity, a day or two afterwards, when there was nothing of importance to attend to, of communicating it to his wife. A debate was held, at which it was agreed that a message should be sent to Malopo's Kloof, inviting young Rudolf Kransberg to pay a visit at Umtongo on the following Monday, and that, shortly before his arrival, Thyrza should be apprised of his visit and its purport.

Mrs Mansen therefore had had a twofold object in sending her out of the room: first, to stop her malapropos remarks about Annchen Vander Heyden, and secondly, that she might be informed respecting Rudolf's visit. Thyrza herself, however, did not anticipate any more important communication than that possibly her stepfather had purchased a new dress for her in Zeerust. She was a good deal surprised when he inquired of her what might be her exact age.

"Nineteen last December, father," she answered.

"Nineteen," he repeated gravely; "it is an early age at which to marry."

"I daresay it would be," she answered, somewhat startled; "but then, I am not going to marry."

"You do not know that," he observed gravely. "An offer of marriage has been made for you—in most respects a suitable one."

"An offer of marriage to me!" repeated Thyrza in astonishment.

"I did not say *to* you, but *for* you," he replied; "the offer will not be made to you just yet."

"And who is to make it?" inquired the damsel hastily.

"You know my neighbour, Mynheer Kransberg of Malopo's Kloof?"

"Yes, but I suppose *he* doesn't want to marry me?" cried Thyrza.

"Why, no, my daughter," returned Ludwig with a broad smile; "he is somewhat past the age of matrimony. Nay, it is his nephew Rudolf."

"Rudolf Kransberg!" again exclaimed Thyrza; "*he* wishes to marry me!"

"Even so," rejoined Ludwig. "Does the idea surprise you?"

"I should as soon have expected the wooden soldier outside your summer-house to make love to me!"

"Nay, Thyrza," said Mansen in a displeased tone, "this does not become you. He is a worthy youth, and deserves due consideration."

"Well, but I may tell him, as soon as he comes—I suppose he *is* coming?"

"He comes to-day," answered Ludwig.

"Well, then, I may tell him I can't marry him, and there will be an end of it."

"By no means; matters cannot be settled so hastily. Do you remember that he came over here about three months ago?"

"Oh yes, when we found out that George was at his uncle's house. I remember that quite well."

"Well, it appears that he came over with credentials from his uncle then, intending to address you. But Mr Margetts, not suspecting his purpose, insisted on riding back with him at once. If he had known the object of his visit, Mr Margetts would not have so taken him away."

Not feeling quite so sure of that, Thyrza remained silent for a minute or two, and then rejoined—

"But if he has put off any renewal of his visit for more than three months, he cannot be very much in earnest about this."

"You do not understand our ways. We do not do things in a hurry. No, Thyrza, you must receive him with all consideration, and must not, at all events, reject him before he makes his offer."

"And how long will it be before he makes it?"

"I cannot say; probably some months. He will come over occasionally, at intervals, and then you will receive him in the proper manner."

"And what is the proper manner?" inquired Thyrza, who was growing more and more discomposed at every fresh detail.

"Why, when he arrives, you will of course shake hands with him, and then he will probably say no more to you till after supper. Then he will remain in the parlour; and then you will wait till we are gone to bed, and then go to him—"

"Gracious, father, you are not serious!"

"Perfectly so, Thyrza. The room will be dark, but you will take a piece of candle with you, which you will light; and the interview between you will last until the candle has burned out. Then you will retire to bed, and he will ride home. That is the usual custom."

"And who is to provide the piece of candle?"

"You must do that. But stop a moment, Thyrza. The candle must be sufficiently long to allow of a proper interview. I have heard of young women taking not more than half an inch of candle—"

"I shouldn't have taken a quarter of an inch—" muttered under her breath—"if it had rested with me."

"I must insist that a proper-sized candle is used—not less than three inches long. Your mother will provide it, and place it on your table. And here is the young man coming," he added; "I hear his horse's steps outside."

Thyrza fled to her room, resolved, at all events, not to encounter her swain before supper-time. Meeting George and Redgy an hour or two afterwards, she confided to them her troubles, and implored them at all events to keep her unwelcome suitor engaged until she was obliged to meet him at supper.

"See him while a bit of candle is burning!" exclaimed Margetts, to whom the custom seemed as *outré* as it had to Thyrza. "Why don't you take a bit of candle as thin as a crown-piece? You'd soon have done with him then."

"Ah, I thought of that," said Thyrza; "but they won't allow it. My mother has looked up a piece of candle long enough for an hour and a halfs interview and laid it on my dressing-table. I must take that with me; and however I am to endure an hour and a half of it I cannot think."

"Well, you must make the best of it," said Redgy. "George, I think you had better take her out for a walk till supper-time. I'll go in and entertain the enamoured gentleman, if he requires entertainment."

On entering the parlour, however, it did not appear that the *soupirant* for Thyrza's favour either expected or desired any entertainment. He had duly arrived, looking very stiff and solemn in his new leather and buckram suit, and, after shaking hands with everybody all round, had seated himself in the corner, where he had remained ever since without speaking a word to any one. So he continued the entire afternoon and evening, until the supper-hour arrived, and he took his place at the table with the others, but carefully keeping the whole length and breadth of the table between himself and the object of his affection. Not a syllable did he utter during the meal; and Thyrza had come to believe that he had changed his mind and did not intend to address her, when suddenly, a few minutes before the party broke up for the night, he moved across the room and whispered in her ear, though loud enough for every one to hear, "I say, we'll sit up to-night!"

The dispersion of the party delivered Thyrza from the necessity of replying, and presently every one had retired to his chamber, excepting Rudolf Kransberg, who remained in the parlour, which was now pitch dark, and George and Redgy, who lingered in the passage.

"I say, George," said Margetts, "shouldn't you like to see the courtship?"

"Well," answered Rivers with a smile, "I must say I should. But of course that is impossible."

"No, it is not," rejoined the other. "Look here: the big dresser runs right through the wall, and there is a cupboard behind that communicates with it, through the cracks in the door you can see everything that passes."

"Wouldn't Thyrza dislike it?" suggested George.

"No. I'll be bound she would be as much amused as we are. It isn't as though she cared a straw for him."

"Well, that is not unlikely," rejoined Rivers. "Come along then. I must own I am curious to see it."

"Creep in here," said Margetts, opening a door in the wall, "and mind you don't make any noise. There are some holes in the dresser through which we shall be able to see."

Almost as he spoke, the door of the parlour opened, and Thyrza was seen standing on the threshold, with the bit of candle in one hand and a match-box in the other. She proceeded to light the former, and placed it in an empty candlestick on the table, and then seated herself—not, as her swain had probably hoped, on the large heavy, wooden-legged sofa which ran along one side of the table, but in the large arm-chair, usually occupied by her mother.

Rudolf, though somewhat disappointed at the position thus taken up, glanced, nevertheless, with approbation at the bit of candle provided, which, in his view of the matter, intimated that the lady was not disposed to abridge the length of the interview. He seated himself in a chair, as near as he could contrive to his inamorata, and looked admiringly at her.

"I say," he said, after a silence of some ten minutes or so,—"I say, I think you are very nice. I admire you greatly."

"You are very obliging," said Thyrza demurely.

There was another pause, after which Rudolf spoke again.

"I say, I mean to come over here very often to see you."

"Indeed?" replied Thyrza with a glance at the candle. Alas! not a quarter of it had yet been expended.

"You don't dislike me, do you, Miss Rivers?" inquired her suitor, after a third and still longer interval.

"I don't know why I should," was the answer.

Deriving some confidence, apparently, from this extremely guarded expression of opinion, Rudolf made a further venture.

"I should like to give you a kiss," he said.

Not meeting with any response, and proceeding perhaps on that most delusive of all proverbs, that silence gives consent, he rose from his place and leaned over her chair, out of which she started with very evident alarm. Believing this to be only feigned reluctance, he pressed forward to urge his entreaty, when suddenly there came a loud explosion. The candle flew all to pieces out of the socket, scattering the tallow in all directions, and the room was left in complete darkness. George and Margetts could hear Thyrza making her escape through the door, while the unlucky lover, wiping the grease from his clothes, made his way to the stable, and rode off as fast as his horse could carry him.

"Redgy, you villain!" exclaimed George, after they had retreated to their room and given vent to their laughter, — "Redgy, you villain, that was your doing!"

"It was the plug of gunpowder, not I," pleaded Redgy. "Mrs Rivers oughtn't to have left the candle all that time on Thyrza's dressing-table."

"Did Thyrza know anything of the trick?" asked George.

"On my honour, she did not."

"Well, it is a good job we are going to-morrow, or there might be a serious row about this."

Chapter Twenty Two

It was a Sunday evening late in December, about nine months after the departure of George Rivers and his friend from Umtongo. George, who wore a suit of clerical black, had just returned from a long ride to Spielman's Vley, where he had passed the day. He was now a deacon, having been ordained by the Bishop of Praetoria a month or two previously. The weather was delicious, but very warm, and George was glad to sit down by his friend's side in a charming little summer-house which they had built under the shade of a tall eucalyptus planted by Mr Rogers when he first came to the Transvaal, forty years before.

"Well, George, what sort of a congregation had you?" inquired Margetts; "and how did you get on with your sermon?"

"I had a very good congregation," was the reply. "The farmer who bought Spielman's Vley of my stepfather is an Englishman, an emigrant from a Berkshire village. He and his wife and grown-up children were all there, and so were nearly all the farm-servants whom he had brought with him. He told me very earnestly how it delighted him to hear the Church service. It was like a voice from Old England, he said, and he couldn't tell me how glad they all were that a clergyman would come over from Umvalosa every alternate Sunday now, instead of once a month."

"And I daresay, when he was in Berkshire, he didn't think much of the Church service," suggested Margetts.

"No, he often didn't go, he told me, and cared very little for it when he did. And it was the same with his labourers. They seldom miss the service here. Well, it is to be hoped that they will not come to neglect it again, now it is once more within their reach."

"But how about the 'natives' service'?" asked Redgy. "Could you get on with that?"

"I am afraid I made a good many blunders," said Rivers, "especially in the sermon. However, nothing but practice will set that right."

"You think an interpreter doesn't answer?"

"No, I am pretty sure it doesn't. You know what Lambert told us about his interpreter, when he first went to preach to the Kaffirs in the Knysna."

"No, I didn't hear the story."

"Lambert said he was puzzled how to address them, when it occurred to him that 'Children of the Forest' was a title that would be sure to take their fancy, and he accordingly began his discourse to them in that way. He thought he had done it rather well, until one of his friends, who had heard him, and who was a good Kaffir scholar, told him that the interpreter had rendered his 'Children of the Forest' as 'Little men of big sticks.' That story determined me never, anyhow, to employ an interpreter."

Redgy laughed. "I think you are right," he said, "and your Kaffir certainly improves. By-the-bye, did you see Hardy? His house is only seven or eight miles off from Spielman's Vley, and I am told he always goes over when there is service there."

"I believe he does, but he was not there to-day. Mr Bacon told me he had gone to Durban—went about a week ago."

"Indeed. Do you know what took him there?"

"I fancy he was sent for to make some report of the state of things in this neighbourhood. You know he now holds an official position of some importance."

"Yes, which you might have had if you had liked it, George. He has the credit of having given them warning at Rorke's Drift in time to prepare themselves for the defence of the place. But it was you who brought them that information."

"I did not want the post, Redgy; and, if I had, Hardy was the person really entitled to it. I did not know the way from Isandhlwana to Rorke's Drift, and could not have found it. And to say the truth, I should not have thought of the garrison at Rorke's Drift, if he had not reminded me of it. No, he fully deserved his appointment, and I am heartily glad he got it. But I believe, when he gets to Durban, he will warn the Government that the Transvaal is not merely in a condition of discontent and disloyalty, but on the verge of an armed outbreak."

"Do you think it goes so far as that, George? An armed outbreak means a war with England, remember. What possible hope can they have in succeeding in that?"

"No reasonable hope, of course. The hundredth part of England's power would be enough to crush them. I don't suppose the Boers could bring 5000 men into the field, and England could easily send five times that number, or twenty times that number, if she chose. The Boers have but little discipline or material of war, or knowledge of strategy. England is a first-rate power in all those respects. It would be as absolute madness for the Transvaal to go to war with England, as it would be for a terrier dog to provoke a lion to fight with it. But, however great the madness, it does not follow that they will not do it."

"What can induce them?"

"Their profound ignorance of the relative strength of the two countries. I was talking with a Boer of some intelligence, who, I found, really believed that Holland was one of the Great Powers in Europe—the equal, if not the superior of England. He knew nothing of history, apparently, since the times of Van Trompe and Admiral Blake. He fancied Isandhlwana had only been redeemed by a desperate and exhausting effort, which would make it impossible for us to engage in any other war for a generation to come. The accidental circumstance that a quantity of newly-coined money had been sent out here to pay the troops was enough to convince him that England was bankrupt, and driven to expend its last guinea. People who know no more than that of the true state of things may perpetrate any act of folly."

"No doubt, George; and I daresay also they argued that the disasters at Isandhlwana and Intombe proved that the English were not so formidable in the field as their own troops had always been. They had repeatedly fought these Zulus, remember, and always with complete success."

"Exactly; no doubt they did, and do, so argue. They were always on their guard, and we were taken off ours, and that made all the difference. But though the Dutch might practise their rude tactics with success on the natives, they will hardly get the English to approach them and be shot down after the same fashion. That is reckoning rather too much on even an Englishman's contempt for his enemy. But they mean mischief, these Boers. They are flocking down this way from all parts of the Transvaal. Whom do you think I saw to-day, of all people in the world?"

"I don't know, indeed—not old Kransberg, I suppose?"

"Not *old* Kransberg, but I did meet the young one—our friend Rudolf. What should bring him here, or Gottlob Lisberg, or Hans Stockmar, or Julius Vanderbilt, or half a dozen other fellows from near Zeerust, whom I have seen about in the course of the last week, unless what they say is true, and they are going to rebel against the English Government."

"It looks like it, I'm afraid. But about Rudolf Kransberg—did you come to speech of him? How did he receive you?"

"I didn't come to speech of him, as he didn't say a single word. He received me as Dido did Aeneas in the infernal regions."

"What! he bears us some grudge for the trick played on him at Umtongo?"

"I am not at all sure that he realises the fact that any trick was played on him. From what Lisberg told me,—Lisberg is very intimate with him, you know,—he fancies the explosion was the work of the Evil One, and that we are in league with him. You know Thyrza wrote us word that he had never turned up at Umtongo again. My mother thought it very odd, but she apparently still believes he is a suitor for Thyrza's hand."

"I suppose Thyrza herself has a pretty shrewd suspicion of the truth."

"I suppose she has, but if she guessed that Rudolf had taken up that notion, she would be quite content to let him entertain it. But the upshot, I fancy, is that Rudolf owes us one, and will pay it if he has the opportunity. He is as thorough a specimen of the sullen Boer as I know, and your sullen Boer is not a pleasant article. But, Redgy," he added, after a few minutes' silence, "there is a matter which I have once or twice wished to speak to you about, but have always put it off. I have a fancy that you really do care for Thyrza, notwithstanding your chaff about her. We are very old friends, and out here, cut off from all the rest of the world, we are like brothers. I wish you would tell me the plain truth about this matter."

"Well, old fellow, where is the use of telling it? I don't see how any one could live as long as I did in your sister's society, and not care for her. She is simply the sweetest and most beautiful creature I have ever seen. But where is the good of my saying this, George? I can't ask her to marry me; I have nothing but a precarious allowance of a hundred pounds a year, and I am not likely to have anything more, unless I can make it myself out here."

"But if Thyrza likes you—"

"I don't know that she does," broke in Margetts. "I have fancied once or twice that she does. But most likely it was all fancy."

"I am only saying, if she *does* like you, she will have something. Umtongo belongs to my mother, not to Mr Mansen."

"But Umtongo will come to you, George," said Margetts, surprised.

"I shall not want it. I shall never marry; and this life here suits me much better than such a farm as Umtongo, though, no doubt, that is a very good farm."

"No doubt," assented his friend. "I see what you mean, and I believe I understand you, when you say you won't marry. But, in the first place,

I hope you are mistaken there; and, in the next, supposing everything else arranged as you wish, Thyrza and I could never deprive you of your inheritance. No, George; I mean to stay here and work as I am doing now. I shall never make a parson; I'm not cut out for that. But I think I shall do well enough at farming and teaching; and, by and by, if your sister doesn't marry a Boer, I may be in a position to ask her."

"Be it so, Redgy. I believe you are right, and this had better not be mentioned again. And here, in good time, comes Mr Rogers. He is back from Newcastle earlier than I had expected."

Mr Rogers, whose acquaintance the reader made in the first chapter of this story, was an extremely worthy man. It would have been well for both England and South Africa if there had been more like him. Left an orphan when quite young, and possessed of a considerable fortune, he had always disliked the ordinary round of English social life, and desired the freer air and habits of a new country. As soon as he could overcome the reluctance of his guardian to the step, he had visited the colonies, and chosen out from among them the border country of Natal and the Transvaal. There he had bought a large farm, — large even for farms in that country, — and built two or three different stations on various parts of it. Spielman's Vley and Rylands were two of these, and here he placed men whose views accorded with his own. Ludwig Mansen, though a Dutchman, had been one of these; and it was with considerable regret that he heard, soon after his arrival in England, of Mrs Mansen's succession to her uncle's property near Zeerust and their removal thither. Notwithstanding his affection for colonial life, he was an Englishman to the backbone, and the blunders made by Colonial Secretaries, one after another, sorely disturbed him. In particular, the gigantic mistake of the annexation of the Transvaal so troubled him, that he made an expedition to England in the hope of persuading the Government to reconsider that disastrous measure. There was no doubt it was, for the moment, advantageous to the Boers, as a sentence of penal servitude would be less unwelcome to a convicted prisoner than a sentence of death. But when the danger of being hanged had passed away, it was not likely that penal servitude would be cheerfully accepted. Foreseeing the inevitable mischief that would ensue, Mr Rogers had urged the repeal, or, at all events, some modification of the decree. But the new Government could not be induced to pay any heed to South African matters, being completely absorbed by domestic and Continental questions; and Mr Rogers went back to Umvalosa, to do the best he could under the circumstances of the case.

On the present occasion he had not returned from Newcastle (whither he had gone, as was his practice, to help in the church services on a Sunday) in the happiest frame of mind. Everywhere he saw the plainest indications of the mischief he had anticipated. Newcastle was full of Boers, who had come in from the more distant parts of the Transvaal, and their feelings and intentions could not be mistaken: not only was revolt designed, but it was close at hand. He greeted George and Redgy with his usual kindness, but his depression and vexation were evident.

"Did you know that your stepfather and mother, as well as your sister, were on the way here?" he asked, addressing Rivers.

"No, sir, I had no idea of it. I haven't had a letter for the last fortnight; and Thyrza, from whom I heard three weeks ago, said nothing of any such intention."

"No; I imagine it must have been a hasty thought. But they are certainly on their way to Newcastle, and will arrive in a day or two at furthest."

"Who told you of it, sir?" asked George. "Perhaps it is some mistake."

"No, that can hardly be. It was Henryk Vander Heyden who informed me. I met him in the street at Newcastle, where he arrived two days ago. Mansen, with his wife and daughter, were to follow him very shortly. Miss Vander Heyden is to travel in their company. Her brother thought it better."

"What are all the ladies coming for?" inquired Redgy. "They are not going to fight the English, anyhow."

"No," said Mr Rogers; "but it may not be safe for them to stay behind. Nearly all the able-bodied men among the Boers will take part in the rising. The Kaffirs and Hottentots would have it their own way, and they might insult or injure the white women. I think Vander Heyden, and your stepfather too, George, are quite right to bring their ladies with them."

"I suppose Vander Heyden is very hot about this," suggested Rivers.

"Yes, he is determined enough, and he is a dangerous opponent to the English. He is a good officer; especially, he understands his countrymen's mode of fighting, and knows from experience what are the faults into which our officers are likely to fall. And he is a desperate man into the bargain."

"How so, sir? I do not understand you."

"Don't you know the story of the girl who was killed by the Zulus not long before the battle of Isandhlwana?"

"Yes; I heard something about it, I believe, from Mr Baylen or Hardy, I don't remember which. Some female relative of his was killed in a very brutal manner. But they are always brutal, these Zulus."

"It was too sad a matter to be much spoken about. The lady, Lisa van Courtlandt, had been engaged to him for some years, and he is said to have been greatly attached to her. She had been murdered just before he came up, and the sight of her mangled corpse drove him, they said, almost mad. It wasn't merely for the purpose of avenging her death that he enlisted in our army—at least, so it is thought. He wanted, poor fellow, to get knocked on the head himself."

"Well, that explains what I couldn't understand before," said Margetts,—"why he was so terribly vexed when it was settled that he was to remain at Rorke's Drift. He was for a time almost beside himself."

"And that, too, may account for his desperate exposure of himself during that night of the encounter with the Zulus," added Rivers. "I never saw a man so utterly insensible to danger; and he hardly seemed rejoiced the next morning at his escape. Poor fellow, he has had a hard lot in life! Well, I agree with you, Mr Rogers; I have no doubt he will fight desperately enough in this outbreak, if it really is going to take place."

"That, I am afraid, there is no doubt of. Vander Heyden told me as much. He wanted to know whether you and Margetts meant to volunteer again to serve in the English army. If you did, he said, you should leave the Transvaal immediately, or you might be arrested. He offered to give you a pass which would carry you across the frontier. That was very kind and generous."

"What did you tell him, sir?" asked Rivers.

"Oh, I said that you were now in orders, and, of course, would not think of fighting; as for you, Mr Margetts, I said I did not know what you might do, but I would ask you, and let him know if you required his help."

"I am obliged to him," said Margetts; "but I have no idea of volunteering again. I consider this to be quite a different matter from the Zulu war, where it was a question whether barbarous or lawless cruelty should be put down. Unless I am myself interfered with, I shall not interfere in this business."

"I am glad to hear you say so," said Mr Rogers. "Then we shall all remain quietly here. I shall invite the Mansens to come and stay at Dykeman's Hollow, and I think they will come. It will be quieter and more comfortable for them than Utrecht or Newcastle, which are overcrowded. I have no doubt Vander Heyden, who has a high command, will be able to secure us from molestation."

Mr Rogers was not disappointed in either expectation. In a few days Mrs Mansen and Thyrza arrived; while Ludwig joined the assembled council of Boers which was now sitting at Heidelberg, exerting himself to prevent the rising which was evidently on the point of taking place. Simultaneously with the appearance of the ladies came a note from Vander Heyden, endorsing a protection from Praetorius for all the inmates of Mr Rogers' household. Not long afterwards the standard of rebellion was openly displayed, and Ludwig joined his family at the Hollow. The Boers in all parts of the Transvaal now took the field with their Westley Richard rifles, and all through the Transvaal the English were obliged to fly for refuge to towns or villages, where they were besieged by the Boers.

Resolved not to provoke the animosity, or even the distrust of his neighbours, Mr Rogers kept himself and all his employés within the bounds of his own domains, not even sending a letter or a message to Newcastle, lest it might be supposed to have some political purpose. He advised his guests also to observe the same prudent demeanour. No doubt Mynheer Mansen was a Dutchman, and one very generally respected; but his wife and stepdaughter were English, and they were the guests of an Englishman; and at this time national feeling, as it might be termed, ran so high that the merest trifle might be enough to cause a general outbreak. The Mansens would have had no inclination to act otherwise than as he advised, even if their sense of what was due to him as their host had not forbade them to do so. They regarded the strife that was in progress as a vexation and a calamity; and whatever might be the issue of it, they were anxious to see an end put to it.

But the ladies felt the time hang heavily on their hands; and when one day had been expended on a visit to George and Redgy's cottage and garden and an inspection of their farmyard and stock, and another to the church and school where he ministered and taught, they were at a loss how to employ themselves, until their host, by a happy inspiration, one day late in January suggested a visit to Kolman's Kop, a most picturesque spot on the very edge of Mr Rogers' estate, from which a wide prospect might be obtained of that part of the Orange Free State known as Harrismith. The road from Bloemfontein to Newcastle ran close beside it, and was visible for a long distance from the summit of the Kop, though the latter was so thickly wooded as to screen any visitors to it from being themselves seen by passing travellers.

To this spot it was agreed that an expedition should be made on the following day; and the whole party, inclusive of Mr Rogers, who acted as guide, set out after breakfast, on horses and mules, having sent some Kaffirs on before them to make the needful preparations.

Kolman's Kop was situated on one of the spurs of the Drakensbergs, not ascending so high as to be bleak or chill, yet high enough to command a magnificent view of the landscape beneath, and there are few countries in the world in which so vast a panorama is visible from the higher lands as in the

Orange Free State. It is not, indeed, an unbroken level, like the low country of the Netherlands, being continually varied by hill and ridge. But these hardly anywhere rise to any considerable height, so that from the slopes of the Drakenberg the eye may range in every direction, until the horizon line melts into the distance. It is a fertile and picturesque territory, watered by noble rivers, whose banks, for the most part, are fringed with foliage, rich with corn lands and fruit orchards, and pastures where sheep and oxen and horses are bred abundantly. The land on that side of the Drakensbergs being considerably more elevated than on that of Natal, the climate is cooler and more agreeable to European residents. A general cry of admiration broke from the visitors as they caught sight of it, and sitting down on the trunk of a fallen tree, they proceeded more leisurely to examine its beauties.

"Well, sir, the Dutch have not much to complain of here, at all events," observed Redgy after a lengthened survey of the scene. "No wonder they halted here when driven from their homes by the English. I should have thought, for my part, that they might have been very thankful to the English for driving them here!"

"Well, so they might, Margetts," remarked Mr Rogers, "if they had thought that the English had been anxious to find out pleasant quarters for them. But I am afraid the English thought of one thing only, and that was clearing them out of their old abodes.

"Yes," he resumed; "the Dutchman has made himself comfortable enough here, if John Bull will only leave him alone. But that John Bull is too philanthropic to do—ha, Mansen?"

"There is no talk of annexing the Free State, is there?" asked old Ludwig with a smile.

"Why, no, Ludwig. The annexation of the other hasn't proved an encouraging experiment, or I think it likely that it would have been proposed."

"Well, sir," observed George, "that annexation took place with the free consent of the Boers, and it was designed in kindness to them."

"Was it?" returned Mr Rogers; "I have my doubts about that latter. No doubt the Boers agreed to it, or rather didn't object to it, at the time. But it was very much like pulling a drowning man out of the water, on condition of his being your bond-servant for evermore. He would agree rather than be drowned, but I doubt whether you could call that his free consent. It was rather his forced consent, to my mind."

"What would you have had England do, sir?" asked Redgy.

"Help the Transvaal out of its difficulties, without insisting on annexation," answered Mr Rogers. "The policy would have been as wise as it would have been kind."

"And you would have given them their independence back when they asked for it after the Zulu war, I suppose?" said Margetts. "Would you give it them now?"

"I should certainly have given it on the occasion you name, when they asked for it. It had then become clear that they did not really desire the annexation; and the only reasonable ground there could have been for it was shown by that request not to exist. I think compliance would have been as wise as it would have been just, and would have gone far to smooth away all difficulties. It is, of course, a very different thing now. England cannot give to armed menace what she has refused to peaceful entreaty. Compliance would be even worse than the previous refusal."

"Well, sir," urged Margetts, "no one, to be sure, could think that the Boers would ever really get the upper hand in a regular war with England. I speak with all possible respect to Mr Mansen, but that is surely impossible."

"No one who understands the strength and resources of the two countries could think it possible," returned Mr Rogers. "But the Boers possess very little information on the subject, and the coloured races still less. They would all think that England yielded now, because her weakness, not her magnanimity, obliged her. But I still trust there will be no war. Enough of this. What is it you have been looking at so intently, Thyrza, for the last ten minutes?"

"I think it is a man on horseback," said Miss Rivers; "but the object is so far off that I cannot distinguish what it is."

She pointed as she spoke to a black speck, on the road that led from Winberg to Newcastle, which was moving towards them.

They all watched it for several minutes, and then Mr Mansen said, "You have a long sight, Thyrza. It *is* a horseman, and he is riding fast. He will pass almost close to us."

"It is an English soldier, or a man who has been one," exclaimed Rivers presently; "there is no mistaking his seat on horseback."

The rider continued to approach until he had arrived almost immediately under the spot where they were sitting. Then George and Redgy started up, simultaneously exclaiming, "It is Hardy, I declare! let us go down and speak to him."

Chapter Twenty Three

Rivers and Margetts hurried down the steep descent without pausing to pick their way, and reached the bottom just as the traveller, whose horse was evidently tired out, passed them at a broken-winded canter, which was the utmost speed, apparently, to which the unlucky animal could be urged.

"Hallo!" shouted George,—"hallo, Hardy, if it really is you! Here are two old friends of yours, who would like to have some talk with you, if you can spare them the time."

The horseman drew his rein in evident surprise.

"What! Rivers, Margetts!" he exclaimed. "Well, this is a piece of good luck. I was just thinking that the best thing I could do would be to ride round by Dykeman's Hollow and ask you to help me. What brings you here?"

"Oh, we have been confined within the bounds of Rogers' property for several weeks, and we made up a party to-day to come here, more for something to do than anything else."

"And why are you confined within the bounds of Dykeman's Hollow?" asked Hardy; "and who has confined you?"

"Well, it is more prudence than necessity," said George. "We don't want to provoke the Dutchmen to attack us."

"You talk riddles," said Hardy, "but I have no time to solve them. Can you tell me where Praetorius,—the great man among the Boers,—can you tell me where he is to be found?"

"I don't know with any certainty," said George; "I expect he has gone southward with the others."

"Southward! what do you mean?" exclaimed Hardy hastily. "What can he have gone south for?"

"Well, he didn't tell me," said Redgy, "but I think I can form a pretty good guess for what he has gone. It is to attack the English troops."

"English troops!" repeated Hardy in evident anxiety and alarm; "what English troops? I did not know that there were any in this neighbourhood."

"We hear that Sir George Colley is marching to the relief of Praetoria with, some say 1000, some 1500 men. Mr Rogers thinks he has got as far as Newcastle, if not still farther north," said Rivers.

"The relief of Praetoria!" again cried Hardy. "Is Pretoria besieged? Do you mean that the rebellion has actually broken out?"

"No doubt of that," replied Margetts; "that is an old story now. The English have for two or three weeks past been besieged by the Boers in all the large towns,—Praetoria, Potchefstroom, Standerton,—and there has been sharp fighting in several places. About the end of December, 250 men belonging to the 94th Regiment were killed or taken prisoners at Bronker's Spruit, near Middelburgh."

"How did that come about?" asked Hardy.

"Well, I suppose Colonel Anstruther didn't know that there was any chance of his being attacked,—didn't know, in fact, that any outbreak was likely to take place,—or his neglect of precautions would seem to be of a piece with what we remember. He was marching, with a number of waggons and 250 men, as Redgy said, along the road, his train being half a mile long, when, at a place called Bronker's Spruit, two Dutchmen rode up to him and handed him a paper, which was found to be a letter from Joubert, who calls himself the Boer General. It stated that war had been declared between the Republic of the Transvaal and England, and called on him to surrender his men and waggons. I suppose Colonel Anstruther hardly thought that the summons was seriously meant; at all events, there was no superior force visible, to which he would be unable to offer resistance, and he only replied by forming his men in column and desiring them to move on, but—"

"But Joubert had planted his sharpshooters under cover everywhere round, and they opened their fire on the soldiers before they knew of their presence."

"That was it, certainly. In ten minutes half the men had been shot down. They were entangled in a marsh, and had not been able to get sight of any enemy to shoot at in return."

"Exactly; and then, I suppose, Colonel Anstruther surrendered?"

"Precisely; that is what he did, and he and his surviving men were taken prisoners."

"He could do nothing else. But I am afraid this will prevent any good being done by my mission. You say this occurred some weeks ago?"

"Yes," said Margetts; "the catastrophe near Middelburgh took place on the 28th of last month, and this is the 28th of January."

"Why, the 28th of last month was just about the time when I set out for Bloemfontein!" cried Hardy. "It is most extraordinary that I never heard this before!"

"What have you been to Bloemfontein for?" asked Rivers.

"I was sent there by the authorities at Natal," answered Hardy, "in consequence of a message from the Colonial Office in England. The Colonial Secretary wanted to come to terms with these Boers. I suppose he thought (as every one else thought) that the annexation had been a most foolish procedure, and that it would be better to come to some reasonable understanding with the Boers than keep up an irritating quarrel with them."

"Small blame to him for that," said George. "Well, go on."

"He thought that Brandt, the President of the Orange Free State, would be a good person to mediate between us and the Boers, and he sent me with a letter to him."

"Did you see him?" asked Margetts.

"Yes; I had two or three very satisfactory interviews with him. He seemed quite sincere in the desire he expressed of preventing bloodshed, and I am the bearer of a letter from him to Praetorius, which, as I was in hopes, would prevent any outbreak of hostilities. He certainly did not know, when I left Bloemfontein, that fighting was going on. I should be almost afraid it will be too late now."

"Is it not extraordinary that no message was sent either from Durban or London, to stop any proceedings until the result of the negotiations with Mr Brandt were known?" asked Rivers.

"It seems so to me, certainly," replied Hardy; "but very likely there are reasons for it, of which I know nothing. Well, anyhow, I had better carry President Brandt's letter to Praetorius. It is only carrying out my orders, and cannot do any harm."

"Not to any one but yourself, Hardy," said Margetts; "but I am not sure it would be safe for you to put yourself in the way of these Boers. The leaders among them seem to behave well enough, but many of the subordinate officers, if one may call them so, are rude and brutal, and might shoot any Englishman who approached them, without inquiry and without listening to any representations."

"You are right, Redgy, I am afraid," said Rivers. "I think Hardy had, at all events, better go with us to Dykeman's Hollow and consult Mr Mansen. He might go with him to Praetorius, and he is so well known to the Boers—indeed, he is one of them himself—that there could be no danger in his company."

"Are the Mansens at Dykeman's Hollow?" asked Hardy.

"Yes, they are Mr Rogers' guests; but they are nearer to us than that. They are up on the Kop yonder, though the trees hide them from our sight. Leave your horse here in Redgy's keeping, and I will go with you up to the Kop."

Hardy accordingly dismounted, and he and George were just commencing the ascent, when three or four men, whose uniform showed that they belonged to the 58th Regiment, came running down one of the narrow passes at the utmost of their speed, close to the spot where the three friends were standing. They had evidently just escaped from some great danger. Their trousers were covered with mud, so that the regimental stripe could hardly be distinguished; their jackets were cut and stained with blood; two of them had lost their caps, and all had thrown away their arms, which would have impeded their flight. As they reached the corner of the road, they came in sight of George and Hardy, and would have turned another way, if the last-named had not called to them.

"Hallo, my lads!" he shouted; "what has happened, and where are you running to?"

Hearing themselves addressed in English, the fugitives stopped, and one of them, a corporal from his dress, answered,—

"There has been a brush with the enemy at Laing's Nek, if you know where that is."

"I know it well enough," returned Hardy; "it is a narrow defile, filled with rocky boulders—just the sort of place where these Dutchmen would take up a position, quite out of sight, and shoot down our soldiers at their leisure. You don't mean to say, I suppose, that you attacked the Boers there?"

"Yes, we did, sir," answered the corporal, "and to our cost. Half our men were killed or wounded in no time, and we couldn't see a single Dutchman to fire at in return. The rest contrived to retreat to the camp, or there wouldn't have been a man left alive. We were cut off by a party of mounted Boers, and offered to surrender to them. But they paid no heed, and fired on us, killing all but two or three. They are after us still, I expect.

They couldn't follow us on horseback up the mountain paths, but they are riding round, I believe, by another road. Can you shelter as?"

"I suppose in strictness we oughtn't to," said Margetts. "But we can't see our countrymen shot down in cold blood; I'd rather take the chance of being shot myself. Come along with me, my lads; you can hide in the caves under Kolman's Kop. The Boers, unless they come from this neighbourhood, won't know anything about them; and they will hardly venture in there after you, if they do. Only we must make all possible haste."

He mounted Hardy's horse and rode off at a trot, the men following him as well as they were able.

Rivers and Hardy watched them as they hurried along under the side of a steep cliff, and then turned into a narrow defile.

"He is right, I suppose," said George; "we are bound not to interfere; but if the laws of civilised warfare are set aside, as it seems they are by these Boers, they cannot expect us to observe them so rigidly as giving these poor fellows up to be shot would amount to. Don't you think so?"

"We have only their word that the Boers would give no quarter," said Hardy, "and it may be that they didn't understand what our fellows said. Still, I can't blame Margetts, if that is what you mean. But we had better make our way to Dykeman's Hollow, hadn't we? I suppose your friends will have gone home by this time."

"All right!" said Rivers; "come this way."

They began climbing the steep path, and were nearly half-way up when they heard voices calling to them, and looking down saw a party of mounted Boers, who were levelling their rifles at them and shouting to them to descend.

"What do you want with us?" called out Hardy in Dutch. "We are not soldiers, and have nothing to do with this war!"

"You are English—I can tell that by your speech," answered the man who had hailed them. "I want to ask some questions of you, to which I mean to have an answer. You had better come down at once, or we will send some bullets to fetch you."

This was evidently no idle threat Half a dozen Boers had already taken their aim, and the path at the point at which the Englishmen had been stopped was without shelter of any kind. There was no help for it.

They had to retrace their steps, and presently found themselves face to face with the leader of the Boers, who proved to be no other than Rivers' old acquaintance, Rudolf Kransberg.

"Ha! it is you, Mynheer Rivers?" he remarked with a scowl. "You are an English soldier, I think, though your companion said you were not."

"I *was* an English soldier in the Zulu war," returned George; "but I left the army at its conclusion, and am now a clergyman of the Church of England."

"I don't care for that. I want to know whether you have seen some runaways from the battle that has been fought at Laing's Nek. We are in pursuit of them, and they must, I think, have passed this way."

"We have told you that we are not belligerents," replied George; "you have no right to question us."

"Ha! I see you will not answer, because you have seen your countrymen, and know where they are. As to having no right, we will see about that. We are at war with the English, and the English are our enemies, though they may choose to say they are not. I shall make you my prisoner. And this person," he continued, turning to Hardy, "who is he?"

"I am an Englishman, like Mr Rivers," answered Hardy; "like him, too, not a belligerent. Your President, Mynheer Praetorius, would not, I am sure, approve your proceedings."

"You think so, hey? Well, you may see him at Laing's Nek, and find out how much respect he will have for your rights?"

"We are quite willing to be taken before him," said Hardy. "We will accompany you to the camp, and answer, without objection, any questions he may put to us."

Rudolf appeared to be somewhat puzzled by this suggestion, but saw no reason why he should not agree to it. Indeed, it had already occurred to him that George Rivers was the stepson of Ludwig Mansen, a man well known to, and respected by, the Boer leaders. Any violence used towards a near relative of his would probably be condemned by his superiors. And he further reflected that he had no kind of evidence that these two Englishmen had really encountered the soldiers, or knew where they were. It was also evidently no use to attempt any further pursuit of the runaways, every trace of whom had disappeared.

"Very well," he said, after a few minutes of silence, "you shall go with us to Laing's Nek, and if the President is still there, and chooses to see you, he will do so. You can ride on the saddles of two of the men, but, I warn you, you will be shot without mercy if you make the slightest attempt to escape."

They mounted accordingly, and the party rode off. George, who understood Hardy's manoeuvre, by which he would get access to Praetorius without attracting general attention, which it was his special object to avoid, made no demur to the arrangement. He further reflected that, as soon as he reached the Boer camp, he could ask for an interview with Vander Heyden, who would, no doubt, at once set him at liberty and grant him an escort to Dykeman's Hollow. Nothing worse, therefore, was likely to happen to either of them than a ride to the Dutch camp and a few hours of detention there; and to this he was so far from objecting, that he was particularly anxious to learn from an authentic source what had really taken place and was likely to ensue.

They rode in profound silence, the Boers being habitually taciturn, and George and Hardy anxious under present circumstances to say as little as possible. Presently the narrow defile running between lofty rocks and along the margin of mountain streams was passed, and they entered the broken and wild country which extends between Newcastle and the border of the Transvaal. After an hour's ride, which would have been protracted to twice that length but for the Boers' knowledge of the ground, they reached the camp, where some five or six thousand men had established themselves. George was at once struck with the difference between it and the camps to which he had been accustomed. There was an utter absence of the military discipline to which he had been used. It bore more the appearance of a great camp meeting, at which every person provided for his own lodging and maintenance; and yet there was a readiness to carry out the orders of the general officers in command, which seemed to take the place of the regular routine of a camp. As they rode over the ground where the battle had been fought that morning, they passed numbers of men employed in the melancholy duties which follow only too surely on an armed encounter. Wounded men were being conveyed on stretchers to the farmhouses and inns, which had been turned into temporary hospitals; others, whose injuries were too severe to permit of removal, were being ministered to on the ground as well as circumstances allowed; while several parties were engaged in digging graves to receive the dead bodies which lay scattered in all directions. One of these companies was working under the direction of Henryk Vander Heyden; and the latter no sooner perceived the two Englishmen than he rode up to them, and, after a friendly salutation, inquired what had brought them to Laing's Nek.

"This gentleman, Mynheer Kransberg,—I am not aware of his military rank,—but he has brought us here as his prisoners," replied Rivers.

"Prisoners! You have not been—"

"We have not been interfering in military matters at all," interposed George. "We had given you our parole not to do so, and, I need not say, have not broken it. We told Mr Kransberg so."

"Then how comes this, Lieutenant Kransberg?" said Vander Heyden haughtily. "Mr Rivers holds a protection which at my instance was granted to him by the President, which exempts him from all interference on the part of the military authorities."

"He did not produce it," said Kransberg sullenly.

"He had no time to do so," interposed Hardy. "But if you would grant me one moment, Commandant Vander Heyden,—that, I believe, is your proper title,—I will explain why the protection was not shown to Mynheer Kransberg. It was because I wished to avail myself of his escort hither. I am the bearer of a letter from Mr Brandt, the President of the Orange Free State, to your President, Mynheer Praetorius, which he was in hopes would prevent the outbreak of war. I regret to find I have arrived too late for that."

"I regret also, Mr Hardy, to say that you have. We have been attacked, and we have driven back our enemies with heavy loss. But we should have preferred to gain our object without spilling of blood."

"Just so," said Hardy; "and you would prefer to gain it now without further bloodshed?"

"Undoubtedly," assented Vander Heyden.

"Then will you obtain me an audience with the President, at which I can still present this letter? If the terms it proposes should be acceptable to him, an armistice may be agreed on, and the question of a settlement between the English Government and that of the Transvaal may be discussed."

"I would take you to him this instant," returned the Dutchman, "were it in my power to do so. But he is not at present in the camp. He has to-day gone northwards on business of urgent importance, nor can I say, without inquiry, when he will return. In his absence I fear the Vice-President and the Commandant-General Joubert could not discuss—certainly could not decide—a question of this importance. But if you will come with me, I will take you to General Joubert's quarters."

"I will go at once; but I should like to ask Rivers what he proposes to do, or rather, what you advise so far as he is concerned."

"He can, of course, return to Dykeman's Hollow if he wishes it, and I will send an escort with him. But I believe they are greatly in want of clergymen to attend the sick and dying in the English camp. Perhaps, if he knew that, he would prefer going there. I need not say he will be at full liberty to do so. But we can speak to him after you have seen Mynheer Joubert. We had better lose no time in going thither."

Hardy accordingly followed Vander Heyden across the rugged and stony ground on which the action had been fought that morning, to a tent— it was the only one in the camp—where the Commandant-General had fixed his quarters. No difficulty was made about obtaining an interview, and Hardy almost immediately found himself in the presence of the rebel leader, as well as in that of another bearded and grave-looking personage, who, he was informed, was Kruger, the Vice-President of the newly-proclaimed Republic.

Hardy looked with interest at the Boer general, who, although he had not at that time attained all the celebrity now attaching to his name, had already achieved some brilliant successes. His family, as Hardy subsequently learned, was of Huguenot extraction, having migrated to the Cape at the time of the Revocation of the Edict of Nantes. But intermarriages with the Dutch in succeeding generations had had their effect, and Joubert had all the appearance of a genuine Boer. Like his fathers, he had followed the calling of a farmer, and had had no experience of warfare, except with native tribes. But he was possessed of rare military ability, and if he had had the advantage of professional training, would have made a great general.

In personal appearance he was of middle height and powerful frame, with an unusually dark complexion, a beard and moustache, and features expressing intelligence and good humour. He was apparently somewhat advanced in years, though he had not passed the vigour of life. He received Hardy with civility, and, after he had heard his story, expressed his regret, as Vander Heyden had done, that the President was not in the camp, so that the matter might be immediately dealt with. Praetorius was expected back very shortly, and then instant attention should be given to it.

"Meanwhile, be assured," he said, "that we desire peace with England, and are willing to concede everything to her, except our national independence. You may not, perhaps, be aware that when the Volksraad declared that the Transvaal Republic was again established, it passed several resolutions, which may well form the basis of negotiations with the agents of the British Government."

"I have only just arrived in the country after an absence of several weeks," said Hardy, "and have therefore had no opportunity of learning what those resolutions were."

"They are soon recited," said Joubert. "The first proclaimed a general amnesty for all past offences. The second ratified all the acts of the British Government up to the date of the proclamation, and the third declared that questions relating to foreign policy might be made matter of special discussion. I think you will allow that these resolutions are not framed in any spirit hostile to your Government."

"I must allow that they are not," replied Hardy. "I should certainly hope that they might form the basis of negotiations satisfactory to both parties. That was also the opinion of the President of the Orange Free State."

"I may add, it is also the opinion of our countrymen in Holland, who have sent an urgent entreaty to the Queen of England that our national independence may be restored to us. The same sentiment has been expressed in other European countries. But I should hardly have thought that such a petition would require foreign support, when it had once been submitted to the English people. They have ever been the first, the most uncompromising of all nations in the assertion of their own liberty. Why should they grudge to others that which they value so highly themselves?"

"You speak well, sir," said Hardy. "I am unable to deny the force of your appeal. We may hope that when the President returns, communications may be opened with the English Government which may lead to a settlement honourable and satisfactory to both parties. But meanwhile, ought not all hostile operations to be suspended? They could not facilitate any negotiations that might be set on foot, but they might seriously impede them."

"If the English general proposes an armistice, it will certainly be agreed to," said Joubert. "On our side we have no need to make any such proposition. If we are not attacked, we shall not ourselves make any attack.

The British have only to do the same, and all fighting will be suspended. But, of course, if we are assailed, we shall repel the assault."

Hardy bowed and took his leave. On returning to the place where he had left George Rivers, he found that the latter had already taken his departure for the British camp, where, as the reader has heard, his services were greatly needed. A few days passed without any resumption of hostilities, when, on the 8th of February, Sir George Colley unexpectedly sallied out of his camp, and the action at Hooge's Chain, between Laing's Nek and Newcastle, on the banks of the Ingogo, was fought, with a result as discreditable and damaging to the English arms as that of Laing's Nek had been.

"What has come to our generals and soldiers I cannot think," said Hardy to George, when he encountered him after the battle on the field, whither both had gone to minister to the wounded and dying. "They seem to me absolutely to court defeat. The only comfort is, that they will hardly make a third attempt after two such calamitous failures."

Chapter Twenty Four

It seemed as if Hardy's anticipations were going to be fulfilled. For more than a fortnight after the disaster on the banks of the Ingogo, both armies remained quietly in their camps, though both were largely reinforced. Negotiations had been opened with the English Government, which bore every appearance of an amicable solution of difficulties. On the afternoon of the 26th of February, Hardy went down to the British lines, with a white flag despatched by Joubert with him, to take some letters to George which had arrived from Dykeman's Hollow. It was some time before he could find his friend, the whole camp being in a state of extraordinary bustle and confusion. Officers and men were hurrying about; one of the guns had been brought out, the horses already harnessed, and the gunners and drivers belonging to it were all in readiness, it appeared, for some immediate movement. Every face bore token that something of grave importance was about to take place.

"What does this mean, George?" asked Hardy as they shook hands. "Sir George Colley cannot anticipate an attack. Everything in the Boer camp, which I have only just left, is quite quiet, and the peace negotiations are proceeding prosperously."

"I cannot tell you, Hardy, what it does mean," answered George. "I hear vague rumours, but they are not to be trusted. One thing, however, is certain, and that is that Sir George Colley cannot get over his defeats by these Boers. I fancy he at first entertained the same contempt for them which English people generally feel. He thought that they were a race of cowards, who would shoot down helpless savages from a safe distance, but dared not face soldiers in a field of battle."

"We have already agreed that that is a mistake," observed Hardy. "Their mode of fighting is quite different from ours. They have no disciplined troops, as we have; and if they were to face us, as Sir George expects, on a field of battle, must inevitably suffer defeat. But they are brave and resolute men, and fight after their own fashion; which is as dangerous and disastrous to our troops as our mode of lighting would be to them."

"Exactly," said Rivers; "and Sir George has chosen to fight after their fashion instead of ours, and these disasters have been the consequence. But that does not reconcile him to them. He is afraid that peace will be made before he has any opportunity of redeeming his military reputation, which he thinks has been terribly damaged by Laing's Nek and the action on the Ingogo. He wants to give them one tremendous thrashing before peace is concluded and the opportunity is lost."

"I can well understand that," said Hardy, "though I think he is quite wrong. But do I understand you to mean that the preparations which I see going on are for another attack on the Boers? Really I do not think that would be a defensible proceeding. If there has been no formal suspension of hostilities, there is a tacit understanding to that effect, which the Boers have most faithfully adhered to."

"I am afraid the preparations do mean that," answered George, "though, of course, I have made no inquiries, nor has any one volunteered the information. I think Sir George means to attack the Boer camp again, though probably he will choose a different quarter from which to assail it."

"It is to be hoped he will, at all events," rejoined Hardy, "unless he wishes exactly the same results to follow as before. Well, we shall soon know what is going to happen, for here come Sir George and his staff. They are evidently about to set out somewhere."

"Come to the high ground on the west of the camp," suggested Rivers. "You can see the whole road to the Dutch lines from it, and some of the waggons immediately under Amajuba hill."

"Amajuba hill," repeated Hardy. "Is that the name of that steep hill yonder, with a flattish top, which completely overlooks the camp? I wonder the Dutch have not occupied it, I must say. Sir George's position here wouldn't be tenable if they did. But then, to be sure, they have no cannon. Well, I may as well go with you as you propose, for, of course, if your conjecture is correct, I should not be allowed to leave the English camp."

They took up their position accordingly, and presently saw the troops, seven or eight hundred in number, move out with the gun which Hardy had seen an hour or two before, the most complete silence being observed. The darkness was already coming on when they set out, and before long it became impossible to distinguish any object, except those close at hand.

"Sir George must intend a night attack," said Hardy; "but, independently of all other considerations, the Boers are less likely to be thrown into confusion by that than our own troops are. They are taught to fight independently of one another. Every man takes up his own position and shifts for himself. If they are disturbed in the middle of the night, they will simply get up,—ready dressed, for they always lie down in their clothes,—take their rifles, pick out the securest spot they can find, and open fire on any enemy they see. Well, George, we had better stay here awhile and see what comes of this. If night fighting is intended, we shall soon know all about it."

Rivers assented. They were as conveniently placed as they could well be for learning what was going on. There was a hollow in the rock large enough to shelter them from wind and rain, if either should come on, and a quantity of moss and heather would make a comfortable bed, if they lay down to sleep. They agreed that they would keep alternate watch through the night, so that nothing that might occur should escape their notice.

The night, however, passed without disturbance, and when the morning dawned it revealed an unexpected spectacle. The British force was clearly to be discerned, by the first beams of the sun, stationed on the top of the Amajuba hill, the ascent of which must have occupied the hours of darkness. It must have been a most difficult and perilous undertaking, and it seemed wonderful that it could have been accomplished in the dark, and without arousing the vigilance of the Boers, who were encamped in the immediate vicinity. There they were, however,—the scarlet uniforms forming bright spots against the background of rock and sky,—and the brass gun, which, by a marvel of engineering skill, had been dragged up the precipitous steeps, sparkling in the sun, as it was fixed in its position, commanding the camp of the sleeping Boers below.

"How in the world can they have managed that?" exclaimed Rivers. "Nothing but a bird, I should have thought, could get up there. The gun, of course they must have hoisted up after them. It is a most daring exploit; but I suppose Sir George has got the upper hand of them now."

"I am not so sure of that," rejoined Hardy. "I grant you this is as bold and venturous a feat as ever has been attempted in war. But I don't know that it will succeed against these Boers. You see, though they have taken possession of the heights, they have not intrenched themselves. The broken masses of rock furnish a cover behind which sharpshooters may hide themselves while they fire on the enemy. But the Boers will be able to fire up at them quite as securely as they will be able to fire down at the Boers. And if the Boers, whose numbers greatly exceed theirs, clamber up on all sides, under cover of the fire of their friends, there is nothing to keep them back. Our men will be overpowered by weight of numbers. I wish I could see them begin to intrench themselves, but there is no sign of it. I hope we are not going to see the Isandhlwana disaster acted over again."

"I suppose they must have been too tired, when they got up there last night to throw up intrenchments," remarked George.

"Very likely indeed," returned Hardy, "but they do not appear to be too tired this morning. If they are wise, they will not begin firing until they have made their position safe."

Meanwhile on the summit of the hill there was triumph and rejoicing. The soldiers had felt keenly the defeats which they had again and again sustained at the hands of an enemy for whom they had entertained a traditional contempt, and who, they were persuaded, if they could once bring them to a fair encounter, would fly before them. But they had been shot down from behind cover, without the chance being given them of returning their adversaries' fire. But here, at last, the tables were turned. They occupied now the vantage-ground from which the foe might be assailed without the risk of suffering retaliation. A genuine British cheer broke forth as the gun opened on the slumbering Dutchmen below, followed by bursts of merriment as the sleepers started up in alarm and confusion, rushing in all directions to find protection from the deadly hail from above. But they did not take to immediate flight, as their assailants had expected. Niching themselves in the hollows of the rocks or behind the mountain ridges, they opened a fire from all directions on the occupants of the hill, obliging these to keep close behind the cover of the rocks as the only mode of escaping the storm of musketry that continued to be poured upon them. No attempt, however, was made to dislodge them, and it was obvious that, if they retained their position on the crest of the hill, the Boer camp must be broken up, leaving the way open for the British troops to enter the Transvaal.

But the English had been once more deceived by the skilful manoeuvring of their enemies. Under cover of a tall cliff which interposed between them and Amajuba hill, the Boer leaders were determining their plan of operations.

"I am sure one of the paths is practicable," Vander Heyden was saying. "It is on the opposite side to that by which the English made their way to the top, and I think it most likely that they know nothing of it. It is completely sheltered from their fire until you are close to the top, and there is a hollow near that where a number of men may be massed. Our adversaries, with their usual contempt for their enemies, have omitted to intrench themselves or fortify their position. There would probably not be more than half a dozen men keeping guard at the point in question. A rush of a dozen or twenty would force the way in, and then the others would follow. As there is no shelter or means of escape except down the steep sides of the hill, they must all surrender or be killed."

"Do you yourself know the way up the path, Vander Heyden?" asked the Boer general.

"Yes," answered Henryk; "I have twice been up to the top that way to make an examination of the English camp."

"Then I think you are the man to lead the assault. What say you?"

"I desire nothing better," returned Vander Heyden, the dark light, which had become habitual with him at seasons of danger, flashing in his eyes.

"Good. Who is there prepared to follow you?"

There was no lack of volunteers; and Vander Heyden's only difficulty consisted in his unwillingness to reject any. Presently the number was made up. Orders were given to the sharpshooters in ambush to pour their fire more hotly on every crevice of the rocks above, so as to engage as much as possible the attention of the garrison.

Then Vander Heyden, rifle in hand, crept cautiously and silently up the rocky ladder, pausing continually to allow those behind him to approach closely to him, until the hollow place, of which he had spoken, was reached, and a dozen of his most trusted followers assembled in it. Then the word was given. The foremost of the party rushed round the corner of the rock, poured in a close fire, and pressed on to force the passage. For the moment they succeeded, but the next a shout was raised, and a bayonet charge met the assailants, bearing them back and almost forcing them down the rocky descent. But more of the Dutchmen had now come on the scene. A second volley cleared the way, and the assailants rushed in in ever-increasing numbers. Presently the whole plateau had become a battlefield, and the English, outnumbered and borne back by the overwhelming mass of Boers, were either shot down, or made their escape by the steep mountain paths, followed by their victorious enemies, who stabbed and shot them down without mercy. If the guns from the camp had not opened their fire and checked the pursuit, it is probable that scarcely any of the British soldiers who had climbed those heights on the previous evening would ever have descended them again, unless as corpses carried to interment.

About the centre of the plateau a group of Boers were gathered round an English officer, who had been struck by a bullet which apparently had instantly killed him. Vander Heyden directed them to take off the leather helmet which partially concealed his features.

"It is he!" he exclaimed, as his order was obeyed. "That is the English general; that is Sir George Colley."

He had scarcely uttered the words when a stray bullet struck him in the breast, and he fell to the ground beside his prostrate enemy. His companions raised him in their arms and earned him down the hill to a room in an adjoining farmhouse, where his wound was examined by a surgeon. The latter shook his head after a brief inspection. The bullet had not touched either heart or lungs; but the internal haemorrhage could not be stopped, and life could not be long protracted. Vander Heyden himself was aware of his condition. He made no other request than that a flag of truce might be sent to the English lines, asking permission for the Reverend George Rivers, who was serving, he was informed, as a chaplain in the camp, to visit him on his deathbed. The request was granted; and in an hour's time after the conclusion of the fight Rivers entered the chamber where he was lying.

Vander Heyden raised himself as well as he was able to greet him, and desired that the room might be cleared.

"George," he said when this had been done, "I am glad you have come. There is no time to lose, for I feel that death is very near. You remember our conversation about my sister many months ago near Intombe."

"It is not likely that I should forget it," answered George.

"I told you two things—first, that my father had forbidden me to give her in marriage to an Englishman; and secondly, that if she did marry one, she would forfeit the whole of her inheritance."

"That is what you said."

"And I said no more than the fact. But I thought even then, and I am now more fully persuaded of it, that my father was mistaken in the resolution to which he came. The English had been harsh and unjust to us. But every Englishman is not harsh and unjust; and if my sister has chosen—as in my heart I believe she has—a generous and upright man, it is hard that she should be denied her wish merely because he was an Englishman."

He paused a moment to recover breath, and then went on.

"Men alter strangely. A twelvemonth ago I thought it impossible I could ever feel as I do now. And if I had married, and had children to follow in my steps, I do not think I could have so altered. But that hope died out and could never be revived, and Annchen's future was all I had to care for. She does not know my change of feeling. When I took leave of her last night, I felt assured that I was parting from her for the last time, though I could not tell her so; but this letter will convey to her my dying wishes. I have drawn up a fresh will, by which everything is left to her and to you. Give me your hand."

They exchanged a cordial grasp. "Now, Rivers," he continued, "we will speak no more of this. But you must remain with me to the end."

There is no need to dwell on what followed. Vander Heyden lingered for an hour, and then passed away quietly, without pain, remaining conscious to the last. When all was over, George gave the order, as his friend had desired him to do, for the conveyance of the body to the burying-ground at Utrecht, where the remains of the hapless Lisa van Courtlandt had been deposited. He himself accompanied the corpse as chief mourner, and saw the funeral rites performed. Then he proceeded to Newcastle, and sought an interview with Annchen, with whom his mother and Thyrza were now staying. They had gone over, by his request, to convey to her the melancholy tidings, and had remained at her earnest entreaty to comfort her.

She did indeed feel unutterably desolate. Her brother and Frank Moritz had been her only near relatives, and of both these she had been bereaved; and the man who, she felt, might have been nearer and dearer than any, was hopelessly separated from her by Henryk's decree. His wishes had always been law to her while he lived; and, now that he had been taken from her for ever, her only satisfaction in life would be to fulfil his pleasure. When the message was brought to her that George desired an interview, she was at first unwilling to grant it. It was possible that he might renew his suit, considering all obstacles to their union as being now removed; and if so, their meeting would be needlessly painful. It was only when Thyrza told her that her brother was the bearer of a letter, which Henryk had sent her from his dying bed, that she consented to receive him.

She was sitting near the window when he entered. Her black dress rendered the dazzling fairness of her complexion more remarkable. Even the look of unutterable sadness seemed to enhance her beauty. He went slowly up to her, took her hand and pressed it to his lips, and then without speaking, placed the letter in her hands. Her tears fell fast over it as she opened it, and it seemed as if they must have prevented her from deciphering its contents; for she twice read it through without appearing to understand its purport. At last a faint flush on her cheek and a strange light in her eye told him that she had realised the meaning of her brother's words. She sat for a few minutes with her eyes fixed on the ground, and then looked up into her lover's face, as if seeking there a confirmation of the wondrous joy that had broken thus suddenly upon her. His smile seemed to satisfy her. She rose and threw herself into his arms.

"Oh, George," she exclaimed, "is it wicked, at a time of sorrow like this, to feel so happy?"

"It is what he wished," answered Rivers. "It was the thought which comforted him at the last."

A few days afterwards, Annchen joined the family circle at Dykeman's Hollow, when it was found that she was not the only bride to whom congratulations were due. George had taken an early opportunity of explaining to his mother and stepfather—to whom the former referred him—the change that had taken place in his circumstances. He was now, or would shortly be, the owner of Pieter's Dorf and Vander Heyden's other property, and, for a resident in that country, a very wealthy man. It was his wish to surrender all interest in his mother's estate in favour of Thyrza. At the same time he pleaded the cause of his friend Redgy Margetts. He had known, he said, for some time past that he was deeply attached to Thyrza, and had reason to believe that she was not indifferent to him. If that should prove to be the case, might not a second marriage take place? Mr Rogers had been consulted, and had declared himself so well satisfied with Margetts, that he was willing to put him into the farm hitherto occupied by George—which was already in a thriving state, with every prospect of improvement. Here he and Thyrza might live, until the time came when Umtongo would be their own.

Farmer Mansen heard his stepson to the end,—he had never, indeed, been known to interrupt any one,—and then answered that he and his wife had already spoken together on this subject, and had no fault to find with Mr Margetts. But it would be impossible for them to accept him as a suitor for Thyrza, because Mynheer Rudolf Kransberg had been received in that capacity, and no decisive answer had as yet been given him. To this George replied that he had had some conversation with Thyrza on the subject, and she had informed him that young Kransberg had never visited her since the day when he himself had left Umtongo, and as that was fully nine months ago, Thyrza had concluded he had abandoned all idea of seeking her as his wife.

"She is too hasty," remarked Ludwig. "Nine months are no unreasonable time for a Dutch suitor to delay; we do not do things in this country in a hurry. She cannot allow the addresses of a new suitor, until the old one has been formally dismissed."

"But, good gracious! how long is that to go on?" pleaded George. "He may pay another visit six months hence, and another a twelvemonth after that. And Thyrza may be an old maid before she has the opportunity of relieving herself from the attentions of her admirer by refusing him."

"You do not understand our customs," said Ludwig sedately. "We do everything deliberately."

This reply George was obliged to transmit to Margetts, by whom, it needs not to say, it was not received with much satisfaction. Redgy, in fact, propounded a variety of schemes for bringing Rudolf von Kransberg up to the scratch, the mildest of which was lassoing him after the fashion of the South American hunters and conveying him in that condition to Thyrza's presence, when she would avail herself of the opportunity of giving her inamorato his *congé*. All these were rejected by George and Thyrza, and the dissatisfaction of the baffled suitor every day waxed more grievous to behold, when one day he chanced to encounter Hardy in the street at Newcastle, and learned from him that Rudolf Kransberg was not only paying his addresses to Gretchen Groetweld, the plump and comely daughter of the Landrost of Lichtenberg, but, it was generally believed, had been accepted by her.

"I met him riding down the street," said Hardy, "dressed in his best holiday suit, and a large nosegay in his buttonhole. He was mounted on a showy horse,—'the courting horse,' as they call it,—which he made amble and prance down the street to the great admiration of the spectators. Presently he drew up at Mynheer Groetweld's door, when the worthy burgess greeted him with ceremonious politeness and requested him to enter. I heard from the Landrost, who delayed a few minutes to speak to me, that Mistress Gretchen is well satisfied with her sweetheart, and the formal betrothal is straightway to take place."

This intelligence, which was presently confirmed by Mynheer Groetweld himself, overcame even Ludwig Mansen's punctilio; and Reginald Margetts and Thyrza were allowed to plight their troth to one another.

Mr Rogers, who had always felt a warm interest in the Mansens, and who latterly conceived a still warmer regard for Rivers and Margetts, was much pleased at the course which events had taken. Notwithstanding the recent death of Henryk Vander Heyden, it was not thought advisable to postpone for more than a few weeks Rivers' and Annchen's wedding; and the Mansens agreed that Redgy and Thyrza should be married on the same day, the chapel attached to Mr Rogers' house being chosen as the place where both ceremonies were to be performed.

The guests were limited to the near relatives of the brides, the only exception being Hardy, who arrived on the wedding morning, bearing the intelligence that the terms between the English Government and the Boers had been finally arranged. The suzerainty of the Queen was to be maintained, but, apart from this, the most complete independence was conceded to the Transvaal Republic, all the terms for which they had stipulated being fully granted.

"Well," said Mr Rogers, "I never thought I should live to regret the reversal of that most mischievous and ill-judged of measures, the annexation of the Transvaal, but I have lived to regret it nevertheless. It appears to me that every blunder that was possible has been made. First of all, advantage is taken of a temporary reverse to impose on a nation a yoke which they are supposed to desire, but which they really dislike. Then, when reasonable and respectful petitions are presented, pointing out that the step is to the injury of both countries, and praying that it might be undone, they are curtly refused. Then, when the aggrieved citizens take up arms to compel the recognition of their rights, an attempt is made to crush them by force of arms, but the campaign is conducted in such a manner as to give them an easy and certain victory. I don't suppose the Tenth Legion of Caesar, or the Old Guard of Napoleon, or Wellington's Peninsular veterans, could have done anything but stand to be killed, if they had been led into action as our soldiers were. And lastly, when the prestige of England has suffered so seriously that a victory (which could easily have been gained) has become imperatively necessary for its restoration, all that had been refused to moderate entreaty is granted to defiant and almost insolent demand! I don't suppose the injury that has been done to British ascendancy in South Africa will be undone in less than fifty years, if it is undone then! Well, things are at their worst now; and when they have come to the worst, then the proverb says they will begin to mend! That must be our comfort, for I am afraid we have no other!"